STUDIES IN HISTORY, ECONOMICS AND PUBLIC LAW

Edited by the
FACULTY OF POLITICAL SCIENCE
OF COLUMBIA UNIVERSITY

NUMBER 499

STUDENT FOLKWAYS AND SPENDING AT INDIANA UNIVERSITY, 1940-1941

BY

MARY M. CRAWFORD

STUDENT FOLKWAYS AND SPENDING AT INDIANA UNIVERSITY 1940-1941

A Study in Consumption

BY

MARY M. CRAWFORD

AMS PRESS
NEW YORK

COLUMBIA UNIVERSITY
STUDIES IN THE
SOCIAL SCIENCES

499

The Series was formerly known as *Studies in History,
Economics and Public Law.*

Reprinted with the permission of Columbia University Press
From the edition of 1943, New York
First AMS EDITION published 1968
Manufactured in the United States of America

Library of Congress Catalogue Card Number: 68-58563

AMS PRESS, INC.
New York, N.Y. 10003

To

MY MOTHER

AND

FATHER

PREFACE

THIS is a study of student spending at Indiana University. It was undertaken in order to determine the patterns of student consumption, to see the variations in spending among different groups on the campus, and to discover the social and economic factors responsible for such variations. The study lies in the general field of consumer economics. It is based on data covering the academic year 1940-41 collected from a sample of 1275 unmarried undergraduate students distributed among the various groups on the campus in such a way as to be representative of the entire undergraduate student body as well as of the individual groups within it to which they belong. Married students were excluded because of the problems involved in estimating their expenses on a basis comparable to those submitted by a single man or woman.

Not only do student budgets differ from family budgets and single person budgets, such as those described in the studies of the Bureau of Labor Statistics and the Bureau of Home Economics, but they have also been studied less frequently and less intensively. Therefore, it is hoped that a study made on the campus of a representative state university will provide material with which student spending at other colleges and universities may be compared. Replies from inquiries directed to the registrars and deans of the institutions belonging to the American Association of Collegiate Registrars and to other college officials revealed that surprisingly little research has been done on the subject of student spending. The majority of the studies in the field have been made not from the viewpoint of prospective students or of college administrators, but rather for the purpose of determining the potential purchasing power of students as an aid to the sale of merchandise or of advertising space. The figures concerning costs published in college and university catalogues are for the most part based upon the estimates of individual faculty members or administrative officials rather than

7

upon data collected from representative samples of the students themselves.

In making this study, the writer has received assistance from so many persons that the length of the complete list prevents its inclusion. Among those persons are the members of the teaching and administrative staffs of Indiana University who helped with the collection of data and the many students whose coöperation made the study possible.

Among the persons to whom the writer's debt is so great that they must be mentioned individually is Professor James E. Moffat, Head of the Economics Department of Indiana University, whose earlier studies of student budgets furnished the inspiration and background for this study. Likewise great is the obligation to Professors Robert S. Lynd and Frederick C. Mills of the Graduate Faculty of Political Science of Columbia University whose encouragement and suggestions at various stages in the development of the study helped immeasurably. To her colleagues, Professors Clausin D. Hadley and Francis E. McIntyre and to Dr. Gerald J. Matchett, now of the United States Department of Agriculture, who contributed helpful advice in dealing with statistical problems, and to Professor Mark C. Mills and Dr. Joseph A. Batchelor of Indiana University and Dr. Dorothy Barrett of Hunter College, who read and criticized the manuscript, the writer is also much indebted.

Finally, it is a pleasant duty to acknowledge the financial assistance received from the Graduate School Research Fund of Indiana University which, with the willing coöperation of Mr. Harold Bly of the University's Central Statistical Bureau made possible the classification of data and the computations required for the study. The writer is also grateful to James Hyndman and Ray La Vallée, graduate assistants in the Department of Economics, and to Selma Liff and Russell Davis, students, who patiently helped in compiling the data used in the study.

MARY M. CRAWFORD.

INDIANA UNIVERSITY.

CONTENTS

TABLES

11

14   TABLES

16   TABLES

CHAPTER I

THE NATURE AND SIGNIFICANCE
OF THE STUDY

THE SPENDING OF STUDENT GROUPS AS A
SPECIAL PROBLEM IN CONSUMPTION

A STUDY of the expenditures of college students is today a much more significant part of the general problem of consumer spending than it was twenty-five years ago. At that time one out of every twenty-four young persons of college age was enrolled in an institution of higher learning; today one out of every seven such persons is so enrolled.[1] The 1940 enrollment in American colleges and universities was estimated to be 1,347,-146.[2] This may be compared with a combined population of 1,235,184 for the states of Nevada, Vermont, Delaware, and Arizona. On the conservative assumption that a full-time student will spend a minimum of $500, the student group can be estimated to spend at least half a billion dollars per year.

Not only has the college group become a larger proportion of the total population; it has likewise become more representative of the different social and economic levels in our society. Among the significant factors that have contributed to this result have been the increasing number of women attending college, the growing number of persons from medium and lower income families that have found it possible to become college students, and the larger number of vocations for which college training has been recognized as an essential preparation.

1 John Roberts Tunis, *Choosing a College* (N. Y.: Harcourt, Brace and Co., 1941), pp. 3 and 4.

2 Raymond Walters, " Statistics of Registration in American Universities and Colleges, 1940," *School and Society*, XVII (1940), 612. The total enrollment of part-time and full-time students in the 652 schools included in Mr. Walter's study for 1940 was 1,347,146. The enrollment of full time students in the 652 universities and colleges was more than 30,000 greater than the total population of Maine.

The attendance of women at college has been stimulated by the changes in our society that have afforded women greater opportunities for freedom in personal development, in cultural attainments, and in the choice between occupation in the home or in the business world. Many jobs from which women were formerly virtually excluded have been opened to them. Satisfactory development or even entrance into many occupations is now materially assisted by college training. The development of scientific study in such fields as nutrition and dietetics in which women have long been occupied has created new opportunities for the college trained women. Furthermore, a larger proportion than formerly of the young women looking forward to marriage and to the occupation of housewives now see in college training a means of enriching their own personal enjoyment and of playing a more significant rôle in the development of their homes and communities.

After 1932-33, the depression gave a new impetus to college attendance in spite of the fact that faith in the generally accepted relation between a degree and a job was somewhat shaken by the presence of graduates out of work and on relief.[3] While some young people who would have ordinarily expected to attend college were prevented from doing so by depressed business conditions, others who might not otherwise have gone went because they could not get jobs. College costs tended to be so reduced that in some instances it was no more expensive to attend college than to stay at home. Emphasis upon courses affording training for specific vocations became more apparent. In the field of business large corporations began to look upon the colleges and universities as their normal recruiting grounds just as the professions had done in the past. With this development

3 Enrollment of undergraduate students at Indiana University on the Bloomington campus during the regular two-semester academic year in the period of 1925-41 was:

1925-26....3653	1920-30....3826	1933-34....3876	1937-38....5267
1926-27....3702	1930-31....3829	1934-35....4324	1938-39....5724
1927-28....3737	1931-32....3790	1935-36....4674	1939-40....6963
1928-29....3724	1932-33....3613	1936-37....5073	1940-41....6759

came the rapidly growing collegiate schools of business which
have attempted to create a professional attitude toward business
careers.[4] Other kinds of vocational preparation and the number
of schools incorporated in a single university gradually increased and brought together students interested in a wider
range of subjects and vocations and with more varied types of
abilities than ever before. The result of this trend was greater
heterogeneity in student bodies.

Since the beginning of the depression also, more students
than ever before have assumed the responsibility of financing
a part or all of their own college expenses. This has resulted in
an increase in the proportion of students who must economize
while in college. It is not uncommon for young men or women
to matriculate at college with funds insufficient to meet the next
installment on their fees, hoping to get along on current earnings. To help students whose parents can give them only limited
financial assistance, many colleges and universities have intro-
duced coöperative housing and boarding facilities, more jobs,
and additional scholarship funds. The federal government has
also made it possible for large numbers of young people to attend and to remain in college. It has done this by means of
funds allotted to universities by the National Youth Administration on the basis of their previous enrollments.[5] These funds
are distributed in the form of monthly wages for certain types
of work on the campus to students who can give evidence of
financial need and of the ability to profit by college training.

During the depression years, changes in social attitudes,
lowered incomes, and a desire to provide vocational as well as

4 At Indiana University the School of Business, established in 1920, has
been the fastest growing unit of the University.

5 In 1934, such funds were distributed for the first time through the Federal
Civil Works Administration Program to non-profit making colleges. On
March 31, 1934 when the Civil Works Administration was discontinued, the
student-aid program was continued under the direction of the Federal Emer-
gency Relief Administration, and became known as the FERA program.
When the program for student aid was extended by executive order by
President Roosevelt, the National Youth Administration was established
within the Works Progress Administration of Indiana University.

liberal arts training for their children have caused more families in the upper income brackets to send their children to state universities than formerly. The pretentious residences and social opportunities now offered by Greek-letter organizations and university dormitories have also attracted to the state universities of the Middle West young men and women who formerly went East to college.

Another reason for the heterogeneity in the types of students and in the consequent patterns of spending on college campuses today, is the publicity that " college life " and college attendance have received in recent years. There are some young men and women who admittedly attend college either because they believe it to be the conventional thing to do, because their friends are there, or because they have heard that college is fun. In recent years, too, the radio, motion pictures, and the press have not only stressed these ideas but have helped to popularize college attendance to such an extent that practically all sections of the country and all types of communities are now represented on university campuses.

Although Bloomington, with a population of 20,000, is a somewhat smaller city than those in which certain other universities are located, it is fairly typical of the towns in which state universities are found in that they are most often located outside the large metropolitan centers.

In respect to the growth of fraternities and sororities Indiana has also been typical. In recent years, also, there have been an increasing number of students from outside the state who have added variety to the composition of the student body. While the extremes in spending are not as great at Indiana as would be found in many other institutions, it is believed that a picture of student spending at that university does offer a cross section view which is typical of many other institutions.

THE BACKGROUND OF THE PRESENT STUDY

There is no record of any formal or systematic study of student expenditures at Indiana University prior to 1925. In that year Professor James E. Moffat became interested in student budgets as a special aspect of consumption and also in their relation to general educational costs.[6] As a result of this interest he instituted a study of the budgets of Indiana students which has been carried on to the present time. For each of the years since 1925 average total expenditures, based upon sampling, have been ascertained and an index number, hereinafter referred to as the Moffat Index, has been constructed. So far as is known, this is the only continuous index of American student spending covering a similar period. Since 1937 the study has been carried on by the writer. In certain of the years special studies were made in which the expenditures of groups within the general sample were compared.

In the construction of the Moffat Index, averages were computed from estimates of expenditures secured from a representative sample of students by means of questionnaires and personal interviews. The averages used were weighted arithmetic means obtained by dividing the sum of the total expenditure of each group by the number of students in that group, multiplying the quotient by the total number of students belonging to that group enrolled in the university, adding the results, and dividing by the total student enrollment. The average for the year 1925-26 was used as the base.

As may be seen from Table 1, the average total expenditure for all students in the sample in 1925-26 was $911, an amount which still reflected the effect of the first World War on prices. In spite of the fact that the next three years fell in the prosperity phase of the business cycle the average expenditures of the students in the samples studied by Professor Moffat were in each year somewhat less than those for 1925-26, amounting to $831.74, $880.74, and $847.23 respectively.

6 James E. Moffat, " Student Expenditures at Indiana University," *Indiana University News-Letter*, XX (Nov., 1932), 1-12; " Student Expenditures and the Depression," *Indiana University News-Letter*, XXII (July, 1934), 1-5; " Student Expenses at Indiana University," *Indiana University Alumni Quarterly*, XIX (Oct., 1932), 476-86; " Student Budgets," *School and Society*, XXXVI (Oct. 1, 1932), 432-4.

The change in business conditions that began in 1929 apparently did not affect the average for 1929-30 which moved up to $877.29.   In the next year the effect of the depression was evident, but the decline was less marked than in the following year, 1931-32, when the average dropped from $837.69 to $729.60.

TABLE 1

Average Estimated Total Expenditures of Students at Indiana University, 1925-41

(Weighted arithmetic mean for 1925-26 = 100)

College Year	Average in Dollars [a]	Moffat Index of Student Expenditures
1925-26	$911.00	100.0
1926-27	831.74	91.3
1927-28	880.82	95.7
1928-29	847.23	93.0
1929-30	877.29	96.3
1930-31	837.69	91.1
1931-32	729.60	80.1
1932-33	582.00	63.9
1933-34	533.15 [b]	58.5
1934-35	553.36	60.7
1935-36	533.26	58.5
1936-37	581.89	65.2
1937-38	630.68 [c]	69.2
1938-39	619.40	67.9
1939-40	642.28	70.4
1940-41	663.40	72.8

[a] These averages were obtained by the methods used by Professor Moffat described on page 21, but in the years 1937-41 the size of the sample used and the number of headings under which the expenditures were listed were increased.

[b] Some of the drop in the average for this year is explained by the introduction of a coöperative dining room and a reduction in dormitory costs in that year (see page 24).

[c] In this year the prices of room and board in the university dormitories and in some of the fraternity chapter houses were increased.

In the latter year, 1931-32, Professor Moffat extended his study of student spending and, from data obtained from 513 students, computed the average expenditures of all students in the sample for 11 different categories in the student budget. Average expenditures were also computed for such groups within the student body as those of all men, all women, the men and women in each of the four undergraduate classes, and students in the College of Arts and Sciences and in the School of Commerce, now the School of Business.

Professor Moffat found from this study that women spent on an average more than men. Both Freshman men and women spent more than the men and women in any other undergraduate class. The highest single expenditure reported by any one student in the group studied was $1,633. The lowest was $280. Organized students spent more than those who were unorganized.[7] Men in the sample spent 28.8 per cent of their budget for food, 16.7 per cent for room, and 10.6 per cent for clothing, while women spent 28.1, 17.4, and 18.5 per cent of their budgets for these respective items.

In the years 1932-33 and 1933-34, when only the average total expenditures of all students in the samples drawn for those years were obtained, the averages dropped sharply to $582.15 and $533.15 respectively. In the latter of these two years, when the average was the lowest for any of the sixteen years during which student expenditures have been studied at Indiana University, Professor Moffat again examined the spending of representative groups within the student body, using the same techniques employed in his study for 1931-32.

In this study for 1933-34, published under the title of "Student Spending and the Depression," Professor Moffat compared the proportions of their budgets spent for different items by the groups examined.[8] From this comparison he concluded that when men curtail their expenditures not only do the proportions of their budget spent for such items as clothing, transportation, contributions, fraternity fees, and incidentals de-

7 The term "organized students" is used throughout the study to refer to members of Greek-letter fraternities and sororities. Non-members are designated as "unorganized students."

8 These 11 items which the student budget was assumed to include were: Food, room, clothing, Contingent fees, books, transportation, medical and dental fees, contributions, recreation, fraternity fees, and incidentals.

crease, but those spent for items for which student costs are fairly stable increase because the total of which they are a part decreases. When women economize the proportions of their budgets spent for food, room rent, contingent fees, and books decrease. Those spent for clothing, medical and dental services, contributions, recreation and incidentals increase and those spent for transportation and fraternity fees remain the same. The latter tendencies suggest that during a depression the amounts spent for the items listed either decrease less or at the same rate as the total expenditure.

Other conclusions reached by Professor Moffat in this study were:

(1) That in depression years men students cut their budgets much more drastically than women.

(2) That the extremes in student expenditures showed only slight variations between 1931 and 1934.

(3) That the reductions in dormitory costs during the depression had helped to lower the living costs of students who took advantage of these changes. (See Table 1, page 22.)

(4) That a large number of students were either partly or wholly dependent on their own financial resources.

(5) That there was good reason to believe that the depression had affected the amount of life insurance carried by students, especially by women.

In 1934-35, the amount of the average, $553.36, showed an increase over the average for 1933-34. The next year, 1935-36, the average dropped back to within eleven cents of the average for the low year, 1933-34.

STUDENT EXPENDITURES 1936-40

In 1936-37, the writer using the methods employed by Professor Moffat, took over the study of student expenditures at the University. In the spring, summer, and early fall of that year business conditions were better than they had been at any time since 1931 and the average total expenditures of all students in the sample for the year increased to $581.89. The next year, 1937-38, in spite of the recession which began in the fall of 1937, the average rose to $630.68.[9] Among the reasons for this rise were the increases in the prices of room and board in the university dormitories and in some of the fraternity chapter houses announced in the spring of 1937 when prices were rising. Prices of clothing were also higher in the fall of 1937 when students were purchasing new clothing for school than at any time since 1931. Several students who were interviewed reported that they came to school in the fall before the decline in business was noticeable and that consequently their spending was in accordance with the upswing that occurred in the earlier months of 1937. It was not until they returned home for the Christmas vacation that they learned of the change in business conditions and began to curtail expenditures. In this same year, the expenditures of NYA students were considered both separately and as a part of those of the student body as a whole.

By 1938-39, prices of several items in the student budget were adjusted in accordance with the declining price level and as a result the average total expenditure for that year dropped to $619.40.[10] The rise in the following year was caused by an increase in the amounts students had to spend rather than by an increase in costs, since the general cost-of-living index showed no increase during the year. The changes in amounts spent occurred in clothing, recreation, refreshments, and cosmetics rather than for fees, room rent, and food.

In 1939-40, the writer revised the questionnaire used for the study and included fourteen headings in the student budget instead of the eleven which had been used prior to that time.[11] The sample included 981 students, or something over one-sixth of the students on the Bloomington campus during the regular

9 Mary M. Crawford, " Student Expenses at Indiana University," *Indiana University News-Letter*, XXVI (Aug., 1938), 2.

10 The United States Bureau of Foreign and Domestic Commerce, *Survey of Current Business*, XXI (May, 1941), 18.

11 These changes involved the inclusion of personal care, laundry and the maintenance of clothing, refreshments, and tobacco, general reading, and the omission of incidentals as a separate item.

academic year. In that year the students had more to spend than in the immediately preceding years, because of generally increased incomes in the state resulting from fuller employment. Their average total expenditure rose to $642.28. The highest individual total expenditure for the year was $1,639.00 by an organized Freshman woman in the College of Arts and Sciences. The lowest amount reported, $209, was spent by an unorganized Freshman woman taking the two-year elective course.

In order to compare the change in student spending from year to year with those found in the Bureau of Labor Statistics index of the cost of goods purchased by wage earners and lower-salaried workers in large cities for the same years the base period for the student index was changed from the single year of 1925-26 to the five year average for 1935-39. A glance at the results shown in the footnote below shows that in general changes in student spending tended to move directly with those in the cost of living but at a more rapid rate.[12] There are several

[12] A COMPARISON OF THE BUREAU OF LABOR STATISTICS COST OF LIVING INDEX WITH THE MOFFAT INDEX OF STUDENT SPENDING, 1925-41 [a]

Year	Index numbers		Percentage by which index numbers rose (+) or fell (−) from year to year	
	Bureau of Labor Statistics [b]	Moffat	Bureau of Labor Statistics Index	Moffat Index
1925-26......	128.2	151.5		
1926-27......	126.1	138.3	− 1.6	− 8.7
1927-28......	123.8	146.4	− 1.8	+ 5.9
1928-29......	122.4	140.9	− 1.1	− 3.8
1929-30......	122.8	145.9	+ 3.3	+ 3.5
1930-31......	115.3	139.3	− 6.1	− 4.5
1931-32......	104.2	121.3	− 9.6	−12.9
1932-33......	93.5	96.8	−10.3	−20.2
1933-34......	93.9	88.6	+ .4	− 8.5
1934-35......	97.0	92.0	+ 3.3	+ 3.8
1935-36......	98.2	88.7	+ 1.2	− 3.6
1936-37......	100.6	96.7	+ 2.4	+ 9.0
1937-38......	102.7	104.9	+ 2.1	+ 8.5
1938-39......	100.0	103.0	− 2.6	− 1.8
1939-40......	100.0	106.8	0.0	+ 3.7
1940-41......	101.0	110.3	+ 1.0	+ 3.3

[a] In this table the weighted means of actual expenditures by students at Indiana University have been turned into relatives on the basis of the average for the years 1935-39 = 100 to make a series comparable to the

reasons for these tendencies in student spending. The retail prices of consumer goods from which the cost of living index is computed change more slowly than wholesale prices, although in general, both move in the same direction. As a result, the incomes of persons employed in producing raw materials and capital goods are affected before the retail prices of consumer goods. Consequently, the rate of change in the incomes of the parents of a large proportion of the students is greater than that in the cost of living index. This is reflected in student spending. In the early thirties, in the trough of the depression, the rate of change in the cost of living was less than in the volume of employment and yearly earnings. This fact together with reductions in the prices of some items in the student budget for which prices ordinarily tended to be fairly rigid accounted for the continued drop in student spending in 1933-34, when the index of the cost of living showed a slight increase.

Professor Moffat's work and its continuation by the writer has provided the background for the present study. But in view of the recent changes in the composition of the student body and the pressures of ten years of financial unsettlement on student spending, it has seemed worth while to appraise the whole problem somewhat more intensively than has as yet been done.

To accomplish the objective of a more thorough and searching study, the schedule used in previous years was revised and expanded in 1940-41 for use in this study. Additional questions were added, designed to obtain information relating to some of the more important factors affecting student consumption and

Bureau of Labor Statistics index of the cost of living set up on that base period. The short method of changing merely the price relatives for the different years as they were affected by the new base average for 1935-39 was used because the original data were not available for some of the years between 1925 and 1936.

b Index of the Cost of Goods Purchased by Wage Earners and Lower-Salaried Workers in Large Cities of the United States (1935-39 = 100). The index numbers in this series for 1925 to 1935 are for December only; that for 1934-35 is an average of the index numbers for November and March of that year. That for 1935-36 is an average of the index numbers for the months of October, January, and April of that year. For the remaining years the figure given in this series is an average of the index numbers for the months of September, December, and March falling within the corresponding academic year.

patterns of spending. For the purpose of securing a stratified random sample, 2820 schedules were distributed to students in all major groupings and all schools of the University in the manner described in Appendix A. Of these, 1389, or 49 per cent of the schedules distributed, were answered and returned. When these were checked for inaccuracies, inconsistencies, and unreasonableness as judged by standards established by personal interviews and when the schedules of married and graduate students had been discarded, 1275 schedules remained to become the basis of this study. These represented 29.04 per cent of the undergraduates enrolled on the Bloomington campus. Further details relating to the methodology of the study are given in Appendix A.

PURPOSE OF THE STUDY

Since a college population consists of young men and women coming to college from communities of different sizes, of members of four academic classes with different orientations to college life, and of persons living in fraternities, sororities, dormitories, and in other types of dwellings the emphasis associated with each of these variables invites analysis. The purpose of this study is therefore to find the answers to questions such as the following:

1. How does average total expenditure vary for students grouped according to these several variables?

2. How does the detail of expenditure within the total vary?

3. What kinds of expenditure show relatively more and relatively less elasticity with increases in the total amount spent?

4. Why do the differences apparent from the three preceding steps of analysis occur?

5. And, lastly, how does the student budget differ from that of single persons in general?

Although the study is concerned primarily with statistics related to student spending, the importance of interpreting the numerical findings has not been overlooked. Variations in spending not only reflect differences in social and economic background but also in personalities and in the immediate problems with which individual students are confronted. Between the sexes there are certain broad differences affecting spending. Expenditures of women are undoubtedly influenced by the fact that many of them are preparing for careers in teaching and for secretarial positions in which personal appearance will play an important part in their success. Many also are thinking quite directly about getting married. The men face the intermediate hurdle before marriage of getting a job and " making good ". But even within these broad sex lines there are big individual differences. Some come from socially ambitious homes where " front " is stressed; some are personally attractive and others handicapped in this respect. There are social canons which the timid struggle to meet and the bold may disregard. In each student is found a unique pattern of stresses and strains which causes him to use his money to try to ease such strains and bolster security. In the chapters which follow an attempt has been made to enrich the statistical material with an interpretation from this broader point of view and to present some of the folkways which affect student spending.

CHAPTER II
TOTAL EXPENDITURES BY ALL STUDENTS AND BY GROUPS

BEFORE proceeding to an analysis of the expenditures for the principal categories into which the student budget is divided, it seems desirable to present an over-all picture of the total expenditures of all the students in the sample and for the principal sub-groups into which the student body may be divided. The significance of variation in expenditures on different parts of the budget by the different groups, for example, will vary with the size of the totals, medians or quartiles of the groups. Such over-all figures are presented in this chapter.

A summary picture of all items in the student budget, the median and quartile expenditures for all students in the sample and for the various component groups are shown in Table 2. The total amounts reported represent the sum of the expenditures listed under the fourteen general categories into which the student budget was divided. These were: rent, food, clothing, personal care, laundry, recreation, refreshments, university fees, textbooks, organization dues, transportation, health, contributions and gifts, and general reading. In the chapters which follow, expenditures for these are considered separately. As may be seen from the table, the groups into which the students in the sample were classified for the purpose of analysis were those according to their sex, whether or not they belonged to a Greek-letter organization, the college class of which they were a member, the school in the University in which they were enrolled, and the type of home community from which they came. In Chapters 3 to 9 inclusive, where the relative amounts spent by these different groups for individual items in the student budget are considered, both the absolute amounts and the proportions of the budget they represent are presented. In the last chapter, these amounts are brought together to show the patterns of spending characteristic of different student groups.

TABLE 2

THE MEDIAN AND QUARTILE AMOUNTS SPENT FOR ALL ITEMS IN THE
STUDENT BUDGET BY GROUPS OF STUDENTS AT INDIANA
UNIVERSITY, 1940-41 [a]

Group	Number of Students	First Quartile	Median	Third Quartile
All students	1275	$514.89	$673.06	$842.83
All men	586	519.58	657.47	799.55
All women	689	509.25	687.63	825.94
Organized men	205	706.63	818.97	977.08
Unorganized men	381	492.59	593.69	745.19
Organized women	236	735.63	873.86	1037.80
Unorganized women	453	455.34	577.27	748.39
Freshmen	446	528.38	693.65	847.06
Sophomores	323	491.39	634.52	832.14
Juniors	291	509.04	673.75	870.65
Seniors	215	533.55	681.43	870.65
College of Arts and Sciences	482	523.58	714.75	906.25
School of Business	519	520.59	663.64	798.33
School of Dentistry	2		650.00	
School of Education	159	472.00	644.44	807.69
School of Law	9	554.17	687.50	795.83
School of Medicine	57	775.00	950.00	1212.50
School of Music	38	543.75	660.00	816.67
Students from farms	351	448.48	570.00	751.60
Students from small towns	400	544.93	786.42	863.41
Students from cities	383	552.46	750.00	892.86

[a] More detailed figures relating to total expenditures and the means for some of the groups in this table are shown in Table 75, page 241, in Appendix A.

An inspection of Table 2 discloses that for the 1275 students in the sample the median total expenditure for the regular two-semester academic year of 1940-41 was $673.06. One fourth of the students spent less than $514.89 and another fourth more than $842.83.

MEN AND WOMEN

The over-all cost of the year at college in 1940-41 for the median man was $657.47 or about $30 less than for the median woman. When forced to curtail expenses, the women are able to reduce their expenses more than men, probably because they can provide more services such as laundry, meals in their rooms, and hair trims. Besides being able to have " dates " without involving any expense to them, they are usually more frequently able to find work, which provides their meals. But, on the other hand, if the woman student has the money to spend, she probably spends more than the similarly affluent man student. Thus we see that although the median over-all expenditure of the women students is greater than that of the men, it is also the women who are able to reduce and expand their expenditures the most when it becomes necessary or possible for them to do so. Their demand for at least some of the items in the student budget is more elastic than that of the men.

ORGANIZED AND UNORGANIZED STUDENTS

The greater amount spent by the organized students is explained largely by the fact that these students had more to spend rather than by greater direct costs resulting from their membership in a Greek-letter organization. The amounts below which a quarter of the organized men and women reduced their total expenditures show that some economy is possible for these men and women. It will be noted, however, that the first quartile expenditures of both groups are greater than the median amount spent by either all women or all men in the sample.

In general the fraternity and sorority members are the pacesetters on the campus in dress and social activities. Desire of leadership and the fear of lessening the reputation of the organization to which they belong which holds a reputation for having well dressed members account for the larger expenditures for dress and personal appearance by some members. Heavy social schedules also affect their expenditures for these items and for recreation and refreshments.

TOTAL EXPENDITURES AS RELATED TO LIVING ARRANGEMENTS

The figures in Table 3 give additional evidence of the greater total expenditures of the organized students. Those living in university dormitories, who include Freshman women pledged to sororities, spend less than the students living in Greek-letter chapter houses but more than students living elsewhere in Bloomington. Since some economy in the expenditure for rent is usually effected by living at home or with other relatives while in college, the total expenditures of the students who have this type of living arrangement give little indication of their economic status. The men and women who live in private homes spend more than those living in student rooming houses. As is to be expected, the students who work for their rooms spend the least. The widest variation in spending is found among the organized students.

TABLE 3

MEDIAN TOTAL ANNUAL EXPENDITURE OF 1068 INDIANA UNIVERSITY
STUDENTS AS RELATED TO THEIR LIVING ARRANGEMENTS
IN BLOOMINGTON, 1940-41 [a]

Type of Dwelling	Number in Sample	First Quartile Expenditure	Median Expenditure	Third Quartile Expenditure
University dormitory ...	453	$561.49	$707.37	$ 845.37
Sorority	143	736.46	866.13	1025.00
Fraternity	136	729.17	854.84	995.24
With Relatives	15	391.67	551.00	675.00
Student Rooming House	144	428.89	509.30	593.02
Private Home	157	446.02	528.72	645.59
Room in Exchange for Work	19	395.00	475.00	581.25

[a] Two hundred and seven of the students failed to indicate where they lived while attending the University.

EXPENDITURES BY COLLEGE CLASSES

The figures in Table 2 show that the median total expenditure in 1940-41 of the Freshmen in the sample was greater than for the members of any of the other college classes. This was largely because of the purchase of new clothing and supplies made by students leaving home for the first time. The expenses incurred by the " rush week " for the women interested in sorority membership and the pledge and initiation fees paid by all Freshmen who joined Greek-letter organizations also helped to raise the median amount spent by the Freshmen. The Sophomores spent the least of any of the four classes, probably largely because the purchases made at the beginning of their Freshman year could still be used the next year. Except for the relatively few Sophomores initiated into Greek-letter societies, there are no exceptional expenses for fraternity and sorority members during their second year in college. The social programs of the Sophomores are usually less full than those of the members of Junior and Senior classes. Seniors spent more than Juniors because of expenses incurred by social and academic events related to their last year in college. There was relatively less variation in the amounts reported by the Freshmen and Juniors than in those of the members of the other two classes.

SCHOOLS IN THE UNIVERSITY

There was no evidence in the sample studied of any marked tendency for either organized or unorganized students to attend any of the schools of the University in disproportionate numbers or of sharp differences in the economic status of the students enrolled in the different schools. In the professional schools such as Law, Medicine and Business there are as might be expected more men than women, since, as a rule, only the specially gifted women are interested in preparation for a lifetime of intensive professional work. The majority of the women who expect to work when they leave college think of such work as lasting over the relatively short period between graduation and marriage. Those who become engaged while in college often want jobs so that they can save for marriage as their fiancés do. The women who choose to marry as soon as they are graduated frequently seek training in college which will enable them to help their husbands either in further professional preparation or in getting established in business. Since in our pattern of culture the man in the family is expected to provide the bulk of the family income, it is more often the men students who are the most interested in specific kinds of training which will prepare them to assume that responsibility.

The women who come to college for reasons other than strictly academic ones are found most frequently in the College of Arts and Sciences. These include girls who feel no economic pressure to work between college and marriage, and those who come to the University for special training as laboratory assistants, home economists or some other definite type of career. The men in this school include those whose parents can afford to give them four years of undergraduate cultural training before they start professional training of some kind. There are also those who are forced to skimp along or work their way through college while they major in such fields as chemistry or physics in the hope of preparing themselves for jobs which promise greater economic security for the future.

There are more men than women in the School of Business, but the difference is not as great as in the Schools of Medicine, Law and Dentistry. This is because courses are offered in secretarial work, a field in which women have been very successful and one in which they can receive training for the kind of a job which bridges between college and marriage. In addition, work is offered in personnel training, retailing, and other fields suited to the abilities and interests of women students. The men include not only the sons of industrialists who are sent for training in business administration so that they may enter their father's businesses, but also men who must depend in the future entirely upon their own ability and training to earn a living.

In the sample of students from the School of Education there were noticeably more unorganized men than organized but the difference between the women was not pronounced. As might be expected, there were also more women than men.

The students in the Schools of Law, Medicine, and Dentistry are predominantly men because these fields are traditionally those of men, and also because women are less interested in preparing themselves for lifetime careers. Once the students are admitted to these schools they tend to move out of their chapter houses, if they are organized, to avoid the distractions of group living.

Talent is probably the most important determinant of enrollment in the School of Music. The number of students from this school as in the case of the Schools of Medicine, Law, and Dentistry was too small to provide any basis for generalizing regarding the proportions of organized and unorganized students found in each. In the sample used the numbers of each were roughly comparable.

The median expenditure of the students in the School of Medicine was the largest and that of students in the School of Education the smallest. The greatest variation in spending shown in Table 2 was among the students in the School of Medicine and the least among the Law students.

STUDENTS FROM FARMS, SMALL TOWNS, AND CITIES

The total expenditures of the students in the sample were also examined to see if the type of community from which the student came affected his spending. The results shown in Table 2 indicate that they did. Students from farms at all economic levels spent consistently less than those from small towns or cities; a fact largely explained by the nature of the farm land and size of many of the farms in Indiana, especially in the southern part of the state. Another explanation is the tendency for families living on farms in Indiana to be somewhat larger than those in other types of communities. Half of these students spent less than $570, an amount only slightly greater than the top expenditures of the lowest one fourth in each of the other two groups. The lowest expenditure of the most extravagant fourth of these students fell between the median amounts spent by students in the other two groups. Of the latter that of students from small towns was the greater. Students from cities showed the greatest variation in their spending and those from farms the least. The modal expenditure of students from farms was $467.30, from small towns $749.58, and from cities $649.58.[1]

1 See Appendix A, page 236 for formula used in computing modes.

STUDENTS WHO EARN PART OR ALL OF THEIR EXPENSES

Fifty-nine per cent of the 1275 students in the sample for 1940-41 earned a part or all of their college expenses. This percentage showed an increase over 1939-40 and 1938-39 when the respective percentages of students who helped to finance their own expenses were 44.5 and 46.9 per cent.[2] All three of these percentages were larger than the 40 per cent shown in the sample for 1933-34, the year for which the index of student spending was the lowest for any of the years studied.[3]

Some of the students who pay their own expenses work while in high school and save their earnings. Others work only during summer vacations. The majority, however, are employed while attending the University, some by the University and others by residents of Bloomington. A few play in orchestras and occasionally travel from place to place to play for dances. A few students return to their home towns on Saturday to work.

A study of the kinds of work done by the university students in Bloomington in 1937-38 showed that approximately one-fourth of the students who worked were employed in restaurants, where they acted as cashiers, cooks, waiters and dishwashers. The kinds of services performed by students in retail establishments included those of clerks, stockkeepers, window decorators, bookkeepers, delivery men and janitors. The kinds of work done by men students in private homes included taking care of a furnace, a garden or a lawn, cleaning, and staying with children at night. Women students cleaned, waited table, cooked, washed dishes, and took care of children.

2 In 1939-40 approximately one of every seven students or 16.3 percent of the sample earned all expenses without any assistance from home. Thirty-two percent of the students in the sample worked while attending the University and nearly 27 percent had worked during the preceding summer vacation. Crawford, *Indiana University News-Letter*, XXVIII (1940), 12 and Crawford, *Indiana University News-Letter*, XXVI (1938), 7.

3 Moffat, *Indiana University News-Letter*, XXII (1934), 5.

THE NATIONAL RESOURCES COMMITTEE STUDY OF THE BUDGETS
OF SINGLE MEN AND WOMEN

In the chapters which follow comparisons are made between student expenditures for individual items in their budgets and the similar expenditures of the single men and women whose budgets were studied by the National Resources Committee.[4] In making these comparisons, however, it is necessary to keep in mind certain important differences in the nature of the data, the methodology, and in the categories into which the budgets are divided in the two studies.

Among the principal ways in which the study of the single men and women, hereafter referred to as the National Resources Committee Study, differs from that of student spending are the coverage of a twelve-month period rather than the nine-month period of the regular two-semester academic year, a wider range in the ages of the men and women in the sample, the use of income data as a basis for classification, greater diversification in the types of communities in which the individuals spend their money, and more varied patterns of living. As might be expected, a larger proportion of the single women in the National Resources Committee Study kept house and prepared their own meals. In the main, the categories of items included in the budgets were the same. Expenditures for automobiles and for tobacco are treated separately in the National Resources Committee Study. University fees and textbooks which are treated separately in the student budget are relatively much more important than the items included under education in the budgets of the single men and women. Organization dues are uniquely important in the student budget. In the budgets of the single men and women, amounts saved and spent for gifts and personal taxes were shown as percentages of total income rather than as proportions of the income spent for the main categories

4 The National Resources Committee. *Consumer Expenditures in the United States* (Washington: Government Printing Office, 1939), pp. 31-43, 81-108. The study was made with the assistance of the Works Progress Administration from data collected by the Bureau of Labor Statistics and the Bureau of Home Economics.

of consumption. Because of the different means by which they were obtained, the writer has felt that a comparison of the absolute amounts of the average expenditures of the single men and women with the median amounts spent by the students would have little significance. For this reason the comparisons in the following chapters are limited almost entirely to those of the proportions of the respective budgets spent for individual items. For, although these percentages are also affected by the differences in methods used in obtaining them, they seem to have some value as a basis for determining the relative importance of the different types of expenditures in the budgets of students as compared with those of single men and women in general. They also throw some light on the answer to the question of whether the same differences in the expenditures of men and women are found among students as may be expected among all single men and women.

The only comparison between the over-all expenditures of the men and women in the two studies that seemed worth while was that of the relative amounts spent by men and women. As shown above, the women students, except for those in the lower quartile, spent more than the men. In the National Resources Committee Study, the single men spent more than the women, probably because their expenditures based upon income depended largely on their own earnings which one would expect to be somewhat larger than those of women. Much of the incomes of the students came from their parents and therefore did not vary between the men and women in relation to their earning capacities.[5]

SUMMARY

The examination of the total annual expenditures of the students at the University shows a wide range and suggests that while some students have no real financial worries, others are continuously faced with the problem of making ends meet and

5 *Ibid.*, pp. 81-83.

are forced to skimp along on less than is needed to provide them with a balanced diet and comfortable living quarters.

The median student in the sample spent $673.06, an amount which was sufficient to provide a comfortable level of living. Women students in general spent more in the aggregate than the men, although among the unorganized students the men spent more. Among the students in the four college classes the Sophomores spent the least. The median student in the School of Education spent less than the students in similar positions in the other schools. Farm students spent less than those from small towns or cities. Men and women who earned none of their own expenses and who obviously came from families in the upper income brackets naturally spent more than those who felt called upon to earn a part or all of their college expenses. The students who received NYA asistance spent the least of any of the groups who paid any portion of their expenses. The total amounts spent also varied among the students living in different types of residences while attending college.

In the chapters which follow, the amounts spent for individual categories in the student budget by the different groups are examined to see how they differ in relation to their total expenditures. The first category examined is that of rent which is discussed in Chapter III.

CHAPTER III
HOUSING

SINCE choice of living quarters plays such an important part in determining patterns and levels of student spending, it has seemed logical to give first consideration to housing expenditures, even though they do not constitute the largest item in the student budget. At Indiana, as at other universities, the students live in a variety of dwelling places. In 1940-41 these included the four university dormitories for women and three for men, listed in Table 4. There were also twenty-one fraternity and eighteen sorority chapter houses, besides a large number of private homes and student rooming houses.[1] In addition, a few students live in small apartments, in hotels, and at the Indiana Memorial Union Building.[2]

TABLE 4

MEN'S AND WOMEN'S DORMITORIES AT INDIANA UNIVERSITY, 1940-41

Women's Dormitories [a]		Men's Dormitories [b]	
Name	Women Housed	Name	Men Housed
Beech Hall [c]	110	North Hall	157
Forest Hall [d]	140	South Hall	92
Memorial Hall	203	West Hall	136
Sycamore Hall	223		
Total	676		385

[a] Dargan House, the dormitory for negro women, is privately owned.

[b] The men's dormitories form the Men's Residence Center.

[c] The name of this dormitory was changed in 1942 to Sarah Park Morrison Hall.

[d] Forest Hall is a coöperative dormitory where each girl takes care of her own room and does a small amount of office work. It does not furnish board.

1 The number of students living in these houses ranged from 9 in one sorority house to 84 in one fraternity house.

2 Only students who work in hotels usually live there while attending the University.

Students differ in their attitudes toward the desirability of different types of housing. The importance to a student of living in a fraternity or sorority house, which is, in a sense, an invitational dormitory, is determined largely by the early conditioning of the student and by his individual interests. The university ruling, effective in the fall of 1940, requiring all Freshman women to live in university dormitories unless excused by the Dean of Women, practically eliminated any question as to where these students live. By the end of the sorority " Rush Week " in September, the majority of Freshmen women know whether they will live in a sorority house or elsewhere during their remaining years at college.[3] After Freshman year the girls pledged to sororities move into their chapter houses, and non-members remain at the dormitories or move to private homes or student rooming houses. Whether or not they leave the dormitories depends largely on such things as whether there is room for them to remain, their financial status, their reaction to group living, and whether they prefer to take their meals at places patronized by men or where they can order *à la carte*.

Fraternity rushing tends to be less formal than that of the sororities, and fraternity Freshmen may live in the chapter houses. Since its opening in the fall of 1940, the new Men's Residence Center, which consists of two new dormitories, North and West Halls, and South Hall, a remodeled one, has become increasingly popular as a campus center of activities for unorganized men in all four college classes. It especially attracts students who either themselves or whose parents recognize the need for balanced meals at regular hours and the social benefits

3 In 1940-41 a period known as " Rush Week " directly preceded the opening of school in the fall. Freshman girls who desired to join a sorority came to the University at that time and lived at one of the university halls where they paid their own expenses. During that period the rushees lived according to instructions laid down by the Panhellenic Association of Indiana University. Before participating in " Rush Week " each girl had to deposit $25 at the Comptroller's Office. Two days before the opening of the University the sororities announced the names of their pledges. The quotas of new members that the sororities could take usually prevented them from pledging all of the girls who came for " Rush Week."

derived from group living. The men who wish to economize on room rent or prefer to eat where they choose and live alone or in smaller groups take rooms in private homes or in regular student rooming houses.

In the following analysis of what different groups of students at Indiana spent for room rent, the amounts spent will be considered in relation to the variables that affect them, such as the relative costs of different types of living quarters, their desirability from the point of view of social attractiveness, the economic status and academic interests of the student, and the kind of community from which he came. But, first before the effect of any of these variables is discussed, the median and quartile expenditures of all of the students in the sample are presented.

EXPENDITURES OF ALL STUDENTS

The median expenditure for room rent in 1940-41 by the 1275 undergraduates in the sample was $110.62 for the school year.[4] This amounted to $55.31 per semester, or $3.07 for each of the 36 weeks in the regular academic year.[5] The interquartile range in the annual amounts spent for rent by all students in the sample in that year was from $94.97 to $144.66. Reduced to a weekly basis this range was from $2.63 to $4.02. Beyond the third quartile the annual expenditures centered around $180 and $200, sums which amounted to $5.00 and $5.55 respectively per week. Only a few expenditures for rent grouped around $72 for the year, which meant a weekly payment of $2. The lowest individual estimate turned in which could be verified was for $54 per year or $1.50 per week. When the expenditures were thrown into a frequency distribution using intervals of $10, the modal interval was $90-99, which indicated a modal weekly expenditure of between $2.50 and $2.75.

4 This yearly expenditure was greater than $106.71, the median amount in 1939-40, because the number of students living in the dormitories had increased rather than because of any general increase in the rents of rooms occupied by students in 1939-40.

5 For the mean and median amounts and the proportion of their budgets spent by all students in the sample and by groups within the sample see Table 76, page 242.

TABLE 5

MEDIAN ANNUAL EXPENDITURES FOR ROOM RENT OF 1275 INDIANA
UNIVERSITY STUDENTS BY TOTAL EXPENDITURE
LEVELS FOR 1940-41

Total Expenditure	Number in Sample	Median Expenditure for Room Rent
$ 200– 399	156	$ 92.18
400– 599	459	93.74
600– 799	237	107.46
800– 999	261	139.44
1000–1199	108	140.00
1200–1399	37	153.56
1400–1599	7	150.00
1600–1799	8	145.00
1800–1999	1	——
2000–2199	2	——

No data relating to student incomes were available, so the
student's aggregate disbursement, referred to in this study as
his total expenditure, was used as a means of designating his
relative economic status. As shown in Table 5, the median
amount spent for room rent changed relatively little as total expenditures increased from $200 to $600. As the total amount
spent moved between $600 and $1000, the sum spent for room
rent rose somewhat more rapidly; but after the total expenditure
reached $1000, the rise in the expenditure for rent was almost
negligible. Regardless of the income of the student, the amount
spent for room rent tends to increase more slowly than his total
expenditure and finally reaches an upper limit beyond which
there is little if any increase. Thus we see that the expenditure
for rent is a relatively less important item in the budget of the
student whose total expenditure is large than in that of the student who spends less. What the student spends for his room at
college depends largely on where he wants to live. Since he
usually prefers to live with young people of his own age, his
rent is determined by the rate charged at the place of his choice.
At most types of residences occupied by students the rents tend
toward uniformity for all students regardless of what the individual student may be able to pay. This tendency is particularly

true at fraternity and sorority houses where choice of the larger rooms depends upon class in college and seniority in membership rather than upon what a member is willing to pay. At the dormitories, the variation is somewhat greater because of the greater variety in the types of accommodation offered. In these residence halls, the charge per occupant in a small double room is the least and that for one of the very limited number of suites of two small rooms with a connecting bath or living room is the highest. In private homes and student rooming houses the prices for different types of accommodation tend to be customary prices that are usually uniform for all students who share double rooms.

For the average student at Indiana University the proportion of the budget spent for room rent was 17 per cent. It should be kept in mind, however, that the student budget differs from the family budget in that it includes no direct outlays for fuel, light, or refrigeration. Whether the student pays for the use of a telephone, water, iron and ironing board, and radio, depends on the type of residence in which he lives.[6]

MEN AND WOMEN

Next, the expenditures for rent by the 586 men and 689 women in the sample were compared to see which sex spent the more. The annual median amounts and interquartile ranges of these two groups were:

Group	Number in Sample	First Quartile	Median	Third Quartile
Men	586	$91.90	$106.58	$143.27
Women	689	97.17	119.83	145.31

As may be seen from these figures, women spent more in 1940-41 for rent than men. The median amount spent by the men was about $4 less than that paid by all students in the sample, while that spent by the women was $9.20 more. This difference between the expenditures of men and women is largely

6 Dormitory students are permitted to have telephones in their rooms, if they pay an extra charge.

explained by the greater proportion of women students living in the dormitories. Other reasons were the greater importance to women of privacy and appearances and the greater safety afforded by living near the campus where rent is usually some-what higher than at dwellings further away.

The median expenditures of men and women living in differ-ent types of dwellings at Indiana University in 1940-41 are shown n Table 6.

TABLE 6

MEDIAN ANNUAL EXPENDITURES FOR RENT BY MEN AND WOMEN
LIVING IN DIFFERENT TYPES OF RESIDENCE AT INDIANA
UNIVERSITY, 1940-41

Type of Residence	Men		Women	
	Number in Sample	Median	Number in Sample	Median
University Dormitories	142	$147.50	399	$138.47 [a]
Greek-Letter Chapter Houses ..	142	123.00	149	126.29 [b]
Private Homes	166	97.10	37	104.78
Student Rooming Houses	107	90.18	73	99.08
All Other Places [c]	29	—	31	—
All Students	586	106.58	689	119.83

[a] The estimates of amounts spent for rent by women living in dormi-tories included those of students who live at Forest Hall, the coöperative dormitory.

[b] The estimates from which this median was computed did not include those of the Freshman pledgees who lived in the dormitories.

[c] This group includes students who commute, whose homes are in Bloom-ington and who live with relatives.

Expenditures for rent represented 16.8 per cent of the men's budget and 17.1 per cent of the women's. The fact that the men spent a smaller proportion of their budget for rent corresponds with the findings of the National Resources Committee. Their study showed that single men spent 23.0 per cent of their budget for rent and single women 26.1 per cent.[7] Both of these propor-tions are larger than those spent by the university students whose budgets cover nine months rather than twelve covered by those of the single persons studied by the National Resources Committee.

7 The National Resources Committee. *Consumer Expenditures in the United States*, pp. 82-83.

UNIVERSITY DORMITORIES

In 1940-41, the number of men and women students living in university dormitories was greatly increased by the opening of two new buildings for men and two for women. As a result of these additions, 676 women students and 385 men were housed in residences of this kind. For the first time, the total number of students at Indiana who lived in university dormitories was greater than that of students living in Greek-letter chapter houses.

In general the rents charged by the University for rooms of similar types in the men's and women's dormitories were the same. The rate per person in a small double room was $2.50, in a regular double room $4.04 per person, and for a single room $5.50.[8] The median annual expenditure for rent by the 318 women in the sample who lived in dormitories was $133.14 per year, an amount about $4 less than the median expenditure of the 137 men housed in the Men's Residence Center. In terms of weekly payments these women paid $3.75 for rent and the men $3.81.

In Sycamore and Beech Halls, the two newest dormitories for women, the rooms are provided with maple furniture of early American design. Each student in a double room has her own bed, desk, study lamp, chest of drawers, chairs and clothes closet. The occupant of a single room has similar furniture and all residents are supplied with an inner-spring mattress, bedspread, draperies, and rug. The wood work in the rooms is white and the walls a pastel shade. Lavatories between double rooms are shared by the four occupants of the adjoining rooms. In Memorial and Forest Halls the furnishings are similar but in the double rooms the allotment of furniture per occupant is not so complete as in the newer dormitories.

At Forest Hall, the coöperative dormitory for women which houses about 140 students, double rooms rent for $90 for each girl per year, or $2.50 a week. No meals are served in this

8 Of the 676 women housed in the dormitories, only 60 occupied single rooms.

dormitory and the rates for rooms do not include bed linen or maid service. Here, each resident is expected to take her turn at answering the telephone, announcing guests, or performing other work at the front desk.[9]

At the two new dormitories for men, West Hall and North Hall, the rates for suites and for double and single rooms are the same as at Sycamore, Beech and Memorial Halls. At South Hall, the oldest residence for men, the rate for a place in a double room is $90 per year, or $2.50 per week, and in a single room $126 per year, or $3.50 per week. The rates for both men and women include maid service for cleaning the rooms, bed linen, and one blanket. Dresser scarfs and towels are provided by the students. The rooms in the men's dormitories are as completely equipped as those in the women's dormitories. In the newer halls each man is provided with an individual study lamp, a large study table, a chair, a bookcase, a chest of drawers, and a mirror.

In spite of the similarity of the rooms in the university halls, variations in the tastes and habits of the students who occupy them are evident. Even in a double room differences can be seen. The bed, bureau, and desk on one side of the room may be extremely neat in contrast to the other half of the room, which may be fairly weighted down with trappings of various descriptions or strewn with garments that have been shed and left lying on the floor and furniture.

In general, women students make a more positive attempt to make their rooms attractive than do men. This tendency is also somewhat greater among dormitory students and those living in chapter houses than among those in private homes and student rooming houses, where the owner of the house frequently supplies pictures and the walls are covered with figured wallpaper. There is also some difference among the students in the differ-

9 In a study made in 1937-38, the writer found that the mean total expenditure for the year of thirty-six, or about one-fourth, of the students at Forest Hall was $531.46 and that of fifty-four, or approximately one-fourth, of the students living at Memorial Hall $659.20.

ent classes. From year to year, students accumulate a variety of possessions which they use to decorate their rooms. Moreover, as upperclassmen some students feel some responsibility for making their rooms look more impressive than they did as Freshmen. On the other hand, the parents and older sisters of students sometimes derive a vicarious satisfaction from planning and actually purchasing additional furnishings for members of their family entering college. As a rule, it is the Freshman women who work for part of their college expenses who decorate their rooms least. Some of the most attractive and popular women students have relatively plain rooms, however, because they are too busy in campus activities to give as much attention to decorating their rooms as the girls who go out less.

In general, the girls who have to economize are more ingenious in making their rooms attractive than those who have more money to spend. In Forest Hall, the coöperative dormitory, a number of girls buy used orange crates for ten cents which they cover with gay colored materials to use for hassocks. They also make many of their pillows and chair covers and bed spreads. A check of the girls living in Forest Hall indicated that the girls from small towns showed the greatest tendency to make things for their rooms. The estimates of amounts spent at the University in 1940-41 for decorating rooms ranged from $1.50 to $20.00.

It also seems worthy of comment that of all the girls who live in dormitories, those in Forest Hall, the coöperative residence, tend to take the best care of the furniture and keep their rooms in the best order. Students living in the other dormitories commented on the way the furnishings in those buildings were abused. One of these girls declared, " It is a positive shame the way the furniture here is treated." This abuse is particularly evident in the smoking rooms.

Fads play a more important part in room decorations among women than among men. Several girls have extensive collections of miniature animals or figures or small pots of plants. Others have their chests of drawers crowded with cosmetics or

arrays of perfume bottles. The more socially-minded have collections of photographs, dance programs, favors, and other sou-
venirs. Some bring familiar possessions from home, such as dolls
or stuffed animals. Girls who have no old toys often acquire
new felt or leather animals in college colors after they come to
the University. In general, the men bring fewer possessions
from home than the women students. Any collections they have
usually consist of such items as pipes, signs, or athletic trophies.

One particular advantage offered by the dormitories is the
part they play in the social life of unorganized students. They
provide dining rooms and drawing rooms in which these students can entertain friends and faculty members in a way comparable to that of members of Greek-letter chapter houses, who
are the social pace-setters on the campus. Besides several small
and less formal rooms in each of the women's dormitories where
women students can entertain their " dates," there is a large
recreational room similar to those found in most of the chapter
houses, where couples can dance or listen to phonograph records
or a radio. In the rooms of the latter type there are usually also
ping-pong tables and soft-drink vendors. The facilities for entertaining in the men's dormitories are very similar to those in
the women's halls.

Other services, comparable to those provided by most of the
Greek-letter chapter houses, which are offered by the dormitories without additional charge are the use of hot plates for
making tea and candy, and the use of electric irons and ironing
boards. In addition, the women's dormitories now provide electric washing machines and hair dryers, which are found in only
a few sorority houses.

The only noticeable variation in rent paid by the dormitory
students belonging to different academic classes was that the
Junior and Senior women tended to spend less probably because as underclassmen they had had an opportunity to find out
which of the low-priced rooms were best and to take steps to
secure them.

The reason for the difference in the median amounts spent by the men and women students is the inclusion among the expenditures of women of the lower rents paid by students living in Forest Hall, the coöperative dormitory, rather than lower amounts paid by the students living in dormitories of the same types as those occupied by the men.

As shown in Table 7, 746 men and 391 women lived in Greek-letter chapter houses in 1940-41. The majority of organized students living in chapter houses but not all of them. For the sake of economy, convenience, or of studying without interruption, almost a third of the fraternity men and a slightly smaller proportion of sorority women take rooms outside their chapter houses, usually in the dormitories or in private homes. Only comparatively few of these students live in student rooming houses.

TABLE 7

PLACE OF RESIDENCE OF THE TOTAL NUMBER OF UNDERGRADUATE MEMBERS
OF THE 18 SORORITIES AND 21 FRATERNITIES ENROLLED AT
INDIANA UNIVERSITY IN 1940-41 [a]

Place of Residence	Number of Men	Percentage of all Fraternity Men	Percentage of all Men	Number of Women	Percentage of all Sorority Women	Percentage of all Women
Chapter House	746	67.82	26.62	391	61.19	24.64
Outside Bloomington	13	1.18	.46			
Out in Town .	300	27.27	10.71	93	14.54	5.86
Dormitory ...	41	3.73	1.46	155	24.26	9.19
Total	1100	100.0	39.26	639	100.0	40.26

[a] This table was computed from the Registrar's figures for the total enrollment of undergraduate students for the regular school year 1940-41.

At the chapter houses, groups of two or three members may share a small study during the day time and sleep in a common sleeping room with the rest of the chapter. Usually the chapter president is expected to sleep in his own room, although sometimes other students move beds from the fraternity dormitory to their own rooms. As has been previously suggested, the right of privacy and uncrowded quarters is a perquisite of seniority in chapter membership rather than a consequence of paying more. This does not mean, however, that the members of all fraternities pay the same amounts. They do not. Costs at any single fraternity or sorority depend on such things as the number of members and whether or not the organization owns its house or leases it. If the organization is in the process of buying a house, the rent charged members is affected by the plan adopted for financing the purchase, the amount still owed, and the contributions of alumni members.

In recent years the number of national organizations having chapters on the campus at the University has increased. In the Middle West, at least, among both fraternity and sorority members, a pretentious chapter house is an important prestige symbol. Since the early twenties the race for preëminence in this respect has gone on not only between chapters on a single campus but even between chapters of the same organization at different universities. The correlation between the pretentiousness of a house and high rent paid by its members is not necessarily close, because gifts from wealthy alumni and parents sometimes help a chapter to pay for expensive property. As a consequence, rents at an impressive mansion-like chapter house with a large membership and no debts may be lower than at some of the fraternity houses where the members live more simply. But, on the other hand, a chapter having a large membership can lease low-rent property and reduce the rent charged its members to relatively small amounts. It is such differences as these that explain the range in the amounts paid for rent by the members of different Greek-letter organizations.

At a fraternity or sorority chapter house, students get more for the rent they pay than just the right to occupy a room or sleep in a common bedroom. They have the use of attractively furnished social and recreational rooms where they can entertain guests and with others act as hosts for dances and parties given by the chapter. Alumni as well as active members of the local chapter give considerable thought to the furnishings of the chapter houses, which as a result provide an impressive social background for their members. This fact, together with the satisfaction derived from the social prestige gained from " being organized," more than overbalances in the mind of the typical organized student any discomfort caused by living in a crowded room lacking privacy.

In 1940-41, the organized students averaged $128.72 for the year, or $3.57 per week for rent. When these amounts were compared with the expenditures of unorganized students, it was found that the median amount spent by the unorganized students was about $25 less per year or 75 cents per week less than the organized. The median amounts spent by both groups and the interquartile ranges of each of these groups are shown below :

Group	Number in Sample	Percentage of Students	First Quartile	Median	Third Quartile
Organized Students [a] ...	441	34.33	$104.66	$128.72	$151.80
Unorganized Students [b] ...	834	65.67	92.83	103.36	142.15

[a] Member of sororities and fraternities.
[b] Non-members of sororities and fraternities.

The median expenditure of 142 men in the sample who lived in fraternity houses in 1940-41 was $123.00 for the year. The first quartile expenditure was $102.19, and the third quartile $154.17. These amounts tend to be slightly less than similar figures for the 149 sorority members, which amounted to $126.29 for the median and $104.54 and $153.13 respectively for the first and third quartiles. The yearly rents charged sorority members ranged from $90.00 to $180.00, amounts practically the same as those paid by fraternity members. As has been explained above, the variations shown in the interquartile ranges of both fraternity and sorority members are probably largely accounted for by differences in the plans used for financing the respective organizations rather than entirely by a greater emphasis on pretentious buildings and furnishings or a demand on the part of the members for comfortable rooms and greater privacy. The larger median expenditure for rent by sorority women than by the fraternity men is probably explained by the greater stress on furnishings and appearances by women, and greater funded debts of some of their organizations. The latter situation arises because in our culture the man in the family usually controls the purse. Membership in a fraternity, if it appears strong, may be a positive business asset. It also provides social advantages and a place to return to when attending football games or other athletic events at the University. For these reasons men will often give $50 or $100 to their fraternity even though they can see no reason why their wives should give comparable sums to their sororities.

STUDENTS LIVING IN PRIVATE HOMES

In 1940-41, approximately one in every four students lived in rooms in private homes in Bloomington while attending college. Living quarters of this type are characterized by great variation in comfort, convenience, and attractiveness, and by desirability from the standpoint of the personal relationships involved. Not infrequently when a family decides " to take students ", they visit second-hand stores to secure a desk or table, a book case, a cot and chairs. The criterion of choice on such occasions is whether a piece of furniture has durability, rather than whether it will lend harmony in the furnishing of the rooms to be rented. But by no means all of the rooms in private homes rented to students are furnished according to such utilitarian standards. Sometimes a son or daughter is married or leaves home to go to work, leaving an attractively furnished room which is rented to a student. Middle-aged and elderly widows and spinsters in very comfortable circumstances sometimes rent a room in their homes to one or two students because they are afraid to live alone or desire company. Some families rent their spare rooms as a means of cutting down their own housing costs; and, in general, such rooms are desirable from the point of view of both comfort and appearance. In homes where students are given lodging in return for staying with children at night, helping with the housework, or taking care of the furnace, they are often housed in the room originally designed for a maid.

Many families prefer to rent their rooms to men students for two reasons: they are not subject to the same university rules as the women students, and they are generally regarded as less trouble. All women students living in private homes are required to live in houses approved by an inspector sent out by the Dean of Women's Office. They are also required to observe the same rules for being in their places of residence at night as the students who live in the dormitories or sorority houses.

The bases on which students who live in private homes select their rooms differ. Some choose them for their individual merits. A smaller number of the more conscientious students prefer rooms located some distance from the campus or houses where there are few or no other students so they will be less apt to be disturbed while studying. It is not uncommon for a man student to take the first room he goes to see, but women are more apt to shop around before engaging a room. One of the greatest handicaps involved in women's living in private homes is the absence of a desirable place in which to entertain men guests when the family with whom they live occupies the downstairs living room. Even where these students feel that the family likes to have them bring in guests, there is often little opportunity to converse privately with their friends.

The median amount paid for rent by the women who lived in private homes was $104.78 per year or $2.69 per week. Although undoubtedly the women paid more extra fees for laundry privileges than men, the greater part of the difference in amounts spent for rent by the two groups was due to the fact that rooms renting for as little as those occupied by some men either were not available to women or that women were not willing to live in as unattractive houses with as few conveniences or as far from the campus as some men were.

The median amount paid for rent by men living in private homes was slightly lower than that paid by women, sometimes running as low as $1.50 per person per week for a room shared with another student. The majority of rooms in private homes available for student women ordinarily rent for $3.50 to $5 per week if occupied by one student, or for $2.50 to $3 per person if the room is shared with another student. A charge of 50 cents per week is made if the bed linen is furnished. For the additional power used to operate a radio the customary charge is twelve and one-half cents per week. Since, with the exception of the people who rent rooms in order to have some one in the house, the private families who rent rooms to students do so to increase their incomes; they tend to make additional charges for extra services. This fact is borne out not merely by the additional charges for linen and radio, but by instances where the number of baths taken or pairs of hose a student is permitted to wash per week is limited unless an additional fee is paid.

STUDENT ROOMING HOUSES

Student rooming houses differ from private homes principally in the number of students living in the house. In private homes the family usually adjusts its pattern of living to include one or two students, while the primary reason for operating the house used for a student rooming house is that it will accommodate several students and provide at least an important part of the income of the proprietor. In the student rooming houses sturdy furniture purchased at public sales or in used furniture shops is the commonest type. Its use by several generations of college students is usually apparent and the wallpaper, draperies, and floor coverings originally chosen for durability are often not replaced until they are completely worn out.

The median amount paid for rent by the 180 students, both men and women, in the sample who lived in these lodgings was $93.64 for the year or $2.60 per week. The first quartile expenditure amounted to $2.30 per week and the third quartile to $2.98 per week. The median expenditures for men who lived in student rooming houses was $90.18 per year, for women $99.09. On a weekly basis their respective expenditures for rent were $2.51 and $2.75. The interquartile range for the men was $78.32 to $100.25 per year and that of women $88.30 to $111.54. Reduced to a weekly basis, these sums amounted to $2.17 to $2.78 for the men and $2.45 to $3.10 for the women. From these figures and a comparison of the median expenditures of students rooming in different types of residences at the University shown in Table 6 we see that the students who live in student rooming houses tend to spend less for rent than do those living in any other types of residence.

RENT AS AFFECTED BY COLLEGE CLASS

As shown in Table 8, Freshmen paid more for rent than members of any of the other three classes.[10] Several reasons may be given for this fact. A larger proportion of Freshmen than of the members of any other class lived in dormitories in 1940-41. It is often not until an unorganized student has been in the University for a while that he learns of the preferable cheaper rooms. Moreover, many of the students who come to college believing that they must live in certain types of dwellings if they wish to " rate " on the campus often change their minds when they observe where some of the socially or academically prominent students live. Besides, by the end of Freshman year, many students have made friends with whom they wish to continue to live during their remaining years at college. Once such a group is formed, the question of where the members can live together or near each other often becomes more important than the prestige of the place in which they live.

TABLE 8

MEDIAN EXPENDITURES FOR RENT BY 1275 STUDENTS AT INDIANA
UNIVERSITY, 1940-41, GROUPED BY COLLEGE CLASS [a]

Class	Number in Sample	Median
Freshman	448	$136.85
Sophomore	323	104.29
Junior	291	106.30
Senior	215	105.92

[a] For more detailed figures see Table 76, page 242.

10 See Table 76, p. 242.

It will be noted from Table 76 that the median expenditures for rent of all men, except the organized Freshman, were less than those of the women until the Senior year, when the organized men jumped ahead of the women. The fact that Senior men often move out of their fraternity houses into more expensive rooms than they have occupied in other years in order to have fewer interruptions while working on advanced courses probably explains why they spend more for rent than the Senior sorority women who usually live in their chapter houses during their last year in college.

The median amount spent by the unorganized Freshman women was the highest for any group and over $40 more than that of the women in any other year. The difference in the rent paid by these women is probably explained by the desire on the part of their parents to place their daughters who are entering college for the first time in safe living quarters. The desire for social prestige for their daughters may have also influenced their parents' choice of rooms for them.

RENT PAID BY STUDENTS IN DIFFERENT SCHOOLS
OF THE UNIVERSITY

The median expenditure for room rent by the students in the College of Arts and Sciences was greater than by students in the Schools of Education, Business, and Medicine, the only others for which the samples collected were large enough to justify any conclusions. Both the medians and the interquartile range in each of these schools are shown in Table 9. Although similar figures for the very limited samples of students from the Schools of Music and Law are also included in Table 9, the inadequacy of the data from which these latter figures were computed makes their significance subject to question.

EXPENDITURES FOR RENT BY STUDENTS WHO EARNED PART
OR ALL OF THEIR COLLEGE EXPENSES

The students who earned none of their own expenses in 1940-41 spent more for their living quarters than those who earned part of their expenses. This fact is shown by the figures in Table 10.

TABLE 9

MEDIAN AND QUARTILE EXPENDITURES FOR RENT BY STUDENTS IN THE
DIFFERENT SCHOOLS OF INDIANA UNIVERSITY, 1940-41

School	Number in Sample [a]	Percentage of all Students in Sample	First Quartile	Median	Third Quartile
College of Arts and Sciences	482	38.13	$96.90	$127.04	$147.50
Education	159	12.58	95.90	112.92	147.60
Business	519	41.06	92.79	105.71	140.42
Medicine	57	4.51	96.67	112.86	143.34
Music	38	3.01	93.00	110.00	147.00
Law	9	.71	82.50	97.50	127.50
	1264	100.00	.	.	

[a] Eleven students in the sample did not designate the school they attended.

The median expenditures for rent by the students who earned less than 40 per cent of their expenses were somewhat greater than those of students who earned a larger proportion and indicate that such students added part of their earnings to the amounts provided by their parents to pay for higher rent rooms than they could otherwise afford. The median amounts spent by the students who earned up to 20 per cent of their college expenses were above the median expenditure of all students (see

TABLE 10

THE MEDIAN AND QUARTILE EXPENDITURES FOR RENT OF 1195 STUDENTS
AT INDIANA UNIVERSITY BY PERCENTAGES OF EXPENSES
EARNED BY THEM, 1940-41

Proportion of total expenses earned	Number in Sample [a]	First Quartile	Median	Third Quartile
None	517	$102.28	$135.73	$149.54
Under 20%	288	98.53	118.64	146.43
20–39%	157	91.87	101.35	128.86
40–59%	89	88.33	96.18	112.50
60–79%	45	91.77	96.46	106.88
80–99%	43	87.50	96.92	113.00
All Expenses	56	82.86	94.74	103.33

[a] Eighty of the students in the sample did not indicate whether or not they earned any part of their expenses.

Table 6, page 46. It was greater than the median amount paid by all sorority members and within $4 of that of fraternity men. As might be expected, the students who earned all of their own expenses paid the least for their rooms. It is interesting to note, however, that the median amount spent for rent by the students who earned any part or all of their expenses was not as low as that of those who lived in student rooming houses.[11]

EXPENDITURES FOR RENT BY STUDENTS FROM FARMS, SMALL TOWNS, AND CITIES

The type of community from which the student came was another factor that affected the rent he paid. As may be seen from the figures below, women from small towns spent noticeably more for their rooms than those from farms and cities.[12] This difference may possibly be explained by the greater stress laid on appearances, space and ventilation by this group. Another reason is the greater homogeneity in the incomes represented by these women than is found among the women from cities where the women from the lower income brackets are often accustomed to cramped living quarters in apartments. Most of the cheaper rooms in private homes or student rooming houses in Bloomington provide bathroom facilities and central heat which even though less attractive than some appeal to the students from farms whose homes have neither furnaces nor running water.

Home Community of Student	Number in Sample	Percentage of Students	First Quartile	Median	Third Quartile
Farm	148	20.02	$91.02	$ 98.57	$114.00
Small Town	263	35.59	97.95	122.66	148.50
City	328	44.38	95.58	115.10	147.31

11 When the rent paid by the NYA students was examined separately, it was found that the women in this group spent more than the men. Their median annual expenditure amounted to $95.86 as compared with $91.89 spent by the men. Both of these amounts were larger than the median amounts spent by the men and women living in student rooming houses. In terms of weekly expenditures the median amounts spent by the NYA men and women were $2.66 and $2.55 respectively.

12 For the purposes of analysis the term small town is used in this study to designate a town having a population of less than 10,000, a city a popu-

The probable reason why the median amounts paid for their rooms by the women from farms and small towns tended to be greater than that paid by the men from these communities was the conservatism on the part of the parents living in rural areas or small towns which affected their choice of living quarters for their daughters.

There was relatively little difference in the amounts paid for rooms by men from small towns and cities. The amounts paid by both of these groups, however, were greater than that paid by farm men, whose first and third quartile expenditures for rent were noticeably below those paid by men from small towns and cities.

The variation in the amounts paid for rent, as judged from their quartile expenditures, was the greatest in the case of students from cities. This is explained by the greater extremes in the income groups represented by these students and the fact that a larger proportion have low incomes than high ones. The least variation in the amounts paid for rent occurred among the men and women from farms.

The size of the community from which the student came apparently had no influence on whether or not he lived at a university dormitory; since 40.99 per cent of the students in the sample whose homes were on farms, 41 per cent of those from small towns, and 41.76 per cent of the students from cities lived in the university halls of residence.

Only 6.3 per cent of the women from farms lived in sorority houses in comparison with 12.03 per cent of those from small towns and 15.59 per cent of those from cities. The percentage of men from farms who lived in fraternity houses was 7.43 and those of men from small towns and cities were 11.86 and 13.36 respectively. The relatively smaller median total expenditure of the students from farms probably explains the difference shown by these figures in the membership of students from farms in Greek-letter societies.

lation of more than 10,000. Not all of the students in the entire sample of 1275 indicated the type of community from which they came.

The proportion of students from farms who lived in private homes was greater than for those from small towns or cities, amounting to 21.17 per cent, in comparison with 10.24 per cent of those from cities and 18.43 per cent of those from small towns. Almost 5 per cent of the students in the sample from farms worked for their rooms in private homes, while only 3 per cent of those from small towns and 1.3 per cent of those from cities exchanged work for lodging in a private home. Approximately 18 per cent of both the students from farms and from cities lived in student rooming houses, and only about 21.1 per cent of these from small towns.

SUMMARY

The detailed figures presented in this chapter show that in 1940-41 the average student at Indiana University spent about $110 for the school year or about $3 per week for housing. Because of the nature of the housing arrangements at the University and the standard rates charged the students who live in each type of residence, the student's demand for housing tended to be less elastic than for many of the other items in his budget. For this reason the student who spent the most money usually allotted a smaller proportion of his budget for rent than did the student whose total expenditure was smaller. In general, women spent more for their rooms than men. Fraternity and sorority members who lived in chapter houses spent more on housing than did the unorganized students in general but somewhat less than the students living in the university dormitories. Below both the dormitory and chapter house residents in their median expenditures for rent were those who lived in private homes and rooming houses.

When the amounts paid for rent were analyzed on the basis of class membership, it was found that Freshmen tended to spend noticeably larger amounts for rent than students in any of the other undergraduate classes. Students in the College of Arts and Sciences spent slightly more on the average for room rent than the students in any of the other schools of the University. It was also found that students who earned all of their own expenses spent less for rent than those who earned less than 40 per cent of their expenses, and both spent appreciably less than the median amounts paid for rent by the students who earned none of their expenses and by all students in the sample. Students from farms tended to spend less for their rooms than those from either small towns or cities.

From this consideration of what students in different groups spend for a place to live while attending the University, we turn next to a discussion of what they spend for their meals and of some of the characteristics of their food consumption.

CHAPTER IV

FOOD

FOOD expenditures tend to occupy the leading place in the budgets of all types of consumer groups. On the basis of the sample studied, it appears that Indiana University students in 1940-41 devoted approximately 27.5 per cent of their total budgets to food, an item approached in importance only by room and clothing, which represented 17.0 and 16.1 per cent respectively.

In the student budget, food is an especially important item; since the amount paid for it is a factor in determining in whose company the meals are taken and the kinds of food consumed. Not only health but social life as well are often influenced by where the student eats. Meal-time provides an opportunity to meet and become acquainted with other students. It is then that many associations are formed which affect the social activities of the student throughout his four years in college.

In this chapter, as in the two preceding, the attempt has been made first of all to determine median expenditures for all students for the budget item under consideration, and to establish its relative importance in the budget.[1] In addition, the general cross-classification used in the study has made possible a comparison of food expenditures by groups of students distinguished by such criteria as sex, membership in Greek-letter organizations, place of residence while in college, enrollment in

1 The problem of what Indiana students spend for food is somewhat complicated by the tendency to have lunch and dinner dates, particularly the latter. This means that all of the food paid for by the men and included under the budget heading of food is not consumed by them alone. Likewise, food expenditures reported by women having "dinner dates" also fail to reflect with absolute accuracy the amount of food actually eaten. Several experiments were made with ways of separating amounts spent for meals for "dates," but in each case the results were unsatisfactory. For that reason the figures relating to food are computed from the estimates of expenditures for meals regardless of whether or not they were consumed by the person reporting them.

the different colleges of the University, and according to the size of the communities from which the students come.

In the case of students living in university dormitories and in fraternity and sorority houses, there is little opportunity to exercise choice in matters of food consumption. The approximately one-third of the student body, who live outside the dormitories and chapter houses do have such an opportunity, however. As a result, it has seemed worth while to devote considerable space to a description and analysis of the habits and patterns of food consumption of the students who " eat out." This generally means eating in the University Cafeteria or coöperative dining room, or at the restaurants near the campus which cater to students. Some attention has also been given to the consumption of certain specific food items which seemed of more than ordinary importance.

EXPENDITURES OF ALL STUDENTS

The median and quartile expenditures for food by the 1275 students in the sample during the thirty-six week school year in 1940-41 were:[2]

First Quartile	Median	Third Quartile
$150.61	$207.28	$240.24

Reduced to a weekly basis, these sums amounted to $4.18, $5.76, and $6.67 respectively, and on a daily basis to sixty, eighty-two, and ninety-five cents respectively.[3]

[2] For the mean expenditure of all students see Table 77, page 243.

[3] The median expenditures for food by all students in the samples for 1938-39 and 1939-40 were $207.38 and $207.76 respectively. These figures and the median for 1940-41 indicate expenditures of a rather consistent amount for the three years. It is interesting to note that national index numbers of food prices for the same periods show only very minor changes. An average of the index numbers for retail food prices computed by the National Industrial Conference Board for the three months of September, December, and March in the years 1938-39, 1939-40, and 1940-41 were 96.6, 96.2, and 97.2 (*Survey of Current Business, op. cit.*, XXI, 162).

Throughout this discussion it is assumed that an expenditure for a week pays for 21 meals and for a day 3 meals.

Since data relating to student incomes were not available, the proportion of the budget spent for food by students in different groups was compared with their total expenditures. This showed that the absolute amounts spent for food tended to increase as the total amounts they spent increased. The rate of increase in the expenditure for food, however, lagged behind that of total expenditure. As a consequence, the proportion of the budget spent for food declined as the amount of the total expenditure increased. This corresponds to the usual behavior of food expenditures found in studies of the general population. As noted at the beginning of the chapter, the proportion of the total budget of the 1275 students spent for food in 1940-41 was 27.5 per cent.[4]

MEN AND WOMEN

Estimates made by the Committee on Food and Nutrition of the National Research Council indicate that women of the ages of those in college, whether moderately active, very active, or sedentary, require fewer calories than men of the same age.[5] There is also a generally accepted belief that men eat more than women, which finds some substantiation in the comparison of the amounts paid for food by single men and women at all income levels studied by the National Resources Committee.[6] Another reason for expecting college women to spend less for their meals than men is that they are practically all of an age at which they may expect to have men take them out for dinner at least occasionally. But in spite of these reasons for expecting greater food expenditures by men, the median and quartile expenditures given below show relatively little difference between the amounts spent by the men and women students at the Uni-

4 This percentage was computed from the arithmetic mean expenditures of the 1275 students in the sample.

5 The National Research Council, *Recommended Dietary Allowances, A Report Prepared by the Committee on Food and Nutrition to Advise on Nutritional Problems in Connection with National Defense* (Washington, 1940), 3, 5.

6 The National Resources Committee, *Consumer Expenditures in the United States*, pp. 81-82.

versity. In fact, the median amount spent by the women was
slightly higher than that of the men.[7]

Group	Number in Sample	Percentage of Total	First Quartile	Median	Third Quartile
Men	586	45.96	$157.39	$206.55	$241.69
Women	689	54.04	145.75	208.08	239.70

There are several explanations, however, why the amounts
spent by men and women at college are more nearly alike than
one would ordinarily expect them to be. The fact that board at
the university dormitories and the student boarding clubs is the
same for both men and women students accounts for the similarity of the amounts spent by the students who take their meals
there. The amounts spent for food at restaurants do not indicate the amount of food, or the calories or vitamins consumed.
In fact, similar expenditures may mean quite dissimilar food
consumption, since women students when interviewed indicated
that they were more particular in their choice of both where and
what they ate than were the men. Attractive surroundings and
service tend to be more important to them than to men. These
preferences usually entail sufficiently greater expenses to coun-
terbalance any additional amounts spent by men for larger
quantities of food. Much of the difference between the amounts
spent for food by the single men and women found by the National Resources Committee is accounted for by the preparation
of their own meals by a larger proportion of the women studied
by the Committee than would be true of college women.

As may be seen from the quartile expenditures given above,
the variability in the expenditures of women for food was
greater than in the case of men. In this variation the women
students tended to veer more in the direction of economy than
of extravagance. The expenditure of men for food represented
28.6 per cent of their total budget, while women spent only 26.5
per cent of theirs for food.

[7] In 1939-40, the median expenditure for food by 432 men at Indiana
University was $209.43 and of 466 women $206.67.

The proportion of their budget spent for food by all single men in the sample studied by the National Resources Committee was 30.1 per cent, almost two per cent more than the men students. But this difference is probably entirely accounted for by the inclusion of the amounts spent for refreshments and snacks in the food expenditures of the single men and their omission in that of the student men, the smaller total expenditure of the student men, and the coverage of twelve months by the budget of the single men as compared with that of nine months by the students.[8] But, in spite of similar conditions the proportion of their budget spent for food by the University women was greater than that spent by the single women.[9]

An analysis of the schedules of 100 students chosen at random from among those whose expenditures for food fell in the lowest quartile showed a preponderance of women and relatively few organized students. Further study of all schedules in the lowest quartile disclosed that the proportion of Freshmen was smaller than that of students in any other undergraduate class. More students in this quartile came from rural areas than from small towns and cities. The majority of men students in the first quartile lived in rooming houses, but the women were divided about equally between rooming houses and the coöperative dormitory, Forest Hall. A large majority of all students in the lower quartile earned at least a part of their own expenses.

When the expenditures for food for the school year reported by all the students in the sample were thrown into a cumulative distribution, the results were as appear in Table 11.

If the dietetically planned meals of the dormitory dining halls is taken as a standard of adequacy, their cost in dollars of $234.00 per year falls in the $200-240 interval. This means that, if this entire interval is regarded as " adequate " roughly 45 per cent of the students eat less than this standard and roughly 25 per cent above it.

8 For a discussion of student consumption of " snacks " see pp. 152-154.

9 The National Resources Committee, *Consumer Expenditures in the United States*, pp. 82-83.

TABLE 11

Cumulative Distribution of 1275 Students at Indiana University
Classified According to the Amount Spent
for Food, 1940-41

Expenditure (in dollars)	Number of Students	Percentage of Students
Less than $120	169	13.25
Less than 160	372	29.18
Less than 200	578	45.33
Less than 240	952	74.82
Less than 280	1230	96.47
Less than 320	1264	99.14
Less than 360	1275	100.00

FOOD EXPENDITURES AS RELATED TO PLACE OF RESIDENCE

The place of residence of a student while at college largely determines the type of place at which he takes his meals. Except for the women living at Forest Hall, the students in dormitories eat in dormitory dining rooms. Fraternity or sorority members ordinarily eat at their chapter houses, even though they may room elsewhere, where, as at the dormitories, meals are contracted for on a semester basis and are planned for them according to generally accepted dietary standards.

Some students who live in private homes or rooming houses are served meals in the houses in which they live or go to the University "Co-op," where meals are also planned for them. But the majority who live in residences of these types take their meals at the University Cafeteria or at restaurants where each meal is purchased singly and the combinations of food consumed must be chosen at each meal. As a consequence, the greatest variation in the character of the meals consumed and in the prices paid is found among students who take their meals at eating places where they must make their own decisions regarding what they will eat. For this reason, the food consumption of these students will be discussed in considerably more detail than that of the students who take their meals in dormitories, or Greek-letter chapter houses which are presented first.

Before discussing the food expenditures associated with various types of living quarters, it has seemed worth while to present a summary table showing median and quartile food expenditures for all students in the sample, classified according to place of residence. These appear in Table 12.

TABLE 12

MEDIAN AND QUARTILE FOOD EXPENDITURES OF INDIANA UNIVERSITY
STUDENTS CLASSIFIED ACCORDING TO PLACE OF RESIDENCE,
1940-41

Place of Residence	Number in Sample	First Quartile	Median	Third Quartile
University Dormitory	541	$159.50	$234.53 a	$245.03
Fraternity	142	216.25	232.73	254.77
Sorority	149	202.79	222.65 b	242.14
Private Home	203	135.00	160.00	190.00
Rooming House	168	110.00	145.00	180.00
Apartment or Residence with cooking privileges	73	120.49	143.11	189.27
All other places c	59	—	—	—

a Food charges for the year were $234.00 at all of the dormitories. The variation shown here is accounted for by the expenditures of Forest Hall girls who tend to economize on food and by the fact that dormitory students eat out occasionally even though their meals at the dormitory are already paid for.

b The estimates from which this median was computed did not include those of the pledgees who lived in the dormitories.

c This number includes students who commute, those who work for their board and did not evaluate cost of meals, and students who take their meals at home.

DORMITORY STUDENTS

The charge for the meals served in both the men's and women's dormitories under the direction of the director of residence halls is $234 for the year. Since this is a uniform rate for all students who eat in the dining rooms of these halls, the amount of the median and quartile expenditure for food by all who eat there is the same.[10] The meals are planned by university dieticians and their assistants who see that they are well balanced and have an adequate vitamin content.[11] Because at all

10 At Forest Hall, the coöperative dormitory, there is no dining room. The girts who live there take their meals at the University Cafeteria, the Coöperative Dining Club, or at restaurants. A few girls work in private homes for their board.

11 During an influenza epidemic in the winter of 1940-41 a large glass of orange juice was served each morning.

of the dormitories the students are allowed second helpings, there is no real need to supplement these meals when judged from the viewpoint of nutritional value or variety.

At the Men's Residence Hall approximately 360 men are served dinner in a two-story room in which the ceiling is beamed and the walls paneled to give it the appearance of a men's club. The chairs are upholstered in red leather and dinner is served on highly polished tables. The dining rooms for the women's dormitories are all located in Beech Hall. In these rooms of colonial design, meals are served on tables similar to those in the men's dormitories. Breakfast and luncheon are served cafeteria-style, but dinner at night is a formal three-course meal at which the students enter and leave the dining room together. They are seated at tables which accommodate from four to ten persons and served by student waiters who earn part of their college expenses in this way. Since the increase in the number of social directors at the dormitories, the university student who lives at one of these residences gets much of the social training that formerly was offered only at endowed private schools. This emphasis upon social training is particularly evident in the dining rooms in the evening, when the students living in the dormitories meet for dinner.

The amounts paid for meals at the dormitories cover more than the mere cost of food. The plain durable dishes used formerly have given way to more fragile and more attractive china. Candles are used regularly for all gala occasions and for buffet suppers on Sunday night.[12] Flowers are used for guest nights in winter, and in the fall and spring they appear on the tables daily. The preparation and serving of meals require the services of a large corps of workers. Several dinners are given at no extra cost to the students each year to which they may invite members of the faculty or other friends. A formal Christmas dinner and the annual dinner for Seniors are given primarily for the students, although a few faculty members are usually

12 In 1941-42 the dormitories discontinued serving an evening meal on Sunday night.

invited. In the dining rooms for both men and women grace is sung before dinner, and current popular songs, college songs, and " old favorites " are frequently sung between courses. The cost of service together with the additional expenses mentioned above account for the similarity in the costs of meals at the dormitories and at the Greek-letter chapter houses.

STUDENTS LIVING IN CHAPTER HOUSES

Social life is also stressed by both fraternities and sororities. The food expenditures of these students cover such costs as the wages of a cook and students to wait table and clean the kitchen and dining room, replacements of china and silver, laundry, candles and flowers. At the sorority houses in particular, the appearance of the table and correctness of the service are stressed. Fancy salads and desserts such as ice-cream pies and other molded specialties are often served on Sundays and guest nights.

Although the amounts charged for food by individual chapter houses vary from one to another, the differences are not great. Within a given house, however, the charge for meals is uniform for all members. Once a student has accepted membership and has agreed to live in the house for the year, his expenditures for food, as in the case of dormitory students, is fixed for that period of time. As a consequence, changes in the prices of food in the market do not usually affect what he pays for meals during that time as much as they may the student who takes his meals at a restaurant. The rates charged by the various chapter houses in 1940-41 ranged between $22.00 and $27.50 per month. The meals themselves are not noticeably different from those served at the dormitories.

The median and quartile expenditures of the students who lived in Greek-letter chapter houses in 1940-41 were as follows: [13]

13 The figures given here are computed from those of the students who ordinarily take their meals at a Greek-letter chapter house. For this reason they differ somewhat from those of all organized students, a group which includes members of fraternities and sororities who do not live in the chapter houses.

Group	Number of Students	First Quartile	Median	Third Quartile
Men who live in fraternity houses	142	$216.25	$232.73	$254.77
Women who live in sorority houses	149	202.79	222.65	242.14

As may be seen from these figures, the men living in fraternity houses paid more for their food than the women living in sorority houses. One reason for this difference given by several fraternity men was that they " had to have steaks oftener and more food than those women eat."

The median and quartile expenditures given below show the expenditures of the relatively small number of organized students who eat elsewhere than in the chapter houses:

Group	Number of Students	First Quartile	Median	Third Quartile
Fraternity men who live outside their chapter houses	47	$181.26	$221.00	$261.25
Sorority women who live outside their chapter houses	16	135.00	180.00	235.50

Fewer initiated sorority women than fraternity men take rooms outside of their chapter houses, primarily because some of the professional schools in which there are mostly men students prefer not to have their students live in a fraternity house during their last years at the University. The difference in the food expenditures of the men and women who live away from the chapter houses seems to indicate that the majority do so because they can live more economically. At least a fourth of the organized students who lived outside, however, spent more than did 50 per cent of those living in the chapter houses. This shows that some of the members who take their meals away from the chapter houses do so not to save money, but to secure greater privacy, quieter surroundings, more room; or because they do work which prevents their returning to the chapter house for meals.

When a cumulative distribution of the expenditures for food by all organized students was compared with that of unorganized students, it was found that more than 50 per cent of the unorganized students spend less than $200.00 a year while only about 13 per cent of the organized students spend less than that amount.

Although the median amounts. spent for food by organized students of both sexes were greater than those spent by unorganized students, the proportion of the total budget of the former spent for food was smaller, amounting to 25.0 and 29.3 per cent respectively.[14]

STUDENTS LIVING IN PRIVATE HOMES

Somewhat more than a third of the students included in the study lived outside the university dormitories and the chapter houses. They are usually referred to as the students who live " out in town." Of these, 203 lived in private homes with families who have one or two spare rooms which they rent to students.[15] As may be seen from Table 12, the median amount spent for food by these students was $160 for the year, $4.44 a week, or 63 cents a day. This median is considerably smaller than the $226.82 spent by students living in Greek-letter chapter houses and the $232.97 spent by students living in dormitories. The first quartile expenditure of the students living in private homes was $135 and the third quartile $190. Thirty-six students in the study lived in private homes where they worked for their rooms. The median expenditure for food for this group was $150 per year, $4.17 per week, or 60 cents per day.

STUDENTS LIVING IN ROOMING HOUSES

One hundred and eighty-seven students living in rooming houses were included in the sample. Of this number 94 per cent were unorganized students. The median amount spent by this group was $144 per year, $4 per week, or 57 cents per day. This

14 For the proportions of their budgets spent by all four groups see Table 77, page 243.

15 Thirty-two of these students were organized and 171 unorganized. The median expenditure of the organized was $217.50 per year and of the unorganized $165.

median was about $4 less than was spent by the unorganized group as a whole. It was $16 less than the median expenditure of the 203 students in the sample who lived in private homes. The interquartile range of the students living in rooming houses was between $110 and $180 per year. The economy of these students shows up more clearly when the variability in their food expenditures is compared with that of all unorganized students in the sample, whose interquartile range fell between $134.77 and $236.36.

STUDENTS WHO HAVE COOKING PRIVILEGES

Seventy-three of the 1275 students in the group studied prepared at least one meal a day for themselves. The facilities used varied from a kitchen in a private apartment to cooking privileges in a private home. Approximately a third of this group prepared all three of their daily meals, while another third prepared only their breakfasts. The rest provided one or two of the remaining meals.

In this group we are dealing with the most economical group of all, whose median annual over-all expenditure for all items while at college was $410.27 as compared with a median of $673.06 for all students in our sample and $574.10 for all unorganized students. Actually, 17 per cent of this group spent less than $400 a year on their college education; 44 per cent spent less than $500; and 62 per cent less than $600. But in spite of the lower median total expenditure of the group, their median expenditure of $143.11 for food in 1940-41 was very similar to that spent by the students who lived in rooming houses. Reduced to a weekly basis this was $3.98, and to a daily basis, 57 cents. The third quartile expenditure of the students who prepared at least one meal a day for themselves fell at $189.27, an amount sufficiently large to suggest that reasons other than sheer economy enter into the decision of some of these students to prepare one or more meals at home for themselves. Some individualists prefer this type of living because they find it difficult to adapt themselves to the restrictions imposed by group living. A few students indicated in interviews that they regarded this mode of living more appropriate for the mature student or one belonging to the campus intelligentsia. In general, however, economy and convenience are the reasons why students prepare their own meals. This group is also noteworthy because of extremes in total expenditures of its members. Six of the 73 students who indicated that they prepared some of their own meals reported total expenditures for all items of $1000 or over. Two of these students spent over $2000.

The first quartile expenditure of the students who prepared their own meals was $120.49 per year, an amount representing only 78 per cent of that spent by students in the first quartile of the sample of all students.[16] The smaller median amount spent by these students is partially explained by supplies such as eggs, chicken, bread, and cake received from home. Considerably more than half of the students who prepared their own meals reported that they occasionally had food sent to them. Only five had it sent as often as once a week and four received it every two weeks. Some students bring canned fruit and vegetables, jellies, and preserves from home, thus reducing their cash outlays for food while at college. While most students are apt to receive food from home, there seems reason for believing that the food sent to students cooking their own food is of a more substantial nature than the incidental sweets received by the average student.

The majority of the students who prepare their own meals live in groups and pool their funds for the purchase of supplies. Because of the ruling against undergraduate women's living in apartments, many more men than women live in this manner. The accounts kept by these men reveal some interesting facts relating to the diets of students who provide their own meals. When questioned, several of these men said they kept records on sheets of paper pinned to the wall, of what each student in the group spent. On these, each member of the group jotted down the items he purchased at the grocery store and the amounts

16 This sum amounted to $3.35 per week or 48 cents per day.

spent. Payments for gas for cooking purposes were recorded in a similar fashion. On the slips that were brought to the writer, great care had been taken during the first few weeks to enter every item meticulously; but as time went on fewer items were entered, and by the end of the semester only amounts were listed. These slips supplied by men who prepared their own meals seemed sufficiently interesting to warrant the inclusion here of a fairly typical one for four male students for a two-week period: [17]

Student A		Student B		Student C		Student D	
Potatoes ..	.19	Bread	.10	Ice	.25	Bread	.20
Meat	.25	Sugar	.49	Milk 1.40		Beans	.15
Cheese	.07	Bread	.15	Ice	.25	Cauliflower	.11
Eggs	.50	Butter	.30	Butter,		Bread	.10
Eggs	.54	Bread,		Sugar,		Sausage ...	.24
Meat	.20	Lunch		Coffee ...	.94	Bread and	
Bread	.05	Meat	.22	Ice	.25	3 eggs ...	.18
Milk	.35	Bread and		Milk	.70	Beef,	
Meat	.45	Butter ...	.43			Lettuce,	
Bread	.10	Gas bill 1.06				Onions...	.91
		Oysters ...	.38			Bacon	.40
Beans	.28	───── ...	.14			Cookies ...	.15
─────	.25	Dressing ..	.17				
Oleo	.25						
Jam	.17						
2 lbs. Pota-							
toes	.17						
Eggs	.27						
Puffed							
Wheat ..	.16						
Veal Chops.	.50						
Eggs	.54						
Onions	.15						
Bread	.10						
Ice	.25 [a]						

[a] The weather was warm during the two weeks covered by this record. In colder weather ice was purchased in 15-cent quantities and less frequently.

It will be noted that, in general, green vegetables, fruits and items for dessert were notably absent from this list. The average

[17] Items mentioned often on other lists included pie, hamburger, and oatmeal. Data collected through interviews indicated that men were willing to buy cheaper brands of food than women and were governed more by price than women were.

individual expenditure of the four boys whose purchases are listed above ranged from $1.40 to $2.25 for twenty-one meals per week, amounts even lower than the first quartile expenditure of all students who prepared their own meals.

Other examples of menus of students who provided their own meals were obtained from two brothers, a Senior taking his first year in the School of Medicine and a Junior in the School of Business. They stated in an interview that they cooked their meals in the room in which they slept, sharing an electric refrigerator in an upstairs hall with a young married couple. Their average weekly expenditure for food for all meals for the two of them was between $4.20 and $4.50, amounts considerably below the median expenditure of all the students who prepared their own meals. Typical menus of these boys were: Breakfast: coffee, toast, and cereal; Lunch: milk and sandwiches; Supper: corned beef, cabbage, peas, and milk; or pork chops, potatoes, and milk. One of these boys who went home frequently brought back much of the food that he and his brother consumed, but the cost of this food was included in their estimates of food costs.

STUDENTS LIVING WITH THEIR PARENTS IN BLOOMINGTON

In contrast with universities located in or near large cities, Indiana University has relatively few students living at home. In our sample 21 students, or only 1.65 per cent, reported that they lived at home or with relatives. Five of these indicated that they paid their parents nothing for their meals. The others said they paid their parents amounts ranging from $72 to $180 for their meals during the school year.

FOOD EXPENDITURES OF GAINFULLY EMPLOYED STUDENTS

As was true in regard to expenditures for rent, there was a marked difference between the median expenditures for food of the students who earned a part or all of their college expenses and those of students who earned none of the money used to finance their college training.

TABLE 13

THE MEDIAN AND QUARTILE FOOD EXPENDITURES OF 1195 STUDENTS BY
PERCENTAGES OF EXPENSES EARNED BY THEM, 1940-41 [a]

Proportion of Total Expenses Earned	Number in Sample	Percentage of Students in Sample	First Quartile	Median	Third Quartile
None	517	43.26	$181.41	$230.54	$245.72
Under 20	288	24.10	169.00	222.60	245.00
20–39	157	13.14	129.16	188.92	235.65
40–59	89	7.45	123.25	155.83	213.75
60–79	45	3.77	121.25	168.12	202.50
80–99	43	3.60	133.75	165.00	208.12
All Expenses	56	4.69	133.33	166.66	209.00

[a] Eighty students failed to indicate whether they earned any of their college expenses.

In the figures above we find that the median food expenditures of students who earn 40 per cent or more of their own expenses in 1940-41 fell between $155.00 and $168.50. That the median expenditure of those who earned 40 to 60 per cent of their expenses was somewhat lower than that of those who were more nearly self-supporting is probably to be explained by the fact that in the former group are included cases of individuals whose support from home is meager but who do not find it possible to work sufficient time to bring their level of consumption up to that which is possible for those who have arranged their schedules in such a way (perhaps taking five years to do four years work) as to enable them to earn a larger part of their expenses.[18]

18 *NYA Students*: The median and quartile expenditures for food by the NYA students in the sample were:

Group	Number in Sample	First Quartile	Median	Third Quartile
NYA Men	93	$127.73	$150.00	$191.67
NYA Women	89	113.75	137.31	163.75
All NYA	183	122.38	147.81	168.53

On a weekly basis this median amounted to $4.11 and on a daily basis to 59 cents. These figures show that NYA students tended to spend notably less for food than the other students who earned a part or all of their own expenses. When the separate figures for men and women were analyzed, it was found that both the median and quartile expenditures for food of the

STUDENTS IN DIFFERENT SCHOOLS OF THE UNIVERSITY

The median annual expenditures for food of the students in the sample representing the different schools in the University are given in Table 14. Here we see a higher median expenditure by the students in the College of Arts and Sciences than in the other schools, which is probably explained by the higher proportion of organized and of women students in this school.

TABLE 14

MEDIAN AND QUARTILE FOOD EXPENDITURES BY 1264 STUDENTS IN
DIFFERENT SCHOOLS OF THE UNIVERSITY, 1940-41

School	Number in Sample [a]	Percentage of Sample	First Quartile	Median	Third Quartile
Arts and Sciences	482	38.13	$148.68	$220.21	$241.35
Business	519	41.06	157.12	205.85	239.77
Education	159	12.58	131.07	202.19	236.97
Medicine	57	3.57	157.50	206.25	241.88
Music	38	3.01	148.75	200.00	239.29
Law	9	.71	142.50	185.00	247.50
	1264	100.00			

[a] Eleven of the 1275 students in the sample did not designate the school attended.

STUDENTS FROM FARMS, SMALL TOWNS, AND CITIES

To determine the effect of the size of the community from which the student came on the amount he spent for food, the expenditures of students in the sample from farms, small towns, and cities were compared. The median amount for food by the 147 students from farms was $156.11 per year, an amount which, while greater than that of the students who prepared their own meals or lived in rooming houses, was less than that of students who lived in private homes. For students from small towns and cities the median expenditures were $225.62 and $221.07 respectively. These latter amounts were similar to the median expenditures of the students living in fraternity and

women students receiving NYA funds were lower than those of the men. When the median annual expenditures for these groups were reduced to a daily basis, they amounted to 54 cents and 60 cents respectively.

sorority houses and only slightly lower than those of students living in the dormitories. For 21 meals per week the median expenditure of students from farms amounted to $4.34, or 62 cents daily. Similar figures for the students from small towns were $6.27 per week and 90 cents per day. The median amount spent by the students from cities was $6.14 per week or 88 cents per day. Although the median amounts spent by the students from small towns and cities were very similar, they were both notably greater than the median expenditure of the students from farms.

TABLE 15

THE MEDIAN AND QUARTILE ANNUAL FOOD EXPENDITURES OF INDIANA
UNIVERSITY STUDENTS REPORTING HOMES ON FARMS, IN
SMALL TOWNS, AND IN CITIES, 1940-41

Home Community	Number in Sample	First Quartile	Median	Third Quartile
Farm				
Men	54	$124.58	$171.67	$224.50
Women	93	108.06	151.88	234.75
Both	147	112.72	156.11	230.96
Small Town				
Men	142	181.50	222.08	247.50
Women	121	157.50	228.75	243.83
Both	263	177.50	225.62	245.65
City				
Men	136	172.00	225.83	252.50
Women	192	152.50	209.41	229.66
Both	328	159.00	221.97	243.54

The median amounts spent for food by women from farms and cities were less than those for men from similar communities. But in the case of students from small towns the median amount spent by the men was less. Of the students from all three types of communities whose expenditures for food ranked in the upper fourth, those of city men were the greatest. Of those whose expenditures for food fell in the lowest fourth, the women from farms spent the least.

HABITS AND PATTERNS OF STUDENT FOOD CONSUMPTION

Four hundred and eleven students, or 32.2 per cent of the 1275 included in the study, reported that they ate at least one meal a day at a restaurant or at the University Cafeteria. Of these, seventy-nine (6.2 per cent) ate only one meal out, 90 (7.1 per cent) ate two meals out, and 242 (19.0 per cent) ate all three meals out. The variation in the habits and patterns of food consumption of these students who regularly ate at public eating places warrants a somewhat detailed description. A study of specific menus reveals a wide variety in choice of food, explained largely, but not entirely, by differences in the amounts which students have to spend. The dietary folkways of the home communities from which students come account for the unusual combinations and choices of foods of some individuals.

Ordinarily, the students who eat out purchase each meal separately. The majority of them must watch unspent balances in order to make their funds last throughout the college year. They are often faced with a dilemma, in that they must choose between quantity and quality of food. This is especially true of men students, who represent the majority of the patrons of the low-priced restaurants. Young people of college age are usually hungry and ready to eat at any time. They are inclined to choose food in terms of appetite rather than in terms of nutritional value. For this reason, they often tend to order such combination dishes as spaghetti and meat balls, chop suey, or meat and vegetable pie, all combinations which provide considerable bulk at low cost. Order slips from one of the low-priced restaurants showed that students frequently ordered meals consisting of three hamburger or frankfurter sandwiches, or a combination of the two kinds and a glass of milk. This meal probably represents the most filling one that a student could purchase for twenty cents.

Students who eat out unconsciously balance the utility from more expensive meals containing the vitamins they need with the utility they would expect from alternative uses of their money. In making a choice, they not infrequently lose sight of the long-run effect of their decisions upon their teeth and their general health and are influenced by what seems expedient at the moment. For the most part they have good health at the time such choices are made, and possible later effects of bad diet seem remote and unreal. Fruit juice, for instance, may seem less important than being able to take a girl to the movies on " date " night.

Information which provided the most interesting material relating to meals of students who ate in restaurants was collected by means of personal interviews and from approximately 500 order slips from eating places popular with the students. One of these restaurants was representative of the lowest-priced group of eating places generally patronized by students. Another was a restaurant at which medium-priced meals are served. Much of the information that follows concerning food consumption of students as related to their place of residence and where they ate their meals was secured from one or another of these sources.

Among the restaurants in a single price-group there are several social factors which explain the patronage by students of particular establishments. One place may be chosen because men prominent in athletics eat there. Another may be chosen by women students because it is frequented by men they already know or would like to know. Men students may choose a restaurant because girls take their meals there.

For the students who are compelled to watch their expenditures most carefully, " splurging " means buying additional food at the place where they ordinarily take their meals. For those students who ordinarily eat at the lowest-priced restaurants, it means a meal at one of the medium-priced ones. It is usually only the more affluent students who, when they want to celebrate, go to one of the restaurants in a third price-group which includes hotels and inns in nearby state parks where the prices of meals range between 75 cents and $1.25.

Organized students tend to patronize one of two of the most popular restaurants serving meals at medium prices, while unorganized students patronize the other one. There was no way of determining how sharp this division of patronage is; but according to statements made by unorganized students who were habitués of one, they would feel out of place in the restaurant patronized by the organized students.

MEALS AT LOW AND MEDIUM PRICED RESTAURANTS

Students tend to group the restaurants which they ordinarily patronize as cheap- and medium-priced ones. But this distinction is apparently based partly on differences in equipment and service rather than price, since the median amounts charged for plate dinners by the restaurants falling in the two groups varied by only ten cents.

It should be pointed out, however, that to a student who spends as little as 55 cents per day for food, a difference as small as five or ten cents may be significant.[19] Important, too, is the difference in prices of single items of food. At the lower-priced restaurants, a student is able to buy such popular items as sandwiches or soup for as much as five cents less per order than is charged for similar ones at a medium-priced restaurant. At restaurants of both types all of the amounts spent by students go for meals and none of it for tips.

In order to reduce the amount spent for food, some students go without breakfast.[20] About one-tenth of the 1275 students

19 Evidence that an increase of even five cents in the price of a meal affected student patronage was shown in the experience of a restaurant which raised prices in the fall of 1941. As a result, the students left in droves and it was forced to return to its old prices. It then attempted to lower its costs by giving each patron only one paper napkin and removing napkin containers from the tables so that as many as fifteen or sixteen could not be used by three or four students during a meal. At the same time the restaurant stopped furnishing a glass of cracked ice with a bottle of Coca Cola. When the price of a vegetable plate was not lowered to its former price, the orders for that type of meal practically stopped.

20 Not many dormitory students miss breakfast, principally because these meals are paid for whether they are eaten or not. When some of those who did not eat breakfast were questioned, they gave two reasons for not eating. One was that the student who did not have early morning classes preferred to sleep. Another, given by women students, was a desire to reduce.

answering the questionnaires said that they ordinarily did not eat this meal. A large majority of those who reported they went without breakfast usually took their meals at restaurants. Considerably more than half of them were girls. Only eighteen lived in dormitories or were members of a Greek-letter organization. Only seven ate at boarding clubs. Practically all of the students who were interviewed gave either convenience or the need to save money as the reason for not eating breakfast.

When the data from the schedules was analyzed, it was found that the average total expenditures of approximately 22 per cent of the students who went without breakfast were below $400. By plotting on a scatter chart the food expenditures of the students who ordinarily do not eat this meal in relation to their total expenditures, it was found that most of the students who went without this meal were students who spent less than $663 per year.

In interviews, some of these students stated that by going without breakfast they could eat dinner or lunch where their friends ate or could do such things as go to the movies or go away for week-ends or buy more clothes, which they could not do otherwise. The students whose average total expenditures amounted to more than $800 probably did so because they preferred to sleep later, as was true in the case of dormitory students whose meals were already paid for.

The breakfast served most often at a representative restaurant in the lowest-priced group included coffee or milk and sweet rolls or toast, and cost ten cents. Only six of the 87 restaurant breakfast order slips that were examined contained orders for a fruit juice, in each instance orange juice. Economy was affected by five of those who took orange juice by omitting any other beverage. In 1940-41, an egg, ham or a serving of hot cakes sold for ten cents each. Fifty-seven per cent of the slips contained orders for coffee, as compared with 37 per cent for milk. The price of milk, coffee, an order of toast, rolled oats, or rolls was five cents.

One student waiter remarked, " One thing that surprises me is that none of the fellows who eat where I wait tables seem to eat any breakfast food for breakfast. Why, at home, we always had some kind of hot or cold cereal or eggs for breakfast. But down here about the only things students order are rolls or doughnuts and coffee. They seem to prefer rolls to doughnuts and coffee to milk."

Data from all sources indicated that the majority of the students who took their breakfasts at restaurants purchased only two items of food.[21] The combinations most frequently chosen were: sweet rolls and milk, rolls and coffee, and doughnuts and coffee. Some students, however, preferred hot cocoa or chocolate milk with rolls or doughnuts.

Breakfast is ordinarily eaten between 7:30 and 7:50 A. M. Fewer students eat breakfast on Tuesdays and Thursdays, because of the smaller number of classes held on those days. On Saturday and Sunday the breakfast trade is usually later. But the students who eat breakfast on Sunday often eat more than on other days, because they have more time.

Data collected from 217 order slips from one of the most popular low-priced restaurants showed that the items ordered most frequently for lunch were sandwiches, soup, milk, and pie. The typical menu for lunch consisted of two hamburger sandwiches, pie, and milk, which could be purchased for twenty cents. Waiters in restaurants of both kinds agreed that a large majority of the students who took their meals in restaurants regularly eat one meal a day that consists of a sandwich and a milk-shake or " coke." A few of the 217 students whose slips from the low-priced restaurant were examined paid as little as five cents for their lunch, which probably meant that they had a sandwich.

At the medium-priced restaurants approximately 10 per cent of the 181 students whose slips were examined paid 45 cents or more for their dinners, while at the lower-priced restaurants only one of the 217 persons whose order slips were examined

21 For a discussion of student consumption of orange juice see pp. 94-95.

paid as much as 40 cents and only 10 paid 35 cents, the modal amount at the medium-priced restaurant.

The price charged for the plate dinner, the type of meal most frequently ordered at the restaurant chosen as representative of the low-priced group on the night the slips were examined was 25 cents.[22] This type of meal included a meat and two vegetables, or a meat, one vegetable and a salad, together with a beverage and bread and butter. At the restaurant considered, if milk were chosen for the beverage; a student could, if he desired, have two glasses, one of whole milk and one of skimmed milk. The plate dinner order permitted the choice of some stewed fruit such as prunes, apples, or peaches in place of a vegetable. Only 40 per cent of the 217 students ordered anything in addition to what was included with the plate lunch.

At all meals, the students who eat at the lower-priced restaurants tend to be in a greater hurry than those who eat at medium-priced ones. As a result, speed on the part of the waiters is stressed by the management. One student waiter said, " We are told that politeness is not so important and that too complete service is not necessary." Another waiter pointed out that speed was necessary for profit. He had been told by his employer that it took 10 breakfasts at 10 cents apiece to make 10 cents in profit. One student waitress said that where she worked the waiters were told not to give a second pat of butter if they could avoid it. The reason given was that butter is the most expensive and least profitable item in the restaurant, costing between 30 and 40 cents a pound. She added, however, that most customers ask for a second serving, especially the men students.

In general, at both the lower-priced and medium-priced restaurants, those who ordered plate lunches or plate dinners seemed to have a better balanced meal and more variety than those who ordered à la carte. When the students who came from the East were interviewed, several of them commented on the

22 Plate dinner is the name given to the type of meal which is similar to but less elaborate than a *table d'hote* meal.

haphazard and planless meals which they saw students order at restaurants. When asked to explain the difference between such orders and those they had seen students order elsewhere, one student from New York City called attention to the fact that, because of the lack of sufficient sunshine and fresh air in that city, concerted health campaigns were carried on in the city schools stressing the importance of vitamins, calories, and minerals in diets. For that reason he felt young people in large eastern cities were perhaps more aware of the need for green vegetables and milk than those at Indiana.

On the basis of the median prices for food at a low-priced restaurant, the amounts spent during a day would amount to 10 cents for breakfast, 20 cents for lunch, and 25 cents for dinner, totaling 55 cents. The typical expenditures in the medium-priced restaurant usually were 10 cents for breakfast, 25 cents for lunch, and 35 cents for dinner, totaling 70 cents.

When food preferences at medium and low-priced restaurants were compared, several interesting differences were found. One tendency which showed up clearly at the low-priced restaurant was for students to order the more filling kinds of meats and vegetables. Those who could not afford " seconds " tended to order potatoes, macaroni, spaghetti, or dried beans of some sort rather than other vegetables, salad, or stewed fruit. Out of 97 dinner slips, only 15 contained orders for spinach, 8 for green beans, and 5 for tomatoes, while fully 80 per cent chose potatoes, and 50 per cent both potatoes and macaroni.

At the medium-priced restaurant potatoes were also the most popular vegetable. Carrots and corn ranked next in popularity. Lima beans, cabbage, and spaghetti vied with each other for fourth place. Here, a salad could be substituted for a vegetable on a plate lunch order, and as many students chose the salad as carrots. As judged from the order slips of medium-priced restaurants, the students who ate there tended to consume more fresh vegetables and fruits than those students who ate at low-priced restaurants.

In 1939-40, any drink, including bottled soft drinks, which was listed on the menu at the low-priced restaurants was served with the regular dinner without extra charge. The next year, the choice was limited to milk, coffee, or chocolate milk. As a result, the milk consumption reported at such places was nearly doubled. For dinner, on the night for which the slips were examined, 37 per cent of the students ordered milk, and an equal proportion chocolate milk. Twenty-eight per cent ordered coffee, while there were only four orders for tea or for " cokes," for which there was an extra charge. At the medium-priced restaurant, 42 per cent of the students preferred coffee and 35 per cent milk; approximately 10 per cent ordered milk shakes or some other ten cent drink. The remaining students ordered tea or no beverage. The difference in the preferences for milk or coffee at the two restaurants is possibly explained by the greater sophistication of the students eating at the medium-priced places.

At the lower-priced restaurants more than twice as many hamburger sandwiches were ordered than of all other types of sandwiches. Tenderloin sandwiches ranked second in choice, and Coney Island and barbecue sandwiches third and fourth respectively. These all sold for five cents each. The majority of students who chose sandwiches usually had two of the same kind. Some students, however, ordered combinations such as one frankfurter sandwich and one hamburger. Ham and egg sandwiches and a few others sold for fifteen cents for two.

At the medium-priced restaurants tenderloin sandwiches, which sold for fifteen cents, and cheese and baked ham, which sold for ten cents each, were more popular than hamburger sandwiches, which were also ten cents. Here, there were no orders for Coney Island or barbecue sandwiches. Instead, ham salad and ham and tomato sandwiches which sold at fifteen cents were ordered.

At the low-priced restaurant chicken noodle, vegetable, and bean soups ranked in popularity in the order listed and each sold for five cents a portion. All of these kinds, except chicken noodle soup, which was fifteen cents, sold at the same price at the medium-priced restaurant. Chili, a ten cent soup, was served five times as frequently as vegetable or chicken noodle at the medium-priced restaurant on the day the slips were collected for the study.

Sliced white bread was preferred by more of the students who ate at low-priced restaurants than any other kind of bread. Rolls were more popular than rye bread, and the latter was preferred to whole-wheat bread. At the medium-priced restaurant approximately three-fourths of the slips called for rolls. Rye bread ranked second in popularity and whole-wheat bread third. Sliced white bread was ordered by only one student.

Pie was definitely a favorite dessert at the low-priced restaurant, being ordered by 75 per cent of those who ordered dessert. Cake, which ranked second in importance, was ordered only one-seventh as often. Because dessert was not included on the plate lunch, it was ordered by only about one-third of the students.

On the day the slips were collected from the medium-priced restaurant, berry cobbler, which was only five cents, was chosen more often than any other kind of dessert. Pie sold for ten cents here and perhaps for that reason it was no more popular than fruit salad or ice cream which sold for five cents.

The study of the order slips from the two types of restaurant revealed clearly certain interesting differences in the food preferences of men and women students. Women ordered less potatos, noodles, and bread than the men. The men drank more coffee than the women. Rolls and milk with a meal are optional at some restaurants, and a vegetable may be substituted. Very few of the men made this substitution, but most of the women did. In addition to these differences several student waiters mentioned certain characteristics of the two groups. In general, they found women inclined to be more particular about their food than men, but that men asked for more and faster service. They also found that women spend more time considering prices than men, and that men decide what to order much more quickly than women.

The number of students who take their meals at the University Cafeteria varies with different meals and different days. Because of its convenient location, many students having "an eight o'clock" drop in afterwards for breakfast. Here the student's breakfast is more apt to include tomato or orange juice, in addition to a roll or toast and milk or coffee, than at the low- and medium-priced restaurants of the types described above.[23]

On Mondays, Wednesdays, and Fridays, the days on which most three-hour classes meet, there are more students at the Cafeteria for lunch than on other days. At noon on week-days in 1940-41, tables were reserved by groups of students who attended the Presbyterian Church and the YWCA and YMCA to provide a common meeting place for members of these groups.

At both lunch and dinner a choice of two soups was usually offered at the Cafeteria for five cents a bowl. The variety of meats depended upon the day of the week and upon the activities on the campus which may have caused the management to expect additional patrons. Cheaper meats such as meat loaf, croquettes, and meat stews sold for around twelve cents, while roast beef and lamb sold for eighteen cents a portion. There was usually a choice of at least four kinds of meat. Apple sauce or stewed fruit was often served with the vegetables, of which there were ordinarily from four to six kinds available. These usually included one or two fresh or frozen vegetables which sold for from six to eight cents a serving. There was always one kind of hot bread. Tea, coffee, milk, chocolate milk, and buttermilk were also always available. A wide variety of salads and desserts were placed at the end of the cafeteria line. Otherwise, the university dietician in charge explained, the students would tend to spend all of their money before they reached the meat

23 After 8:00 A. M. breakfast is not served cafeteria-style. From that time on it is served from the fountain counter in the cafeteria dining room by student waiters.

and vegetables. A meal which included a serving of one of the higher-priced meats, two vegetables, a salad, a dessert and a beverage cost something over 45 cents. For meals similar to those served on plate lunches at the low-priced and medium-priced restaurants, which included a cheaper kind of meat, either one vegetable and a salad or two vegetables, sold for around 25 cents. The findings of a study of the average amounts paid for breakfast and lunch at the Cafeteria showed them to be 13 and 19 cents respectively. The range in average expenditures for three meals for a day at the Cafeteria in 1940-41 was between 50 and 90 cents. According to the dietician at the Cafeteria, students can eat balanced meals for these prices; but often fail to do so either because they have not been trained to consider food values or are unwilling to sacrifice the food they like best for the kinds that are best for them. Evidence that many of the students who eat at the Cafeteria are aware of the need for vegetables, however, is found in their comments as they pass the vegetable counter. It is not uncommon to hear a student say, " I guess I ought to have some, but I won't today." [24]

Fewer students ordinarily patronize the Cafeteria at night than at noon. This difference is probably largely because many students live some distance from the Cafeteria and prefer to have their meals nearer their rooms. On the nights that a student orchestra plays in the cafetera dining room, however, the number of student patrons is usually increased.

One interesting sidelight on the food preferences of the students who take their meals at the University Cafeteria was reported when rising food prices made it necessary to discontinue the practice of giving a free serving of potatoes with each meat order at the Cafeteria and to impose a charge of five cents for a serving. The demand dropped perceptibly, although when potatoes were served free with meat at least 90 per cent of the stu-

[24] About two hundred girls were questioned to find out whether they had eaten any new foods since they had come to college. Several said that they had. A summary of the kinds and numbers of students mentioning each is: broccoli, 5; cauliflower, 5; Brussel sprouts, 5; egg plant, 4; asparagus, 3.

dents ordering meat took them. Even co-eds who talked much
of reducing ate them regularly when they were free. But when
a charge was made for potatoes, the co-eds began to comment
frequently on their fattening qualities, and a few even shuddered
when they passed them at the cafeteria counter.

The Ship Room in the Memorial Union Building is traditionally a men's grill where both *table d'hote* and *à la carte*
meals are provided. For some time the women students had
complained because they were not permitted to eat there and
had no place in the building where they could be served at
tables. As a consequence, in 1940-41 women students were permitted to have meals there occasionally.

Twenty-eight of the students covered by the study took all of
their meals at the Coöperative Dining Room maintained in the
Memorial Union Building under the supervision of the University.[25] This eating place is designed to serve the needs of students who need to economize on food expenditures and to provide properly planned meals at a minimum cost.[26] In 1940-41,
eighteen meals were offered for a six-day week for $2.40 to
students who were willing to work approximately two hours a
week.[27] This rate of payment was the lowest for which a student

25 These meals are contracted for by the week rather than by the semester.

26 The *menus* served on March 21, 1942 reported by a student who ate at
the Cooperative Dining Room were:

Breakfast (choice of three items)	Lunch	Supper
One glass of milk	Chile Soup	Hamburger and spaghetti
One bowl of cereal	Four crackers	Two slices of bread
One half glass of grape-fruit juice	One pat of butter	One pat of butter
One sweet roll	One glass of milk	One glass of milk
One pat of butter	Peach cobbler	Cabbage salad with pineapple
		Chocolate salad

27 In 1941-42 students who patronized the dining room for three con-
secutive weeks could exchange approximately six hours of work in the fourth
week for $1 in credit toward their meals for that week. " Self Help, Scholar-
ship and Basic Budgets, Indiana University, 1940-41." *The Indiana University News-Letter.*

at Indiana University could secure a meal. When 75 cents was allowed for meals on Sundays, when the Coöperative Dining Room was closed, the cost of meals for the students who ate there on week-days was about $113.50 a year, or $56.75 per semester. In order to purchase meals at this dining room a student must purchase a weekly ticket in advance on Friday noon.

STUDENT CONSUMPTION OF SPECIFIC FOOD ITEMS AND MILK

Obviously, detailed study of student diets lies in the field of nutrition. It has seemed to the writer, however, that some information relating to student consumption of fruit, fruit juice, and milk, all items of food now generally recognized as desirable in a balanced diet, might have a place in a study of what students spend for food. Another reason for singling out these specific items for study was that their consumption is not restricted by religious background and, less than most, by the section of the country from which the student comes.

THE DAILY CONSUMPTION OF FRUIT AND ORANGE JUICE

One of the most marked dietary differences between those who ate in fraternity or sorority houses or dormitories and those who ate in restaurants out in town was the customary inclusion of orange juice in the breakfast menus of the chapter houses and dormitories. A check of student breakfast orders from two commercial restaurants revealed that only one student in thirty ordered fruit juice, and that practically none of them ordered fruit, while most of the students from the dormitories and sororities reported daily consumption of either fruit or orange juice for breakfast.

Of all Freshman students who answered the inquiry as to whether they ordinarily consumed either of these items for breakfast, 74 per cent replied in the affirmative. This proportion was larger than that in any other class because all of the Freshman women live in the dormitories. Only 63 per cent of all the Sophomores who replied to the question relating to their consumption of fruit or fruit juice gave an affirmative answer.

The fact that only 84 per cent of the sample of organized students reported a daily consumption of fruit juice is explained by the fact that many of the fraternity students who take their meals away from the fraternity houses do so for reasons of economy. Only 60 per cent of the unorganized students consumed fruit juice for breakfast daily, in spite of the number of both men and women belonging in this group who lived in the dormitories.

The omission of orange juice in the menus of students who take their meals at restaurants is obviously an economy measure. This beverage usually sells for ten cents a glass, an amount that would double the cost of breakfast for students who are accustomed to paying only ten cents for their breakfast.

Most of the students who were interviewed were aware of the need for fruit or tomato juice in their diet. Two girls explained their patronage of a restaurant that is inconveniently located for them by saying that pineapple juice was served there for five cents a glass. Several other students said they had arranged to go to a particular restaurant, which they had formerly considered too far out of their way, because it had announced that it would serve tomato juice for five cents a glass. One boy said, " Mother sends me down a sack of oranges about every week. She worries for fear I don't get enough orange juice."

THE DAILY CONSUMPTION OF MILK

About 82 per cent of the 1275 students in the sample reported that they drank at least one glass of milk per day. Of these, about 19 per cent stated that they usually drank only one glass of milk a day, 26 per cent reported two glasses a day, and more than 22 per cent consumed three glasses per day. Slightly more than 10 per cent drank four glasses daily, and almost 8 per cent averaged more than four glasses a day. A larger proportion of Freshman than Senior women drank milk each day, while among men the reverse was true. The greater consumption of milk by the organized students suggests that this item of food is one on which the students who have the least to spend economize. Since the students living in the university dormitories can have milk at every meal, it would seem to be the unorganized students who take their meals at restaurants or the University Cafeteria who consume the least milk per day and bring the proportion of unorganized students who drink milk daily below that of sorority and fraternity members.[28]

SUMMARY

The conclusions that seem warranted from the foregoing analysis of the food expenditures of different groups of students on the Indiana University campus may be summarized as follows: The median food expenditure of 1275 students in 1940-41 was $207.28 for the school year, $5.75 per week or 82 cents per day. The food expenditures of men and women in the sample were very similar and, while men probably ate more than women, they were willing to eat at cheaper places.

Food expenditures varied with place of residence and manner of living. Members of Greek-letter societies spent more for food than non-members but slightly less than students living in the university dormitories. Within the dormitories as within particular chapter houses, the rates paid for board by individual students were uniform. Below the expenditures of the students in the dormitories and the chapter houses were those of the students living in private homes and student rooming houses. Lowest of all, but by a margin of only a few cents, were the median expenditures of those who prepared their own meals.

Among the students buying their meals singly, such as those eating at the University Cafeteria and other restaurants, were found some who took their meals at the lower-priced establish-

[28] The percentages of the organized and unorganized men and women in the four undergraduate classes at Indiana University in 1940-41 who consumed one or more glasses of milk per day were:

	Organized		*Unorganized*	
	Men	Women	Men	Women
Freshman	89.66	89.17	67.12	76.14
Sophomore	73.47	90.78	67.12	75.79
Junior	89.36	83.33	83.78	77.08
Senior	91.66	81.08	87.84	69.12

ments and ordinarily spent as little as 55 cents per day. Many eating at the medium-priced restaurants spent around 70 cents a day. At the University Cafeteria, where a wider range of choice was available, the amounts spent per day varied between 50 and 90 cents. Although fruit juice, usually orange juice, was regularly served in the chapter houses and in the dining rooms of the dormitories and two-thirds of the students in the sample reported daily consumption of some kind of fruit juice, an examination of a large number of breakfast order slips from restaurants catering to student trade disclosed only one order of fruit juice out of thirty breakfasts. Eighty-two per cent of the students in the sample reported that they drank at least one glass of milk per day. In the case of those who were forced to economize on food a high degree of elasticity of demand was evident. A difference of five or ten cents in the cost of a meal might determine quite definitely both where they would take their meals and what they would eat.

When food expenditures were studied in relation to the schools of the University in which the students were enrolled it was found that those in the College of Arts and Sciences spent somewhat more than those in any of the other schools. As might be expected, students who earned part or all of their expenses spent less than those who contributed nothing toward their own support. For reasons suggested in the chapter, those who earned about half their expenses tended to spend least of all for food. The median food expenditures of the students from farms were less than those from either small towns or cities.

From the foregoing consideration of what different groups of students spend for their meals, their consumption of certain items of food, and the food consumed by the students who eat at restaurants and consequently have a choice of food at each meal, we turn next to a discussion of what these groups spend for clothing.

CHAPTER V

CLOTHING

IN a recent study of consumer spending published by the Bureau of Labor Statistics the following statement appears:

. . . persons of both sexes in the 16 to 29 age group tend to place more emphasis on personal appearance than they do at any other period in their lives. It is a common observation that grown daughters are likely to spend more for clothing than do their mothers, particularly if they are in school or if they have gainful employment.[1]

Since the students in the present study fall within the age group mentioned above, it would be expected that clothing would represent an important item in their budgets.

The movies and modern methods of merchandising have played an important part in lessening the differences in the types of clothing worn on individual campuses as well as at colleges and universities in different parts of the country. This change is particularly true in regard to the functional type of sports clothing worn by women students for work and play. Skirts and sweaters worn with or without blouses, flat-heeled shoes, and colored half socks have become the almost universally accepted costume for such purposes for women.

Among women at Indiana University and elsewhere, the greater uniformity in school clothes has not, however, eliminated the possibility of the reflection of individual personality in dress. In spite of greater standardization this difference is still seen through the choice and combinations of colors and specific items of wearing apparel and the materials from which garments are made. Appearance has remained the paramount criterion in the choice of clothing, but standards of attractiveness have

---

1 Bureau of Labor Statistics, Bulletin No. 648, *Family Expenditures in Selected Cities, 1935-36. Vol. III Clothing and Personal Care* (Washington: Government Printing Office, 1941), p. 24.

changed and are influenced by a greater demand for comfort. High heels in a class room now tend to be frowned upon as in poor taste.

The costumes worn to classes by university men are perhaps more varied than those of women students. In general, these men fall roughly into three groups, those who usually wear a very collegiate type of sports clothes and more or less pride themselves on being careless about their dress; those who are reasonably neat but not fastidious and usually wear a necktie and a sweater or coat on the campus; and those meticulous about their appearance at all times and to whom a reputation for being well-dressed seems important.

In making this study, the collection of data relating to expenditures for clothing presented the greatest difficulty of any of the items in the student budget. In answer to a question relating to which expense was the hardest to estimate accurately, a majority of the students who returned the questionnaires checked clothing. However, since one of the purposes of the study was to answer the question of what are representative total amounts spent during a college year by different groups of students at Indiana; it seemed best to include clothing rather than to omit this item, as has been done in some studies of spending made at other schools. Of necessity the expenditures for clothing tend to represent a budget for twelve months rather than for the thirty-six weeks in the regular academic year because items such as socks, underwear, and cotton dresses purchased for summer wear are later worn at college.

Another problem encountered was that of determining how much of the price paid for a durable item should be included in the estimate for clothing for one year. After considering various means of obtaining significant estimates, it was decided, in the case of the purchase of an article of clothing which the student expected to wear for more than the current year, to compute the amount included in the estimate by dividing the price paid for a garment by the number of years the student expected to wear it. For example, if it was the second and last winter the student expected to wear a coat for which he had paid $50, the amount for this item included in his estimate of clothing expenditures would be $25.

EXPENDITURES BY ALL STUDENTS

Since the median and quartile amounts spent for clothing by women differed so much from those of men, it was felt that the median expenditure for all students in the sample would have little significance.[2] It did seem worth while, however, to see what happened to the amount spent for clothing as the total amount spent for all items in the student budget increased. For this reason the following table was prepared.

TABLE 16

MEDIAN EXPENDITURES FOR CLOTHING OF 1266 STUDENTS BY
TOTAL EXPENDITURE LEVELS FOR 1940-41

Total Expenditure	Number in Sample	Median Expenditure for Clothing
$ 200– 399	20	$ 35.50
400– 599	426	51.95
600– 799	415	90.70
800– 999	250	162.50
1000–1199	105	240.75
1200–1399	36	315.75
1400–1599	7	568.75
1600–1799	5	825.50
1800–1999	1	875.00
2000–2199	—	——
2200–over	1	975.00

From these figures it is apparent that the amount spent for clothing rose as the total expenditure increased. After the student's total disbursement reached $400 the amount he spent for clothing rose at a more rapid rate than his total expenditure until the latter reached $180.00. Beyond $1400 the increase in

2 The median expenditure for clothing for all students in the sample for 1940-41 amounted to $74.78. The interquartile range was $44.20 to $147.86. When the 1275 cards were sorted for clothing expenditures, nine cards were rejected because of inconsistencies in punching. For the mean expenditure for clothing by all students in the sample and other groups studied see Table 78, page 244.

the total expenditure was explained almost entirely by purchases of clothing.

EXPENDITURES BY MEN AND WOMEN

The age factor previously mentioned is probably the most important reason why clothing is such an important item to college students, especially to women. The fact that men students have control over the marriage proposal and have been conditioned to rate women primarily in terms of " attractiveness " has made women students much more clothes-conscious than men and anxious to improve their appearance and personal charm. Criteria of prestige for men are different. At a similar age they tend to become interested in future success. Having and earning money is important. They begin to focus hard on a career and usually face the prospect of a delay of a few years before marriage. All of these things, plus roads to campus prestige by means of athletics and other extra-curricular activities, tend to make clothing a secondary factor in establishing men on the campus. Women's extra-curricular activities stand them in less good stead than in the case of men; and, to the extent that they do, there is apt to be a higher correlation than is true in the case of men between personal attractiveness and the achievement of campus leadership. Because women usually marry at a younger age than men and college women are ready to marry without the necessarily delaying hurdle of finding work which men face, college and the marriage quest are linked more immediately for them than for men. As a result, college is a more active period of mate seeking for women than for men. Preparation for a career more often represents to women insurance against economic dependency in case they do not marry or their marriage fails. Those who come from smaller communities often expect to find at college a better opportunity for meeting men than their home towns afford. All women at college, however, find that they must compete with other women for male attention and must therefore dress not only to attract men but so that they will stand out in contrast to other women. For the occasional woman who is outstandingly physically beautiful, clothes may be somewhat less urgently necessary; but for the majority, clothes must be made to play a much more actively assisting rôle. All of these circumstances cause women to face a greater and more immediate need than men to dress well while in college.

In general, business exploits the importance of women's dressing well to the utmost. Furthermore, the recent emphasis on price-lining and the swifter copying of expensive models in cheap price-lines rapidly diffused even to small communities has made the entire country both more style-conscious and more desirous of being " style-right." But the woman of moderate or low means has been robbed of part of the advantage inherent in the attractive low-priced garments now found in the market by the fact that, with cheaper dresses, there has developed the mandatory habit of having a greater number so as not to be seen too often in the same dress.

In 1940-41, the median college woman at Indiana University spent $111.14 for her wardrobe as against the median male expenditure of $57.93. This difference in the amounts spent for clothing by college men and women was greater than that found between the single men and women at all income levels studied by the National Resources Committee.[3] The levels of the clothing expenditures of university students who had to economize varied less than those of the students who had the most to spend. This is partly because the social programs of the latter group tend to be more restricted. Many of these women also make a large part of their clothing and have fewer duplicates of the same items in their wardrobes.[4] The fact that the third

3 The National Resources Committee. *Consumer Expenditures in the United States*, pp. 81-82. The findings of this study showed that the average annual expenditure of single men at all the income levels included in the study was $98 and that of the single women $138.

4 About 22 percent of 682 women in the sample made at least some of their own clothing. The majority of these students spent less than the median total expenditure of all students.

quartile expenditure for clothing of women students was more
than twice as great as that of men reflects the tendency for
women to spend a large proportion of any surplus income they
have over that required for necessities for clothing.

Group	Number in Sample	First Quartile	Median	Third Quartile
Men	584	$35.69	$ 57.93	$104.30
Women	682	53.48	111.14	212.57

Women spent 20.4 per cent, or slightly over one-fifth of their
total budget, for clothing; while the men spent only 10.7 per
cent of theirs. Clothing ranked third in importance in the budget
of women and fourth in that of men. But although the men
spent only about half as large a proportion of their budget for
clothing as the women, they spent more for recreation and refreshment (See Table 92, page 258). This suggests that women
spent what they saved on those items for clothing. In general,
the men students recognize these differences and accept them.
In interviews, several intimated that they considered the preëminence gained from dating an attractively dressed co-ed sufficient
reward for sharing their incomes.

For the reasons discussed earlier in the chapter, it seems
probable that the expenditures of men and women reach a peak
disparity while in college. Except in families having incomes of
over $5000, the average expenditures of husbands and wives in
all areas studied in the recent Consumer Purchase Studies were
much more nearly the same than the median expenditures of
men and women in this study. In the light of these findings, it
seems probable that after marriage the disparity between the
amounts spent by men and women tends to disappear.

EXPENDITURES OF ORGANIZED AND UNORGANIZED STUDENTS

The comparison of the median and quartile expenditures for
clothing of the members of Greek-letter societies and non-
members shown in Table 17 proved particularly interesting.

From these figures it is evident that membership in a fraternity or sorority influences the amount spent for clothing, even
though it is usually the students who have the most to spend

TABLE 17

MEDIAN AND QUARTILE EXPENDITURES FOR CLOTHING BY ORGANIZED AND
UNORGANIZED MEN AND WOMEN AT INDIANA UNIVERSITY, 1940-41

Group	Number in Sample	First Quartile	Median	Third Quartile
Men				
Organized	205	$ 54.58	$ 94.16	$139.94
Unorganized	379	27.58	48.30	72.44
Women				
Organized	230	107.34	203.32	304.00
Unorganized	452	46.86	77.76	154.84
	1266			

who join these organizations. In the case of both organized
and unorganized students the median expenditure of the women
was greater. Almost 7 per cent of the unorganized and over 25
per cent of the organized women studied reported that they
spent $300 or more per year for clothing. Some of the larger
amounts spent by unorganized women were by transfer students
who had been members of sororities at other colleges but were
not affiliated with the chapter of their respective sororities at
Indiana and for this reason were grouped with the unorganized
women in this study. In some instances the expenditures for
clothing of these women represented an attempt to compensate
for not being organized while at the University. Occasionally,
a girl who is not asked to join the sorority of her first choice
refuses to join any other and consoles herself by attempting to
become a campus pace-setter in matters of dress.

EXPENDITURES BY COLLEGE CLASSES

As shown in Table 18, class membership affects the student's
clothing expenditure. Freshmen spend relatively more for clothing than do upperclassmen. Going off to college as a Freshman
is a big event and naturally causes the student to outfit himself
for the new world he is entering more extensively than in any
succeeding year. The new student entering college for the first
time depends somewhat on personal appearance as a means of
obtaining the approval of the new group. Often, self-conscious

in a new environment, he leans on material aids such as clothing and physical adornment in seeking greater security. Later, as he finds himself accepted by his associates for his personality or admired for some skill or ability, clothing becomes less important. As an upperclassman, he also is less afraid to wear what he chooses for fear his associates will think he doesn't know any better.

TABLE 18

THE MEDIAN AND QUARTILE CLOTHING EXPENDITURES OF 1266 STUDENTS IN THE FOUR UNDERGRADUATE CLASSES, 1940-41

Class	Number in Sample	First Quartile	Median	Third Quartile
Freshman	443	$48.91	$99.09	$200.62
Sophomore	321	40.16	66.33	137.92
Junior	289	42.46	74.25	135.91
Senior	213	38.47	67.94	115.74

A comparison of the median clothing expenditures of both organized and unorganized Freshman women shown in Table 78, page 244, with those of other classes suggests that the sorority "Rush Week" in September of 1940 was also a factor that affected the amounts spent for clothing by Freshmen and Sophomore women.

Larger amounts spent by Freshman and Sophomore organized men shown in Table 78 suggest that the "rush" for men, which in 1940-41 was extended over a longer period of time and was less formal than that of women, may also have affected the clothing expenditures of men in those two classes. Although the majority of their pledgees are Freshmen, both fraternities and sororities usually invite a few Sophomores to become members each year.

The Seniors spent the least for several reasons. Unlike high school, graduation calls for less new clothing than does the Junior year, for example, when new formal dresses are purchased by many women students for the Junior Prom. Competition for offices for which clothing might be an aid are over by

Senior year and the students are often too occupied by the duties of their offices to emphasize dress as in previous years. For students seriously interested in preparing themselves for jobs academic work leaves less time for social activities.

EXPENDITURES BY STUDENTS IN THE DIFFERENT SCHOOLS OF THE UNIVERSITY

The median expenditures for clothing by students in the College of Arts and Sciences in 1940-41 was $106.06, an amount almost $40 greater than that spent by students in any other school. This was because of a relatively greater enrollment of organized students and because the two-year elective course falls in this school. The latter group includes a large proportion of the students who come to college for reasons other than strictly academic ones.

As shown in Table 19, the median amounts spent by students of the professional schools, in which the students tend to concentrate harder on definite preparation for earning a living, were noticeably less than those spent in the College of Arts and Sciences, in which the proportion of organized women was greater.

TABLE 19

MEDIAN AND QUARTILE EXPENDITURES OF 1266 STUDENTS IN
DIFFERENT SCHOOLS ON THE BLOOMINGTON CAMPUS
OF INDIANA UNIVERSITY, 1940-41

School	Number in Sample	First Quartile	Median	Third Quartile
Arts and Science	482	$51.85	$106.06	$210.21
Business	519	40.19	65.95	114.79
Education	159	41.09	69.50	162.50
Medicine and Dental....	59	42.65	59.41	115.00
Music	38	32.86	55.56	96.67
Law	9	20.00	50.00	80.00
	1266			

EXPENDITURES BY STUDENTS WHO WORK

Table 20 shows, as might be expected, a fairly regular progression in the median expenditure for clothing as one progresses from the group earning all their college funds to those earning none.

TABLE 20

THE MEDIAN CLOTHING EXPENDITURES OF 1195 STUDENTS BY
PERCENTAGES OF EXPENSES EARNED BY THEM, 1940-41 [a]

Proportion of Expenses Earned	Number in Sample	First Quartile	Median	Third Quartile
None	517	$58.15	$117.12	$212.98
Less than 20	288	45.32	83.08	143.16
20–39	157	37.96	55.87	98.75
40–59	89	32.39	50.38	77.73
60–79	45	35.00	52.67	88.75
80–99	43	29.58	46.92	75.00
All	56	27.06	45.45	72.00

[a] Seventy-one of the 1266 cases used in the clothing analysis failed to indicate whether they earned any of their college expenses.

There appears to be a fairly coercive minimum central tendency for the student to spend from $45 to $55 regardless of whether he earns all or anything down to 20-40 per cent of his college expenses. Only among the students earning less than 20 per cent of their way does the minimum amount begin to rise sharply.[5]

EXPENDITURES OF STUDENTS FROM FARMS,
SMALL TOWNS, AND CITIES

Table 21 shows that the type of community from which a student comes also affects his expenditures for clothing. Students from farms spent less than those from small towns or cities for several reasons. Their consistently lower expenditures for all items in the student budget indicates that in general they tend to have less to spend. Part of the smaller amounts spent by

5 The median expenditure for clothing by the NYA students was only $27.20 per year, an amount less than the median amount spent by any other group of students who earned any part or all of their own expenses. Further evidence of the extreme economy practiced by these students in their clothing expenditures was found in their first and third quartile expenditures, which were $19.50 and $37.80 respectively. The median NYA woman in the sample spent $29.29 and the median man $26.32. One fourth of the NYA men spent less than $13.95 for clothing and one fourth of the women less than $23.08. This difference gives further evidence that the minimum amount that women can spend on clothing is considerably greater than that of men students.

women from farms is explained by the fact that more of these women made a part of their own clothing than did the women from other types of communities. Still another reason for the lower expenditure for women from farms may be found in their greater tendency to purchase clothing from mail order houses. The median expenditure for clothing by women from small towns was more than that by women from cities. This was because, as was mentioned in Chapter II, the extremes in the incomes of students from cities showed wider variation than among students from small towns and a larger proportion had low incomes than high ones.[6] Another possible explanation of the greater expenditure by women students from small towns is that these girls are frequently the only girls from their home towns in college and are the social leaders at home and pacesetters in dress. The median and quartile amounts spent by men students from cities were higher than those of men from farms or small towns, probably because of the more formal type of clothing worn by city men rather than because of differences in the incomes of the men from the other types of communities.

TABLE 21

MEDIAN AND QUARTILE CLOTHING EXPENDITURES OF 739 INDIANA
UNIVERSITY STUDENTS FROM FARMS, SMALL TOWNS,
AND CITIES, 1940-41

Group	Number in Sample	First Quartile	Median	Third Quartile
Men				
Farm	55	$29.64	$ 48.13	$ 69.50
Small Town	142	36.02	59.68	107.38
City	136	41.07	66.09	115.00
Women				
Farm	93	38.61	56.54	109.29
Small Town	121	70.00	150.00	258.33
City	192	53.57	111.54	215.56

HABITS AND PATTERNS OF STUDENT CLOTHING CONSUMPTION

The amounts paid for a few specific items in the wardrobes of men and women students were also examined although no

6 This statement is based on the total expenditures of these students which were taken as an indication of income.

attempt was made to cover the complete wardrobes of either sex.[7] The only items for which it was felt the students would remember the price, either because of the frequency with which they were purchased or because the amounts paid for them were great enough to be remembered easily, were considered. The objectives in studying the prices that students customarily paid for specific items of clothing was to determine what priced items students at Indiana tended to buy; whether women students spent more for clothing because they paid more for such items as hats, shoes, coats, hose, etc., or because they purchased more of each; and to determine whether organized students purchased higher priced clothing or more of it than did non-fraternity members. Frequency distributions of the prices paid by all men and all women in the sample and by the four groups of organized and unorganized men and women were set up to see if the items purchased fell about any central prices and in order to find the median amounts paid by each group.

Sweaters.—A check of three classes showed eighty per cent of the women wearing sweaters. There are several reasons for the popularity of sweaters among college students. They are comfortable, easy to get into, require relatively little care, and are generally accepted as " smart." They are made in such a wide variety of colors, weaves, and styles that they permit the students who own several to have a wide variety in costume. For even the most " exclusive " student the utilities offered by this type of garment for campus wear more than offset the fact that practically every student on the campus owns at least one sweater. Some of the girls in the sample owned as many as eight or ten. The more affluent students depend on variety in colors, styles, and qualities to develop prestige in everyday dress. In 1940-41 pastel shades were the most popular, and slip-ons the most generally accepted style.

7 These were the actual prices paid rather than the part of the total cost included in the clothing expenditure for the year (see page 99).

The low price at which sweaters are sold makes them a means by which the students who must economize most can keep abreast of the fashions. The woman student who has the least to spend for clothing gains self-assurance from being able to appear in a sweater of the latest fashion which looks so much like that worn by women who can afford expensive clothing that the average man couldn't tell the difference. With care, even an inexpensive sweater wears fairly well.

Table 22 shows that the median price paid for a sweater by men at Indiana University in 1940-41 was $3.98 and by women $2.98. The latter amount, which was also the modal price for both men and women, was paid by more than 72 per cent of the women and by 46.8 per cent of the men. From the data examined, it was found that women usually wore their sweaters longer than men. Organized men and women wore them a shorter time than the unorganized, probably because of the greater pressure on the organized students to adopt new styles.

There was no difference between the median prices paid by organized and unorganized men, but in the case of women the sorority members tended to pay about two dollars more for a sweater than non-members.

TABLE 22

PRICE PAID FOR SWEATERS BY 1180 STUDENTS AT INDIANA
UNIVERSITY, 1940-41

	Men		Women	
Price	Number in Sample	Percentage of Students	Number in Sample	Percentage of Students
$1.00	3	.57	28	4.29
1.98	63	11.93	188	28.83
2.98	181	34.28	255	39.11
3.98	144	27.27	104	15.95
4.98	122	23.11	55	8.44
5.98	10	1.89	8	1.23
6.98	2	.38	3	.46
7.98	1	.19	4	.61
8.98	2	.38	7	1.07
9.98	0	0	0	0
	528	100.00	652	100.00

Thus, we see that women, whose median total expenditure for clothing was greater than that of men, paid less per garment for their sweaters. We therefore conclude that any part of their greater expenditure that can be attributed to the purchase of sweaters must be explained by the purchase of more sweaters rather than of more expensive ones, since women tended to wear their sweaters longer than men.

Skirts.—A frequency distribution showing the number and percentage of women paying different prices for skirts is shown in Table 23. The median price paid by 645 women for skirts suitable to be worn with sweaters was $4.38. The median price paid by organized women for a skirt of this type was $4.45 and the median for the unorganized was $3.78. A majority, centering between 59 and 61 per cent of women in each group examined (organized, unorganized, Freshman, Sophomore, Junior, and Senior), ordinarily wore a skirt from 12 to 18 months.

TABLE 23

PRICE PAID BY 645 WOMEN STUDENTS OF INDIANA
UNIVERSITY FOR SKIRTS, 1940-41

Price	Number in Sample	Percentage of Sample
$0– .99	0	0
1–1.99	5	.78
2–2.99	84	13.02
3–3.99	209	32.40
4–4.99	168	26.05
5–5.99	100	15.50
6–6.99	45	6.98
7–7.99	21	3.25
8–8.99	8	1.24
9 or over	5	.78
	645	100.00

Men's Shirts and Women's Blouses.—There was considerably more variation in the kinds of blouses worn by women than in the kinds of shirts worn by men. This difference existed largely because many women made their own blouses and experimented with new patterns and because women often purchased fancy blouses for dress. As may be seen from Table 24, over one-fifth of the women customarily wore blouses costing less than $1.[8] Around 10 per cent paid less than $1.50 for them and about 39 per cent paid from $1.50 to $1.99. At the other extreme less than 2 per cent of the women were accustomed to paying $4.00 or more for their blouses. The median amount spent for a blouse by all women in the sample was $1.76. The difference between the prices paid by sorority women and nonmembers was negligible; although the former wore their blouses longer, probably because the higher priced ones they purchased stood laundering better.

Table 24 shows that over 10 per cent of the men students usually paid less than $1 for a shirt. Only 3.5 per cent paid $2.50 or more. The median price paid by all men was $1.64.[9] Almost 15 per cent of the men said they usually wore a shirt less than a year. About 40 per cent reported that they expected a shirt to last a year or more, and around 25 per cent thought their shirts lasted from two to two and one-half years. Obviously, the number of shirts owned by a student affected how long he expected one to last. A considerably larger proportion of Freshmen and Sophomores purchased shirts costing less than $1.50 than did upperclassmen, although the modal price interval for all classes was $1.50 to $1.99.

Almost 22 per cent of the organized men and 40.2 per cent of the unorganized men paid less than $1.50 for a shirt. The median amount paid by fraternity men was $1.54 and by nonmembers $1.51. Slightly less than 24 per cent of the organized men paid $2.50 or more for a shirt, and only 13.39 per cent of the non-members.

From this examination of prices paid for women's blouses and men's shirts, we see that the differences in amounts paid by

8 These were probably blouses costing 89 to 98 cents and purchased from mail-order houses or ones made at home.

9 This median was computed on the basis of class intervals because of the wide variation in the prices paid for men's shirts.

TABLE 24

PRICES PAID BY 544 MEN FOR SHIRTS AND BY 202 WOMEN
FOR BLOUSES AT INDIANA UNIVERSITY, 1940-41

Price	Men		Women	
	Number in Sample	Percentage of Sample	Number in Sample	Percentage of Sample
$ 0– .49	1	.18	2	.99
.50– .99	56	10.29	40	19.80
1.00–1.49	131	24.08	18	8.91
1.50–1.99	292	53.68	78	38.61
2.00–2.49	45	8.27	4	1.98
2.50–2.99	12	2.21	44	21.78
3.00–3.49	0	0	3	1.49
3.50–3.99	0	0	10	4.95
4.00 and over	7	1.29	3	1.49
	544	100.00	202	100.00

men and women and organized and unorganized students were small. For this reason any differences between the clothing expenditures of men and women or members of Greek-letter organizations and non-members that can be attributed to either of these items would be explained by the tendency for men to own a smaller number of shirts than the number of blouses usually owned by women students.

Shoes.—Co-eds at many universities were relatively slow in adopting the comfortable, flat-heeled sports shoes that students in women's colleges have worn almost exclusively for classes for more than a score of years. But by 1940-41 shoes of this type were quite generally worn at Indiana University on week days. Rubber-soled, saddle-strap oxfords of brown or of white combined with brown, blue, or black, which were among the first styles to be adopted, were still worn. Low-heeled, leather-soled oxfords in brown or in combinations of white and brown, sandals, or the type of oxford with soles reinforced to form heels known as "wedgies" were popular in that year. Only a few women continued to wear high-heeled shoes to classes.

In 1940-41, the women at Indiana University tended to prefer variety in color and style in their shoes to quality and durability.

As a consequence, they were inclined to buy cheap shoes that could be discarded after a short time rather than more expensive ones that would wear better and have to be worn longer.

TABLE 25

Prices Paid for Shoes by 564 Men and 643 Women Students at Indiana University, 1940-41

	Men		Women	
Price	Number in Sample	Percentage of Sample	Number in Sample	Percentage of Sample
$1.98–2.97	4	.71	10	1.49
2.98–3.97	73	12.94	88	13.08
3.98–4.97	113	20.04	175	26.00
4.98–5.97	250	44.33	202	34.47
5.98–6.97	49	8.69	76	11.28
6.98–7.97	27	4.78	38	5.65
7.98–8.97	28	4.96	31	4.61
8.98 and over	20	3.55	23	3.42
	564	100.00	643	100.00

Table 25 shows that the modal amount paid for shoes by the women students fell in the class interval of $4.98-5.97. The median expenditure was $5.22. The median organized woman ordinarily paid $6.34 for her shoes and the median unorganized women $4.88. The modal price interval for the unorganized women was $3.98-4.97 and for the organized women $4.98-5.97. From these figures we see that membership in a Greek-letter society had relatively little effect on the price paid for shoes by women. However, the organized women purchased more pairs than the unorganized.

In the same year the majority of men were wearing either brown or black leather oxfords to classes, often shoes purchased and worn previously with business suits for semi-formal occasions. The economy effected by wearing out these shoes which were no longer in good enough condition for dress occasions tended to prevent the complete adoption by men of rubber or crepe-soled moccasin or saddle styled sports shoes for school year. The majority of men interviewed said that when they were able to do so, they liked to keep a relatively new pair of black or brown oxfords for " best " so that they could be worn without having to stop to shine them if they were needed in a hurry. About a fourth of the men said they usually could not afford to have more than one pair of shoes at a time. The median price paid by all of the men in the sample for their shoes was $5.35 per pair.

A larger proportion of women than of men discarded a pair of shoes at the end of six months, either because they purchased cheap shoes which didn't wear well or because the designs were fads which were replaced in quick succession by newer ones. In general, when women purchased shoes of durability comparable to that of the shoes worn by the majority of the men they were able to wear them longer than the men. The women also tended to own more pairs of shoes at a time than the men, probably because the median price paid by men was greater than that paid by women.

When both men and women were considered on the basis of organization, several differences were observed in their respective shoe purchases. Only about five and one-half per cent of all the organized students ordinarily paid as little as from $2.98 to $3.98 for a pair of shoes, while 16.9 per cent of the unorganized students bought shoes in that low price range. Another sharp contrast in the buying patterns of the organized and unorganized students appeared in regard to the purchase of shoes priced at $3.98 to $4.97. Shoes falling in this price range were worn by only 12.7 per cent of the organized students while they were worn by 29.6 per cent of the unorganized students.

Socks and Hose.—In spite of the widespread adoption of half-hose for sportswear by women college students in 1940-41, silk stockings continued to be an important item in their wardrobes. As may be seen from Table 26, the variation in the amounts paid for silk hose was fairly wide, although the prices paid tended to center sharply around 79 cents and $1 per pair.

TABLE 26

PRICES ORDINARILY PAID FOR SILK HOSE BY 609 WOMEN
STUDENTS AT INDIANA UNIVERSITY, 1940-41

Price	Number in Sample	Percentage of Sample
$ .49	8	1.31
.59	37	6.08
.69	74	12.15
.79	172	28.24
.89	49	8.05
1.00	138	22.66
1.25	43	7.06
1.35	88	14.45
	609	100.00

The median price reported was 89 cents, and the modal price
79 cents. The lowest price reported was 49 cents per pair and
the highest $1.35.

Table 27 seems to indicate that at least a small part of the
difference in the clothing expenditures of organized and unorganized women students is accounted for by the difference in
the prices they pay for silk hose, since the median price paid by
the former group was $1 and that of the latter 79 cents. The

TABLE 27

PRICES ORDINARILY PAID FOR SILK HOSE BY 227 SORORITY WOMEN AND
382 NON-MEMBERS AT INDIANA UNIVERSITY, 1940-41

Price	Organized		Unorganized	
	Number in Sample	Percentage of Students in Sample	Number in Sample	Percentage in Sample
$ .39	1	.44	2	.52
.49	1	.44	4	1.05
.59	4	1.76	33	8.64
.69	12	5.29	62	16.23
.79	49	21.59	123	32.20
.89	21	9.25	28	7.33
1.00	77	33.92	61	15.96
1.25	17	7.49	26	6.81
.1.35 or over	45	19.82	43	11.26
	227	100.00	382	100.0

median price paid for hose by Freshman, Sophomore, and
Junior women was 89 cents, and by Seniors $1. The modal
price in all classes was $1, although similar numbers in each
class paid 79 cents.

As would be expected, the men paid less for their socks than
the women paid for hose. The amount of the median price paid
by the men was only 30 cents, and the modal price 35 cents or
three pairs for a dollar. Eleven men paid as little as 10 cents per
pair, and only three paid as much as 90 cents. The data collected
showed that men students not only tend to pay less for their
hose than women, but that they also replaced them less frequently. The number and percentage of the men paying various
prices for their socks are shown in Table 28.

TABLE 28

THE PRICES ORDINARILY PAID FOR SOCKS BY 396 MEN
STUDENTS AT INDIANA UNIVERSITY, 1940-41

Price	Number in Sample	Percentage of Sample
$ .10	11	2.78
.20	72	18.18
.30	127	32.07
.40	103	26.01
.50	72	18.18
.60	1	.25
.70	3	.76
.80	4	1.01
.90	3	.76
	396	100.00

Fraternity men tended to pay more for their socks than non-
members, probably because they had more to spend rather than
because higher priced hose had any prestige value for them. The
median price paid by these men was 40 cents and their modal
price 50 cents. Only about 2 per cent paid less than 20 cents or
as much as 90 cents or more for their socks. Both the median
and modal price paid by the unorganized men was 30 cents.
About 3 per cent of these men paid less than 20 cents per pair
and none of them as much as 90 cents.

The fact that men not only pay less for their socks than
women do for their hose but also wear them longer shows that

this difference helps explain the greater amounts spent by women for clothing. Sorority women pay higher prices than non-members because the quality of hose is a prestige symbol among them.

Coats

Light Weight Coats.—Most students own some kind of a medium-weight coat suitable for wear in the spring and fall. It may be a leather jacket, a reversible, a " finger-tip " gabardine or corduroy coat, or a more formal one of camels hair, tweed, or some other woolen material. In the past two years, women students have worn tweed coats with linings which were attached with zippers so that in milder weather the lining could be detached and the coat made to serve as a spring or fall wrap as well as a winter one. It is not uncommon for a woman student to own both a sport coat and a dress coat of medium weight. The women who have more to spend on clothing usually prefer to have several sports coats of lesser quality instead of one or two expensive coats.

To determine the relative popularity of the different kinds of light-weight coats worn on school days in the fall, the coats of fifty women students and as many men students were checked on their way to convocation.[10] The results are shown in Table 29.

Over 40 per cent of the women paid from $10 to $19 for light weight coats and almost 37 per cent between $20 and $29. A smaller proportion of the men purchased coats in the first of these price ranges and a larger proportion of men than women paid from $20 to $30. Almost the same proportion of men and women bought coats priced at less than $10. A larger proportion of men than women paid from $30 to $50 for these coats.

10 These programs are ordinarily given on Tuesday or Thursday morning at 10 o'clock. The Commons and the library are closed at such times, so that unless the student goes to his room or to a restaurant off the campus he is apt to go to the Auditorium to hear the program. Because of this it was believed that a tabulation of 100 men and women on their way to the Auditorium would provide a representative sample.

TABLE 29

TYPE OF LIGHT WEIGHT COATS WORN TO CONVOCATION BY 50 MEN AND
50 WOMEN STUDENTS AT INDIANA UNIVERSITY, 1940-41

Type of Coat	Number of Women	Number of Men
Leather jacket	2	11
Reversibles	10	
Full length natural shade camel's-hair coat	14	1
Bright-colored short wool jacket	7	
Full-length tweed coat	12	5
Natural shade gabardine "finger-tip" coat	3	
Blue or black "dressmaker's" coat	2	
Trench coat of natural shade twill or gabardine		21
Corduroy jackets		9
Business man's type of top coat		3
	50	50

But more women than men bought coats costing $50 or over.

The median price paid by the men for a light-weight coat was $23.54, an amount slightly higher than $21.45, the median spent by women.

TABLE 30

PRICES PAID BY 209 MEN AND 631 WOMEN AT INDIANA UNIVERSITY
FOR LIGHT WEIGHT COATS, 1940-41

Price	Men		Women	
	Number in Sample	Percentage of Sample	Number in Sample	Percentage of Sample
$ 0- 9	9	4.31	29	4.60
10-19	64	30.62	253	40.10
20-29	89	42.58	231	36.61
30-39	40	19.14	84	13.31
40-49	5	2.39	15	2.37
50-59	2	.96	16	2.54
60-69	0	0	3	.47
	209	100.0	631	100.0

The median price paid by the sorority women was considerably higher than that paid by non-members, amounting to $25.20 as compared with $18.86, the median price paid by the unorganized women. Among the men, the median price paid by fraternity members was $34.44 and by the non-members $21.50. About 22 per cent, or almost twice as large a proportion of the organized students as unorganized, paid as much as $30 or more for a light weight coat. Almost the same proportion of men as women reported that they usually wore a spring or fall coat only one year.

From these findings we see that not only sex but membership in a Greek-letter society is a factor which seems to affect the prices paid for this kind of coat.

Winter Coats.—A small majority of the women paid less than $40 for a winter coat for which the expenditure was usually the heaviest for any single item in their wardrobes. Above that amount the distribution was spread over $20 class intervals up to $240. An amount beyond $100 was in practically all instances paid for a fur coat which was definitely a prestige symbol on the campus.

TABLE 31

PRICES PAID FOR WINTER COATS BY 546 MEN AND 641 WOMEN
STUDENTS AT INDIANA UNIVERSITY, 1940-41

	Men		Women	
Price	Number in Sample	Percentage of Sample	Number in Sample	Percentage of Sample
$ 0– 19	67	12.27	65	10.14
20– 39	422	77.29	296	46.18
40– 59	48	8.79	105	16.38
60– 79	3	.54	53	8.27
80– 99	4	.73	17	2.65
100–119	2	.37	53	8.27
120–139	0	0	14	2.18
140–159	0	0	16	2.50
160–179	0	0	5	.78
180–199	0	0	3	.47
200–219	0	0	14	2.18
	546	100.00	641	100.00

A slightly lesser proportion of Freshman women than those in other classes paid over $100 for a coat; which indicated a tendency for families who can afford to do so to purchase a fur coat for a daughter when she enters college, so that she can wear it during the four years. Girls who purchased coats costing less than $30 usually expected to wear them two years, while those who paid $100 or more usually expected to wear their coats four years or more.

Table 31 shows a strong concentration of the expenditure for a winter coat by men students in the $20-39 class interval. The median amount paid was $29.76. More men spent amounts falling below this class interval than above it. The distribution of the prices shows a narrow range in the amounts paid by men for winter coats. About one in three in each of the upper classes indicated that he expected to wear his coat from two to three years, and about two in five said from three to four years. In the Freshman year approximately one of every two men said he expected to wear his overcoat from two to three years, and one in three from three to four years.

The median amount spent by all men in the sample was $29.74 which was about 20 per cent less than $37.18, the median amount paid by women students. Although the tailoring and materials are often superior in men's coats, the fur commonly used on the collars of women's coats tends to make them cost more. Only about 10 per cent of the men paid more than $40 for a winter overcoat.

TABLE 32

MEDIAN EXPENDITURES FOR WINTER COATS BY 545 MEN AND 661 WOMEN
STUDENTS OF INDIANA UNIVERSITY, 1940-41

Group	Number in Sample	Median
Men		
Organized	350	$29.05
Unorganized	195	30.15
Woman		
Organized	220	53.69
Unorganized	441	34.98

A winter coat was one of the few items of clothing for which the unorganized man spent slightly more than the fraternity man. The median sorority woman, however, spent noticeably more for her winter coat than the median non-member. For both men and women the length of time a student expected to wear his winter coat tended to vary directly with the price paid for the coat. In the case of fur coats purchased by women students fairly long periods of time were indicated.

Suits.—Table 33 shows that about one in every two of the 550 men reporting ordinarily purchased suits costing between $20 and $29.99. About two in every five paid $30 to $39.99. The highest priced suit mentioned, by only one student, cost between $60 and $69.99. The median price paid for a suit by the 550 men who reported was $29.77. The median price paid by the unorganized men was $25.22 and by the organized men $34.33. The modal interval in which the prices paid by the men in the Freshman, Sophomore, and Junior classes fell was $20 to $29.99, but for Seniors was $30 to $39.99, a difference explained by the greater emphasis placed on clothing by men students who are beginning to look for jobs.

TABLE 33

PRICES PAID FOR SUITS BY 550 MEN AND 311 WOMEN STUDENTS AT INDIANA UNIVERSITY, 1940-41

Price	Men		Women	
	Number in Sample	Percentage of Sample	Number in Sample	Percentage of Sample
$ 0– 9.99	3 a	.55	23	7.40
10–19.99	16	2.91	154	49.52
20–29.99	262	47.64	102	32.80
30–39.99	223	40.55	23	7.40
40–49.99	43	7.82	3	.96
50–59.99	2	.36	3	.96
60–69.99	1	.17	1	.32
70 or over	0	0	2	.64
	550	100.00	311	100.00

a The suits purchased by these men were possibly second-hand garments.

About 40 per cent of the men reported that they ordinarily wore their suits two years. Thirty per cent said three years.

Only thirteen per cent indicated that they generally discarded a suit at the end of a year. It was not uncommon for one suit plus "cords" and sweaters and a leather jacket to constitute the complete wardrobe of a man student. Over 59 per cent of the organized men reported that they ordinarily wore a suit two years, and about 22 per cent said three years. Over 47 per cent of the unorganized men wore one two years and 32 per cent three years.

The modal interval of prices paid for suits by women was lower than that of men, amounting to $10 to $19.99. The median price paid for a woman's suit in 1940-41 was $18.60. About one out of every two of the 311 women who owned suits in 1940-41 paid between $10 and $20, about one in every three paid between $20 and $30, and about one in fourteen paid less than $10 for a suit. At the other extreme were two girls who reported that they paid as much as $70 for their suits. Slightly more than half of the women said they expected to wear a suit two years, and about one quarter said three years. The modal length of time for wearing a suit indicated by sorority women was two years and by the unorganized women three years. In general, a larger percentage of unorganized women than organized wore their suits longer than three years.

The median amount spent for suits by the men was over $11 more than the median amount spent by the women. But only about 50 per cent of the women reported that they owned a suit. The differences in the amounts spent by organized and unorganized men and women were about the same.

Hats.—Hats were worn less by both men and women students at Indiana University in 1940-41 than in former years, but, nevertheless, they were items of expenditure for most students, particularly the co-eds. Styles in women's hats change rapidly, and to be the first seen in a new style gives the woman student an opportunity to win a reputation as a style leader. For more co-eds the becomingness or "smartness" of a hat is more important than its quality or price. While the tendency toward emulation in hats, as among other types of clothing at college, is great; there is perhaps more individualism in the choice of hats than in most items.

In general, the prices paid by co-eds for their hats in 1940-41 were low, the median price being only $3.28 (see Table 34). One in every three co-eds paid from $2 to $3, and about one in every four from $3 to $3.99. Relatively few paid as much as $6 or over. The median price paid by organized women was $4.81, and by unorganized women $3.16.

TABLE 34

MEDIAN AMOUNTS PAID FOR HATS BY MEN AND WOMEN
AT INDIANA UNIVERSITY, 1940-41

	Men		Women	
Group	Number in Sample	Median	Number in Sample	Median
Freshman	248	$2.96	127	$4.21
Sophomore	137	3.44	120	5.17
Junior	152	3.69	86	5.24
Senior	103	4.56	75	4.24
All Organized	215	4.81	146	5.34
All Unorganized	425	3.16	262	4.51
All	640	3.28	408	4.92

About three in every five women wore their hats only one season and about three in every ten ordinarily wore them two seasons. Less than four per cent of the women reported that they expected to wear a hat more than two seasons.

In general, men students paid more for their hats than women but wore them longer. About 44 per cent of the men said they usually expected to wear a hat only one year, 42 per cent said two years, and about 14 per cent said three years or more. No data were collected relating to the relative number of hats owned by men and women, but it seems probable that women purchased more hats than did the men during the school year. The median amount spent for a hat by men in 1940-41 was $4.92. Thus we see that, contrary to common opinion, the men tend to pay more for their hats than the women. This suggests that, in general, the expenditures of men for hats would help to narrow rather than widen the differences between their total expenditures for clothing and those of women if it were not for the fact that women buy more hats than men.

Evening Clothes.—A college woman had to be plain indeed not to look attractive in the style of evening dress popular on college campuses in 1940-41. In general, these were made with full swing skirts, bodice blouses, puffed or no sleeves, and flattering low neck lines.

The average woman student eager to make herself attractive spends considerable time planning her evening clothes. This is especially true when the number of evening dresses she owns is limited and the occasions on which she requires them are many. To vary the appearance of a single gown, she changes the accessories worn with it. Snatches of conversations between women students overheard on the campus or in a dormitory when they get together at night gives evidence of the importance attached to evening clothes in the minds of college women. Their interest lies not only in the clothing that they themselves wear, but also in that worn by the women with whom they must compete for escorts and male attention.

In the fall and winters of 1939-40 and 1940-41, silk and rayon in white, black, and a variety of colors, and figured patterns were favorite materials for evening dresses. In the spring, lingerie materials such as dotted swiss, batiste, organdy, pique, and other cotton materials were popular in both print patterns and plain colors. Not infrequently dresses of this kind were made at home at a rather nominal price. Some were made by students in the classes in clothing in the department of home economics.

Almost 26 per cent of the 692 women students said they ordinarily expected to wear an evening dress only one year, and about 40 per cent said two years. Nearly 20 per cent indicated that they usually wore a dress of this kind three years, and 6.11 per cent said four years. Only 2.60 per cent reported wearing an evening dress longer than four years, although several women admitted that they had dresses which they had worn six or seven years. About the same proportion of organized as unorganized women said that they ordinarily wore an evening dress from one to three years; but almost twice as great a proportion of the organized as the unorganized wore a dress of this kind as long as four years. In comparing these figures, however, it must be kept in mind that the organized women tend to have a somewhat greater need for evening dresses than the unorganized women and as a consequence tend to have more at any one time than the unorganized women.

In spite of the great importance of evening clothes in the minds of the typical " co-ed " at Indiana, Table 35 shows that the prices paid for evening dresses in 1940-41 were relatively low. Over 67.6 per cent of them paid less than $20. Of these, 21 per cent paid less than $10 and 46.6 per cent from $10 to $19.

TABLE 35

Prices Ordinarily Paid for Evening Dresses by 657 Women
at Indiana University, 1940-41

Price	All Women		Organized		Unorganized	
	Number in Sample	Percentage of Sample	Number in Sample	Percentage of Sample	Number in Sample	Percentage of Sample
$ 0– 9........	138	21.00	18	8.0	120	27.78
10–19........	306	46.58	85	37.78	221	51.16
20–29........	190	28.92	106	47.11	84	19.44
30–39........	18	2.74	12	5.33	6	1.39
40–49........	3	.46	3	1.33	0	0
50–59........	1	.15	0	0	1	.23
60–69........	1	.15	0	0	0	0
70–79........	0	0	0	0	0	0
80 or over	0	0	0	0	0	0
	657	100.00	224	100.00	433	100.00

Sorority women spend more for evening dresses than non-members, partly because they tend to have more money to spend for them and partly because they go to more social events of the kind which require evening clothes. Moreover, a larger proportion of the organized students come from cities or larger towns and consequently have greater need of " formals " while at home during vacations. Many come from families which are social leaders who belong to the " country club " groups in their home communities. The median amount spent for an evening dress by the sorority girls in the sample was $28.49 and that of non-members $14.37. For all girls the median amount paid was $16.23.[11] The proportion of the sorority members and non-members paying different prices for their evening dresses are shown above in Table 35.

TABLE 36

THE MEDIAN AMOUNTS SPENT FOR EVENING DRESSES BY WOMEN IN THE
FOUR UNDERGRADUATE CLASSES OF INDIANA UNIVERSITY, 1940-41

Class	Number in Sample	Median
Freshman	257	$16.61
Sophomore	141	16.12
Junior	159	17.23
Senior	100	15.51

Table 36 shows that Freshman women paid more for their evening dresses than the Seniors and Sophomores and less than the Juniors. The Seniors paid the least and the Juniors the most, probably because the Junior Prom is generally regarded as the peak social event during the four years of college.

Only 251 of the 584 men in the sample or 42 per cent owned a dress suit. Of those who did the majority had a " tux " rather than " tails ", since men at the University attend formal " proms " in tuxedos. Although college men do not spend as much time discussing what they will wear to dances as women, they are concerned about their personal appearance on such occasions and spend more time getting ready for them than is generally supposed.

Table 37 shows the prices paid by 249 men students for their evening suits in 1940-41. The median price paid by all of these

11 The women who paid less than $10 made their own evening dresses.

men was $31.50, an amount considerably higher than the median price paid by women students for an evening dress. The aggregate expenditure for evening clothes by men for the four years in college tended to be greater, however, because one " tux " sees most men students through college, while relatively few women students would be willing to attend dances if they had to wear the same dress during the four years.

As may be seen in Table 37, the difference in the amounts paid for evening suits by organized and unorganized men was not large, primarily because of the standardization in the prices. For moderately priced suits of this kind the price tends to center around $30 to $35. Prices beyond these amounts rise rapidly and for the most part go beyond a level that the average college student can afford to pay. The median amount spent by the 88 unorganized men who reported what they paid for their evening suits was $29.55 and that of the 163 organized students $32.50. This difference is perhaps explained by the fact that more un-organized than organized students purchased used dress suits rather than by differences in prices paid for new suits.

TABLE 37

PRICES ORDINARILY PAID BY 251 MEN STUDENTS AT INDIANA
UNIVERSITY FOR EVENING SUITS, 1940-41

Price	All Men		Organized		Unorganized	
	Number in Sample	Percent-age of Sample	Number in Sample	Percent-age of Sample	Number in Sample	Percent-age of Sample
$ 0– 9........	3	1.20	2	1.23	1	1.14
10–19........	3	1.20	2	1.23	1	1.14
20–29........	105	41.83	61	37.42	44	50.00
30–39........	97	38.65	66	40.48	31	35.23
40–49........	32	12.74	25	15.34	7	7.94
50–59........	8	3.18	5	3.07	3	3.41
60–69........	2	.80	2	1.23	0	0
70–79........	1	.40	0	0	1	1.14
	251	100.00	163	100.00	88	100.00

To provide a better opportunity for the comparison of the prices paid for different items by the six different groups of students discussed above, the summary Table 38 is presented.

TABLE 38

MEDIAN PRICES PAID FOR SPECIFIED ITEMS OF CLOTHING BY SIX GROUPS OF INDIANA UNIVERSITY STUDENTS, 1940-41

Group	Sweater [a]	Skirt	Blouse or Shirt	Shoes	Hose
All Men	$3.98		$1.52	$6.63	$ .25
All Women	2.98	$4.14	1.53	5.25	.89
Organized Men	3.98		1.54	6.99	.40
Unorganized Men	3.98		1.51	5.75	.30
Organized Women	2.98	4.45	1.55	6.34	1.00
Unorganized Women	1.98	3.78	1.51	4.88	.79

[a] $2.98 and $3.98 are the customary prices for sweaters in the shops usually patronized by Indiana University students.

TABLE 38—*Continued*

Group	Light Weight Fall or Sport Coat	Winter Coat	Suit	Hat	Evening Dress or Dress Suit
All Men	$23.54	$29.76	$29.77	$4.92	$31.50
All Women	21.45	37.94	18.60	3.28	16.23
Organized Men	34.44	29.05	34.33	5.34	32.50
Unorganized Men	21.50	30.15	25.22	4.51	29.55
Organized Women	25.20	28.85	23.42	4.81	28.49
Unorganized Women ...	18.86	26.26	16.58	3.18	14.34

SUMMARY

A student's expenditure for clothing tends to reflect his economic status more accurately than that for either food or rent, the other two major items in his budget. With care and some minor additions, clothing can be made to last through " lean " years without much expense; but the possibility for reducing expenditures for food and room are more limited. In good years and for students with large incomes the potentialities for additional expenditure for new clothes and better qualities of material and workmanship are practically limitless. The minimum amounts spent for clothing by students at Indiana University are somewhat greater than those spent by the young people considered in the Consumer Purchase Study made recently by the Department of Labor.

The women at the University spent considerably more than men students. Moreover, as the absolute amounts spent by the two groups increased and as the total expenditures rose; the difference between the amounts spent widened. The minimum to which a woman student could reduce her clothing expenditure amounted to about $10 more than that for a man student. The largest expenditures reported were those of women students, and in most instances included the amount paid for a fur coat. Membership in a Greek-letter society had a greater influence on what a student spent for clothing than on what he spent for housing or for food. Differences in the median amounts spent for clothing by organized and unorganized women were about the same as between the corresponding groups of men. The variations between the median and third quartile expenditures of both groups of women were greater than between those of the men.

Students who earned more than 20 per cent of their expenses tended to spend $45 to $55 dollars for clothing, while the amounts spent by those who earned less than that proportion rose rather sharply. Further evidence that clothing was one of the items in the budget on which a student could economize most was shown in the small expenditures of the NYA students.

The students who spent the most for clothing were enrolled in the College of Arts and Sciences rather than in the professional schools. Freshmen and Juniors spent more for clothing than Sophomores and Seniors, largely because of the tendency to buy new clothes to come to college in the first place and the need to replenish a wardrobe after being there for two years. The data examined showed that both men and women from farms spent less for clothing than those from either small towns or cities because, in general, they had less to spend and also because women students from farms were able to reduce their expenditures by making part of their clothing at home. The median woman from the small towns spent more for wearing apparel than the median woman from a city, but among the men those from cities spent most.

When prices paid for several specific items of clothing were examined, it was found that the median amounts paid by men for shoes, hats, sweaters, suits, light-weight coats, and evening clothes were greater than those paid by women. The latter paid more for their winter coats, blouses, and hose. There was less variation in the prices paid by students in the different groups for specific items of clothing than in the number of garments of a given kind which were purchased. In general, a winter coat was the most expensive item in the student wardrobe and in some instances represented as much as two-thirds of a student's total clothing expenditure. The differences in the amounts paid by organized and unorganized students for most of the articles for which prices paid were considered was not great. For practically all items the amounts paid tended to center around one or two customary prices rather than to be distributed evenly in successive price intervals.

Although relatively less important from the standpoint of absolute amounts spent than certain other budget items not yet considered, personal care and laundry are logically so closely related to clothing that it has seemed best to treat the expenditures for these services in the next chapter.

CHAPTER VI
PERSONAL CARE AND LAUNDRY

WHILE expenditures for personal care and laundry represent a relatively small proportion of the student budget, the items included tend to have a disproportionate importance in the minds of students because of their relation to personal appearance and hence to popularity and social activity. Among the goods and services for which expenditures are discussed in this chapter under the heading of personal care are shaves, hair cuts, hair waves, hair ornaments, cosmetics, and toilet articles. Included in the treatment of laundry and the maintenance of clothing are the amounts paid for laundry, cleaning and pressing services, shoe shines, shoe repairs and postage for mailing laundry.

The co-ed at a state university usually pays more attention to her make-up and the way her hair looks during the daytime on school days than does her sister who attends a woman's college and who is inclined to save her greatest efforts for weekends when men come to the campus. In the case of the girl in a co-educational institution, there are usually men in her classes, whom she either already knows or hopes to know. Her hair and nails and her use of lipstick must stand scrutiny at all times, even though she appears in class in a slip-on sweater and dirty white shoes. The men at the University may be grouped according to the stress they place on personal care in a manner similar to that related to their mode of dress described in Chapter V. Although smart toilet articles and tonsorial services have some prestige value for the men students, they spend relatively more on cleaning and pressing, shoe shines, and laundry.

EXPENDITURES FOR PERSONAL CARE

The figures below show that the median expenditures for personal care by the men and women at the University in 1940-41 differed less than is generally assumed.[1] The median amount

1 For the mean expenditures of men and women students for personal care see Table 79, page 245.

spent by each was lower than the average amount spent by either single men or women at all income levels studied by the National Resources Committee which were $17 and $25 respectively.[2]

Group	Number in Sample	First Quartile	Median	Third Quartile
Men	586	$6.52	$ 9.17	$13.72
Women	686	7.72	11.23	18.26
	1272			

Reduced to a monthly basis, the median expenditure for the men at the University was $1.02 and the interquartile range $0.72 to $1.52. The median monthly expenditure for the university women was $1.25, the first quartile $0.86 and the third $2.03. As judged from the extent of the interquartile ranges of both the men and women, the demand of each for the items listed under the heading of personal care is fairly elastic beyond certain minimum amounts required to purchase such necessities as soap, tooth brushes, and dentifrices. It was on luxury items that the student who felt the need to do so economized. Gifts of toilet articles, which are popular gifts among college students, also helped to reduce their expenditures for items listed under personal care.

The men spent 1.5 per cent of their budget for personal care, a percentage slightly higher than the 1.4 per cent spent by the single men studied by the National Resources Committee.[3] The student women's expenditures for personal care represented 1.6 per cent of their budget as compared with the 2.3 per cent spent by all single women.[4] In the budgets of the men students, personal care ranked in eleventh place in order of importance. In those of women, whose median total expenditure was greater than that of the men, it held tenth place. Among the twelve

2 The National Resources Committee. *Consumer Expenditures in the United States*, pp. 81-82.

3 The National Resources Committee. *Consumer Expenditures in the United States*, pp. 82-83.

4 *Ibid.*, p. 83.

headings under which the disbursements of single men and
women were listed personal care ranked tenth in importance in
the budgets of the men and sixth in that of the women.[5]

EXPENDITURES BY MEN

Men at college today provide a share of the market for the
nationally advertised toilet goods made or recommended especially for men. These include hair tonics, cold creams, and skin
lotions for use after shaving. College men are also vulnerable
to advertisements urging them to use specially compounded per-
fumes, face powders, mouth washes, and deodorants.

The men in the sample were not asked to state the amounts
they ordinarily paid for barber shop services, because of the
practically uniform rates of 20 or 25 cents for a shave and 50
cents for a hair-cut which prevail in Bloomington. Also, since
personal interviews showed that very few men went to a barber
shop for a shave except before formal dances, no question was
asked relating to how often they had such service. The reason
given for being shaved before dances was to prevent their faces
from being cut and blemished for the dance. The men interviewed averaged one hair-cut every two to four weeks. Occasionally a man had a shampoo when he had his hair-cut before
a formal dance, but most of the sums included under the heading of personal care by men were spent for hair-cuts, razor
blades, shaving cream, soap, and dentifrices. It was only on very
special occasions or in the instance of the student of exceptional
means that money was spent on such luxury services and goods
as manicures and fancy cosmetics. Sophomore men true to their
traditional carelessness in dress and appearance spent less of
their budget on personal care than the men in any other college
class. Junior men spent little more than the Freshmen whose
expenditures ranked second in amount. The Seniors, who are
interested in finding jobs, spent the most.

5 *Ibid.*, pp. 82-83.

EXPENDITURES BY WOMEN

The most important items for women students among those listed under the general heading of personal care were shampoos and waves. Although only about a third of the women who returned questionnaires indicated how often they were accustomed to going to a beauty shop to have their hair shampooed and waved, the frequency distribution of these students presented below gives some significant data relating to the student use of such services.[6]

The number of girls who reported hair waves would doubtless have been greater if many of the women students had not been surprisingly adept at pinning up their hair at night so that it would curl as they wanted it to the next day. Girls living in dormitories and sororities as well as in the private houses where groups of girls live helped each other. Those who were not skillful in making curls or putting on nail polish sometimes traded other kinds of services such as pressing or laundry work for help with their hair. There was frequent borrowing of

TABLE 39

DISTRIBUTION OF 280 WOMEN STUDENTS AT INDIANA UNIVERSITY
CLASSIFIED ACCORDING TO THE FREQUENCY WITH WHICH THEY
HAD THEIR HAIR SHAMPOOED AND WAVED, 1940-41

Time interval	Number in Sample	Percentage of Students in Sample
Once a week	55	19.64
Every two weeks	64	22.86
Once a month	36	12.86
Only for dances	125	44.64
	280	100.00

6 In his study made at the University of Pennsylvania, W. P. Kuenstler found the Freshman and Sophomore women in his sample tended to visit beauty parlors about once a month, Juniors about twice a month, and Seniors only once every two months. About 4.7 percent of the women in the sample went only once a year to get permanents. See Walter P. Kuenstler, "The Buying Habits of Women Students on the University of Pennsylvania Campus" (Unpublished Senior Research Thesis, Wharton School of Finance and Commerce, U. of Penn., 1940), p. 46.

136   STUDENT FOLKWAYS AND SPENDING

" bobbie pins " and hair nets. Most of the women who did have
their hair curled at a beauty parlor, as well as those who curled
it themselves, sometimes slept with their hair bound in a hair
net for several nights to keep from mussing their curls.

As may be seen from Table 40, both the modal and median
price paid for a shampoo and wave by the students who answered the question relating to the price paid for waves was 75
cents. The lowest price mentioned for a wave without a shampoo was 35 cents and the highest price reported for both was
$1.50.

TABLE 40

Prices Paid by 243 Women Students at Indiana University
for Shampoos and Waves, 1940-41

Price	Number in Sample	Percentage of Students in Sample
$ .50	80	32.92
.75	95	39.09
1.00	61	25.10
1.25	6	2.47
Over $1.25	1	.41
	243	100.00

In 1940-41, the prevailing style of hair dress of women students on the Indiana campus was a " long bob." Only the girls
who were fortunate enough to have naturally curly hair and a
few individualists who wore their hair straight did not have at
least one permanent wave during the year. Some had as many
as two or three, and many had end curls even more frequently.
A few girls said the only time they patronized a beauty shop was
when they went to get a permanent wave.

Among the cosmetics and toilet articles purchased by practically all women students were nail polish, rouge, lipstick, face
powder, soap, cleansing tissues, and tooth paste. The majority
also used cold cream, hand lotion, perfume, and bath powder. A
smaller number used mascara. The colors of liquid nail polish
worn in 1940-41 were so varied that some students owned as
many as a dozen shades. The importance attached to the choice

of color for a certain costume or occasion was, in the opinion of some women, as great as the choice of the dress to be worn. Moreover, the process of changing polish was a time consuming one. Although less rouge was worn in 1940-41 than in some of the immediately preceding years, the use of lipstick was more generally adopted than previously. But, in general, less lipstick was applied at one time than in the year before.

At different times a given brand of cosmetics becomes popular on the campus and enjoys a prestige value. Local beauty parlor operators stock such products and, while they work on their hair, acquaint their customers with the names of the college celebrities who use them. Because of the popularity of shower baths at college, students tend to increase their consumption of soap and lessen their use of bath salts.

Among the women in the different classes the Seniors spent the most for personal care, primarily because they tended to have their hair curled at beauty parlors more frequently than the women in other classes. One reason for their doing so is the importance attached to grooming on the part of applicants for jobs by placement bureaus and faculty members who help the majors in their departments find positions. Another reason why the Senior women spend more to have their hair waved is because they usually hold the most important offices in academic and social organizations and are therefore more conspicuous. Still another reason for the greater expenditures for personal care by the Senior women is found in the following comments of a man student:

In her first year at college, the typical Freshman girl learns merely the fundamentals of how to cause various members of the male species to jump through hoops like a trained dog. She still looks fairly young and innocent, most of the time, but those days are numbered.

After the first year, the college co-ed leaves the amateur class of Delilahs and really goes to work. Her quota on fraternity pins jumps to three per semester and she now has her eyes on several extra-curricular activities, usually acquired through the help of some unsuspecting male.

In her Junior year, she begins to visualize herself as a " roddess," which is almost as silly a word as " rod." [7] Then there is that matter of swinging several votes for the Junior Prom candidate. By this time she is in politics deeper than James Aloysius Farley.

Usually the co-ed reaches her peak in " manhandling " during her final year in college. If she is lucky, she may be successful in luring some draftdodger into the fold permanently. After four years of sifting, culling and threshing, she has a hard time finding any kind of a husband, let alone one that she approves of. Such a state of affairs probably is brought about because of her Brutus-like tactics while she was in the process of getting a sheepskin.[8]

Fifty-five per cent of the Sophomore women reporting went to a beauty parlor to have their hair washed and waved only when they were going to a dance; a fact which helps explain a lower average expenditure for personal care by the women in this class than in any of the other three.

EXPENDITURES BY ORGANIZED AND UNORGANIZED STUDENTS

Except for their first quartile expenditures the sorority women spent more than the fraternity men for personal care. Among the unorganized students the first quartile and median expenditures of the men were greater than those of women but the third quartile amount spent by the women was greater than

TABLE 41

EXPENDITURES FOR PERSONAL CARE BY ORGANIZED AND UNORGANIZED
MEN AND WOMEN AT INDIANA UNIVERSITY, 1940-41

Group	Number in Sample	First Quartile	Median	Third Quartile
Men				
Organized	205	$7.78	$11.02	$16.09
Unorganized	381	6.26	9.50	12.99
All Men	586	6.52	9.17	13.72
Women				
Organized	233	7.61	13.34	23.05
Unorganized	453	4.80	8.74	14.23
All Women	686	7.72	11.23	18.26

7 Rod and roddess are terms sometimes applied on the Indiana campus to students prominent in extra-curricular and social activities.

8 *Indiana Daily Student*, Oct. 1, 1941.

that of the men. The ranges in expenditures of both sorority women and non-members were wider than in those of the men.

The probable reason why the first quartile expenditures of the unorganized men were higher than those of the unorganized women was that even the men who economize most have to have their hair cut at least once a month and purchase soap, razor blades, and dentifrices. The women students can wash and curl their own hair and reduce their expenditures for soap, dentifrices, face powder, rouge and lipstick by purchasing them at the five- and ten-cent stores. In the case of the unorganized students the difference between the median amounts spent by the men and women for personal care was less than between their third quartile expenditures. Both of these, however, were less than was found between the amounts spent by sorority and fraternity members in similar positions. The greater differences between the median and third quartile expenditures of the fraternity and sorority members than between those of non-members suggest that their demand for the items included under personal care is more elastic than that of non-members.

The amount spent for personal care represented 1.6 per cent of the budget of organized students and 1.5 per cent of that of unorganized students. This similarity in the proportions of their budgets spent by the two groups was true because, although the absolute amount of the median expenditure by unorganized students was less than that spent by sorority and fraternity members, the total expenditure of the latter groups was sufficiently greater to make the percentages of the totals the same. In the budgets of the unorganized men and women the expenditure for personal care ranked in tenth place and in that of organized in twelfth place.

When the expenditures of the women were analyzed on the basis of college class membership, it was found that the organized Senior women spent considerably more than either the organized or unorganized women in any of the other undergraduate classes.[9] In each of the four classes the organized

9 For the median amounts spent by the organized and unorganized men and women in the four college classes see Table 79, page 245.

women spent more than the unorganized. This difference suggests that the social pressure on unorganized students for maintaining a good appearance is not so great as on organized students whose sorority sisters like to have the members of the chapter known as well groomed, attractive girls. Such a reputation is believed by some members to put the girls belonging to the sorority at a premium for dates and make possible more desirable social contacts. A larger proportion of sorority women than of non-members had their hair waved at a beauty shop once a week, while more of the non-members waited two weeks between trips to the beauty parlor or until they were going to a dance. It was a more common practice among the unorganized than organized women to wash their own hair and pay from 35 to 50 cents to have it waved. The majority of those who went to a beauty parlor for both services paid 75 cents.

EXPENDITURES BY STUDENTS IN THE DIFFERENT SCHOOLS OF THE UNIVERSITY

The median amounts spent by the students in the sample enrolled in the different schools in the University are shown in Table 42. In considering these figures, however, the reader should keep in mind that, because of the relatively small number of students from the last four schools listed, the significance of the median expenditures of the students from these schools is questionable.

It is interesting to note that the median amounts spent for personal care by students in the School of Education was greater

TABLE 42

MEDIAN EXPENDITURES FOR PERSONAL CARE OF 1266 STUDENTS ENROLLED IN DIFFERENT SCHOOLS AT INDIANA UNIVERSITY, 1940-41

School	Number in Sample	Median
Arts and Sciences	482	$ 9.97
Education	159	10.17
Business	519	8.33
Music	38	9.99
Law	9	16.25
Medicine	57	10.87
Dentistry	2	—
	1266	

than that of the students in the College of Arts and Science, even though the students in the latter school spent considerably more on clothing. This variation may possibly be accounted for by the emphasis placed on the need for careful grooming on the part of students who expect to become teachers and the student's realization that recommendation for a job may be influenced by personal appearance. In the School of Business where students are also aware of the importance of good grooming in obtaining a job, the median amount spent for personal care was pulled down by the predominance of men students.

EXPENDITURES BY STUDENTS FROM FARMS, SMALL TOWNS,
AND CITIES

There was much less variation in the expenditures for personal care by men students from different types of localities than in those of the women. In the case of the latter both the median and quartile expenditures of the women from small towns were the greatest and those of women from farms the least. The greater amounts spent by the women from small towns is explained by the fact that beauty services are particularly important in small towns in Indiana where the beauty parlor tends to be a meeting place for women and the beauty services they offer a prestige symbol. For these reasons and because the services can be obtained at a relatively low price at shops that are easily accessible, most of the girls from small towns who go to college tend to regard beauty shop services as a " must " item in their college budget.

TABLE 43

Expenditures for Personal Care of 642 Indiana University
Students from Farms, Small Towns, and Cities, 1940-41

Group	Number in Sample	First Quartile	Median	Third Quartile
Men				
From Farms	55	$6.08	$9.20	$14.27
From Small Towns ..	142	6.90	9.76	14.39
From Cities	136	7.40	10.74	14.36
Women				
From Farms	92	4.47	7.77	11.88
From Small Towns ..	121	6.55	11.39	19.13
From Cities	192	5.72	10.78	16.81

EXPENDITURES FOR LAUNDRY AND THE
MAINTENANCE OF CLOTHING

About two out of every five of the 1086 students in the sample who answered the question relative to whether or not they laundered any of their own clothes while at college said they did. In the years prior to the general adoption of silk and jersey underwear and nightgowns by women, laundry represented a much more important item in their budget than it has since. Muslin and nainsook nightgowns and petticoats could not be rinsed out very satisfactorily in a bathroom at night, because of the bulk of the garments and the need for boiling them to keep them white. As a consequence, the laundering of clothing while at college was formerly so difficult that women usually found it necessary to send their clothing out to be laundered, and the amounts spent for laundry were consequently relatively greater than in 1940-41. But even when cotton materials first began to be replaced by rayon and silk for use for undergarments the number of items worn and their weight and fullness continued to make the task of laundering difficult. By 1940-41, however, the reduction in the size and number of items worn by women and the change in the nature of the materials used in their clothing made it fairly easy for women students to launder them in the bathrooms of the houses in which they lived. By that time it was also customary for electric irons and ironing boards to be provided for the student use in the private homes which rented rooms to women. At the women's dormitories there were electric washing machines and drying rooms which the students could use with no extra charge. These changes together with the popularity of sweaters, which were easily washed and required no ironing, made possible considerable reduction in the amounts women spent for laundry.

For men, this reduction has not been so great as for women, although there has been some. In 1940-41, they no longer wore stiffly starched collars. Many had adopted knitted slip-on sweaters and sport shirts which reduced the number of cloth shirts they wore. Changes in the kinds of underwear they wore also lessened the bulk of their laundry.

Another change that has affected the expenditures of both men and women students in recent years has been the greater tendency for students to send their clothes home to be washed with the family laundry. Although the railroad facilities out of Bloomington made such a practice feasible for most students earlier, it was not generally adopted until inexpensive laundry containers made of canvas and heavy paper or leather were put on the market. These boxes made it easy for a student to pack his laundry for mailing without having to stop to hunt a container, wrappings or string. The greater use of automobiles also often made it possible for a student to find someone who was going to his home to take his laundry. In 1940-41, approximately three-fourths of the men in the sample mailed their clothing home to be laundered and nearly 55 per cent of the women. In general, these students made a practice of sending their laundry every other week rather than each week. Freshmen in the fraternity houses attend to the mailing of most of the laundry sent home by the members in the upper college classes.

Interviews with students revealed that while a desire to lessen their expenditures for laundry was probably the greatest single reason for sending clothing home to be washed, it was not the sole reason. Their clothing was usually mended while at home, and a laundry box provided an excellent opportunity for parents to send the student such things as candy, fruit, or cakes. In general, the students who did not launder their own clothing at college sent it home to be washed, since only approximately 8 per cent of the unorganized students stated that they had their clothing washed by Bloomington laundresses or laundries. It was not uncommon for men students to send their shirts to a Bloomington laundry and the remainder of their laundry home.

EXPENDITURES BY MEN AND WOMEN

As may be seen from the figures below, the men in the sample paid more for the laundrying of their shirts, the pressing and cleaning of their suits, and the shining of their shoes than the women spent for laundry, cleaning, and care of shoes. This was largely because the demand of men for most of these services was less elastic than that of women, since they were more dependent on others to launder and press their clothing than women.[10]

Group	Number in Sample	First Quartile	Median	Third Quartile
Men	585	$6.82	$11.49	$20.10
Women	684	4.25	8.62	14.61

When reduced to a monthly basis, the median man spent $1.28 and the median woman $.96. The interquartile range for the men was $0.76 to $2.23 and for the women $0.47 to $1.62. The men spent 2.1 per cent of their budget for these items and the women spent 1.4 per cent of theirs.

About one in every two of the 626 women who answered the question on the schedule relating to whether they laundered their own clothing at college replied that she did. In sharp contrast, only about one man student in thirty admitted doing his own laundry. Interviews with some of the men convinced the writer, however, that it was not uncommon for a man to wash out a pair of socks, a pair of shorts, or an undershirt. When funds were especially low and a clean shirt was needed, a few of them sometimes even washed and ironed a shirt.

About half of a group of fifty students who were interviewed on the subject found dry cleaning cheaper in Bloomington than in their home towns and as a consequence had their clothing cleaned there. The other half took or sent their garments home to be cleaned, either because they found the rates cheaper or because their parents paid for their cleaning at home. The charges for cleaning a dress reported by the women who had their cleaning done in their home towns ranged from 35 cents to $1. The prices reported by the women who had dresses cleaned in Bloomington centered around 75 cents. The men students who

10 For the mean expenditures for laundry, see Table 80, page 246.

were asked what they spent for shoe repairing reported slightly larger amounts for a semester than the girls who averaged between 50 cents and $1. In order to economize on shoe repairs some students have metal plates put on their heels to prevent their wearing down.

EXPENDITURES OF ORGANIZED AND UNORGANIZED STUDENTS

The median amount spent for cleaning, laundry, and care of shoes by the fraternity men was almost twice as much as that spent by non-members. Reduced to a monthly basis, the fraternity men spent $2.10 and the unorganized men $1.10. On a similar basis the sorority girls spent $1.32 and the non-members $0.82. The difference between the median amounts spent by sorority women and unorganized women was not as great as in the case of men. Because of the larger total expenditures of the organized students, the proportions of the budgets of the organized and unorganized students spent for laundry and the maintenance of clothing were similar, amounting to 1.8 per cent of the organized students and 1.6 per cent of the unorganized. The fact that more unorganized than organized women made a practice of laundering their own clothing while at the University is probably partly explained by the fact that more of the unorganized women have been accustomed to laundrying at least a part of their own clothes at home. Another reason why

TABLE 44

EXPENDITURES FOR LAUNDRY AND MAINTENANCE OF CLOTHING
BY ORGANIZED AND UNORGANIZED STUDENTS AT
INDIANA UNIVERSITY, 1940-41

Group	Number in Sample	First Quartile	Median	Third Quartile
Men				
Organized	204	$8.45	$18.87	$27.60
Unorganized	381	6.18	9.88	17.63
All	585	6.82	11.49	20.10
Women				
Organized	229	7.00	11.85	19.74
Unorganized	455	3.54	7.40	12.50
All	684	4.25	8.62	14.61

more of the unorganized than organized students did their own laundry while at college was that the facilities for laundering available to the unorganized students are, on the whole, better at the dormitories than at most of the Greek-letter chapter houses. Although the unorganized students living in houses out in town are often required to pay extra if they use the bathroom to launder their clothes, the charge is usually less than it would cost to mail their clothing home and have it returned.

SUMMARY

As a result of an analysis of student expenditures for personal care and laundry we may conclude that the man who is forced to economize is usually unable to reduce his expenditures for items under this heading as drastically as can a woman who has to curtail her expenses. But the woman whose total expenditures are greatest spends considerably more for personal care than the man in comparable circumstances. The difference between the median expenditures of men and women students is less than is generally assumed. Because of the larger total expenditure of women students, the amount they spend for personal care, even though it is a larger absolute amount than that spent by the men, represented a proportion of their budget similar to that spent by the men for this item.

Organized men and women spend more than unorganized students for personal care, but the differences in the case of both men and women are narrower between the first quartile and median expenditures than between the third quartile amounts. The range in expenditures of the organized students was much broader than that found in the expenditures of unorganized students.

The median woman student from a small town spent more than those from farms or cities for personal care, but among the men there was relatively little difference in the amounts spent by the students from the three types of communities. When the expenditures of the students in the different colleges in the University were considered separately, it was found that students in the School of Education spent the most. This was probably because those students are especially aware of direct relation between their personal appearance and recommendations for teaching jobs.

Changes in the kind of undergarments worn by women students has made it easier for an increasing number of them to do a large part of their own laundry at college. Because of the economy effected by mailing laundry home to be washed with the family clothing, the majority of students who do not launder their own clothes mail them home or send them by someone going to their home towns. Except for men who have shirts laundered at Bloomington, relatively few students pay to have their laundry done in Bloomington; and those who do so tend to be the students who have the most to spend.

The expenditures of all the students in the sample for the items included under the general heading of laundry and maintenance of clothing centered around eight or nine dollars. The men spent noticeably more than women for these items because they were more dependent on others to provide such services as pressing, laundry, and shoe shining. As the men's total expenditures increased, the amounts spent for laundry and the other related items increased more rapidly than in the case of women. The sorority women spent slightly more than unorganized men for laundry and the maintenance of clothing but considerably less than the fraternity men. The unorganized women spent the least and showed the least variability in their expenditures. From the standpoint of their respective expenditures for both personal care and laundry it may be seen that personal care is a relatively more important item for women than laundry; but that the reverse is true in the case of men.

This discussion of personal care and laundry completes the consideration of the expenditures related to personal appearance. We turn next to an investigation of the amounts spent by different groups of students for recreation and refreshments, items which have for the most part been treated together because of the difficulty encountered in attempting to separate them.

CHAPTER VII
RECREATION AND REFRESHMENTS

UNDER the heading of recreation and amusement the students were asked to group their estimated expenditures for tickets for such activities as dances, concerts, spectator sports including athletic events, lectures, the theater, and the movies, as well as amounts spent for any equipment used during leisure time such as radios, phonograph records, photographic supplies, and sporting goods. Amounts spent for beverages of all kinds, candy, ice cream, fruit, and midnight " snacks " were listed under refreshments. In order to avoid using an additional heading, expenditures for tobacco were also listed under refreshments.

Before proceeding to the discussion of the amounts spent by different groups of students, it has seemed worth while to describe some of the typical recreational habits of Indiana University students which usually entail expenditures.

RECREATIONAL OCCASIONS AND CUSTOMS

As would be expected at a co-educational school, the students tend to think of recreation in terms of a " date," which in turn ordinarily involves the purchase of some kind of refreshment.[1] One of the commonest kinds of dates is popularly known on the campus as a " joeing date." [2] These usually occur at the University Commons or at some restaurant near the campus either

1 Data collected by means of a questionnaire distributed by Professor Clausin D. Hadley of the Economics Department at Indiana University showed that 33.5 percent of the 176 students who returned questionnaires did not regularly have as much as one date a week. Thirty-five and eight-tenths percent averaged one date per week and 18.8 percent averaged two per week. Six and three-tenths percent said they ordinarily had dates three times a week and 2.9 percent four or more times. The remaining students in the sample either answered the questionnaires inadequately or were married. Great care was taken to distribute the questionnaires used in this study so that a representative sample might be collected.

2 " Joeing " is a term used to apply to time spent by a student drinking soft drinks or conversing with friends when he should be studying.

between classes or during hours ordinarily set aside for study. In warm weather, a " coke " or frosted chocolate is usually purchased for refreshment, and on cold days hot coffee or chocolate. If the man student is feeling affluent, the couple may also order sandwiches. Since a larger proportion of the unorganized students work than of those who are organized, dates of this kind tend to be more popular among the latter. Evidence of this fact is found at the places patronized by organized students where refreshments are served, which tend to be more crowded during the " joeing " hours than are those preferred by unorganized students.

Sometimes students go " dutch treat " on dates. Rather than not go to the Commons or stay home in the evening because the man with whom she ordinarily has dates is " broke " or hasn't received his allowance from home, a girl may prefer to pay for her own recreation and refreshment. Although this practice is usually most common among students who " go steady," the most casual acquaintances may drop in the commons for a " coke " and pay for their drinks individually.

The cost of a movie date depends on the movie attended and upon what refreshments are purchased on the way home. In Bloomington, the price of two movie tickets at night varies from 40 to 66 cents. Sandwiches or a cold drink for two usually costs from 10 to 40 cents. Unless the couple gets a late start and there is danger that the girl will not reach her place of residence by the time she has to be in, couples usually walk to and from the movies.[3]

3 The women students are required to be in the house in which they live by 10:30 every night, except Friday and Saturday nights when they may stay out until 12:30 A. M. In a study made by the writer in 1939-40, it was found that organized Junior men were the greatest cinema devotees on the campus, having an average attendance of 1.55 shows per week. The difference among all of the groups was not great, since only the unorganized Freshman men averaged less than one movie per week. There was practically no difference between men and women in attendance, as the men averaged 1.17 shows per week and the women 1.19.

Walking dates which are most popular in the spring and fall usually also involve the purchase of a "coke" or ice cream. They most often occur in the middle of the week when the couple has nothing else to do or when the man student is too " broke " to buy tickets to any form of amusement. Dates for the record hour when classical music is played in the Union lounge are sometimes followed by movie dates, but at other times the couple may stay in the lounge to talk and before going home drop by the Commons for a cold drink.

The Bloomington churches provide carefully planned social and religious programs for the students at the University. These include a variety of evening meetings and of parties. Men and women students who meet for the first time at these often become accustomed to attending them together. The parties given by the church organizations usually cost the students about 10 or 15 cents per person.

In 1940-41, dates at the dormitories were more popular than they were before recreation rooms were provided. In some of these rooms there are ping-pong tables and shuffle boards, as well as radios and machines for playing records. In spite of the fact that candy and " cokes " can now be secured from vending machines in the dormitories, most couples like to break the evening by going to some restaurant or to the Commons for something to eat.

Most of the picnics and outings that students attend are planned by some campus club. For these, food is purchased by a food committee with funds raised by means of a levy of from 25 to 50 cents imposed on the students who attend. Ordinarily the place chosen for the picnic is within walking distance of the campus. Occasionally, however, the assessment is raised so that a bus or hay wagon can be hired to take the picnickers to a state park in one of the adjoining counties. On private picnics it is a common practice for the girls to supply the food and the men the transportation.

Couples bowl at different times during the day. A game costs 15 cents per person or 30 cents per couple. The number of games played at one time averages two, making the cost 60 cents, an amount that limits the number of dates of this kind. Some couples stop to bowl on their way to the movies, others play before lunch or dinner.

Usually, even the most popular girls buy their own season tickets for athletic events which in 1940-41 cost $7.50. But on these occasions the men who take them to the games have to spend money for "cokes" and candy or other refreshments to eat during the game and possibly for a taxi to and from the stadium or gymnasium. After a football game, the fraternities and sororities as well as the dormitories often have coffee hours or buffet suppers to which a man can take his date. Later in the evening the co-eds usually expect to be taken out for dinner or to a dance.

At Indiana, as at other state universities, dances are generally regarded as the most important social events by both men and women. As a consequence, they are both numerous and varied in kind. The amount charged for the tickets depends on the nature of the dance and the orchestra. Men usually pay all expenses, except at the annual Dames' Ball for which women pay all of the costs. The dances are generally classified according to whether they are formal or not and whether there is a campus or off-campus band. Almost without exception they are held at the Memorial Union Building, the dormitories, or at a fraternity or sorority house.

Informal dances held at the Union Building and sponsored by the Association of Women Students cost $1.00 per couple in 1940-41.[4] Except for refreshments purchased in the Commons, the cost to the men who attend is limited to the price of the ticket. For these dances flowers and taxis are usually omitted, although a man may send a gardenia for his girl's hair.

Formal dances are the most expensive dates. Although the Junior Prom and other annual dances cost less than on many

4 The Association of Women Students is an organization designed to bring about greater unity among the women students at the University. In 1941-42 the price of these dances was reduced to sixty-six cents per couple.

campuses, they are the most expensive of all university dances at Indiana. A Prom ticket costs $5.00 for a couple. Those for others of the more formal dances range down from that price to $2.00, depending on the band secured. For these dances, flowers are generally regarded as a necessity. In fact, they are so important that some men hesitate to invite a girl to a dance rather than ask her and not be able to send her flowers. The average price paid for a corsage for these dances is around $1.50 or $2.00. For " Orchid Dances," when all the girls receive orchids from their escorts, the men are able to purchase the flowers for $2.00 or $2.50, a price which is less than is usually charged for a single flower of this kind.[5] If the man calls for a girl in a taxi and takes her home in one, the cost for the round trip is 50 cents.   If he walks to her home and calls a taxi from there and rides only as far as the girl's home after the dance, his taxi bill to and from the dance is reduced to 30 cents. If he takes the girl to dinner before the dance, an additional dollar or two is added to the cost of the evening. "Cokes" during intermissions may cost 20 cents more. If sandwiches are purchased on the way home or the couple attends a breakfast after the dance, another fifty cents or a dollar is spent. Thus we see that the total over-all cost of a formal dance to a man at the University ranges from $3.50 to $9.00.

In 1940-41, a new auditorium was opened at the University with a gala series of concerts, lectures, drama, and opera. Because of the opportunity presented by these programs for the students to see and hear persons of international reputation for a nominal amount, a large percentage of the student body purchased books of tickets at prices varying from $2.40 to $4.00. In most instances the women purchased their own tickets but their seats were often reserved next to those of the men with whom they were accustomed to attend such entertainments.

In addition to the refreshments purchased on dates, both men and women students buy food to eat between meals and for

5 For these dances the price of an orchid is not included in the price of a ticket.

parties in their rooms. In recent years the kinds of food eaten at such times has changed. Fuller social and academic programs than formerly have left less time for cooking. Although electric stoves are supplied in the dormitories, relatively few women students nowadays find time to make fudge. Electric corn poppers have become popular because of the speed and ease with which corn can be prepared. In 1940-41, however, the majority of the students purchased ready prepared food for " snacks " to nibble while studying or for mid-night parties in their rooms.

It is not uncommon to hear Freshmen discussing the purchase of food to take to their rooms between meals. They are less accustomed than the upperclassmen not to be able to raid the kitchen when they come in from classes. As a consequence, they tend to be somewhat more interested in more substantial kinds of this supplementary food than upperclassmen. Tenderloin and hamburger sandwiches, milk, fruit, and doughnuts are among the most popular kinds of food that men purchase to eat between meals.[6] Because of the variety of cakes and crackers now sold at restaurants and drug stores, however, men students now tend to buy more different kinds of food than formerly. The girls, more wary of fattening sweets, tend to buy such things as potato chips, pickles, olives, and cheese crackers. In recent years many students, both men and women, have made a practice of ordering sandwiches or ice cream from a drug store or restaurant or from some student who earns part of his expenses by preparing and delivering hot coffee and sandwiches at night. Because women are not permitted to leave their homes on school nights after 10:30, this method of securing food sometimes makes it possible for them to obtain food after that hour; although in general after the dormitory and sorority doors are locked at closing time they are not opened to admit food.[7]

6 The men students sometimes have as many as sixteen hamburgers sent in at one time for four men. Some men purchase a bushel of apples to keep in their rooms.

7 The habit of having midnight refreshment is probably as old as the University. James D. Test in a letter written to his mother on Sunday, February 10, 1845 stated that on the preceding night he had come home

In 1940-41, vending machines for " cokes," nuts, and candy were placed in the dormitories. The revenue from sale of these items was used to purchase books for the dormitory libraries. As a result of the accessibility of " cokes," many dormitory students adopted the habit of meeting in the smoker for refreshments before going to bed, after they finished studying or came in from a date at night. This fact and the popularity of " cokes " during " joeing " dates help to account for the statements made by three girls in interviews that they had drunk more " cokes " during the school year of 1940-41 than in all of their years at home. Part of the popularity of this soft drink is simply that its purchase supplies a reason to go to the Commons, a restaurant, or the smoker in the dormitory where students meet acquaintances and make new ones.

The proportion of the 1275 students in the sample for 1940-41 who indicated that they smoked was 36.8 per cent. Of those who smoked, 19 per cent said they purchased an average of one package of cigarettes a day. Only one or two packages a week were consumed by 13.4 per cent of the students and three packages per week were smoked by 14.3 per cent. From four to seven packages per week were smoked by 30.4 per cent of the students in the sample, and eight or more packages by 8.3 per cent. The median number of packages consumed by the students who reported that they smoked was five packages per week.

EXPENDITURES BY ALL STUDENTS

Refreshments and recreation together, in 1940-41, accounted for a median expenditure of $39.43 for the school year or $1.10 a week for the average student at Indiana University.[8] Of this amount the students estimated that $21.83 was spent for recreation, an amount sufficient to permit the purchase of a student book of tickets for the basketball and football games played at

from Society (Athenian) and taken his usual refreshment of a glass of milk and half a mince pie. (Woodburn, James A., *The History of Indiana University, 1820-1902*, Bloomington: Indiana University, 1940, p. 151.)

8 For the mean expenditures for recreation and refreshments see Tables 81 and 82, pages 247 and 248.

Bloomington during the year, tickets for the concert series, a movie ticket a week or two movies a month, and a few dances during the year. The median estimated annual expenditure for refreshments was $17.60. This amount would permit a purchase of an average of about two packages of cigarettes and four " cokes " a week, although it must be remembered that not all students purchased these particular items. In the budget for all students the amount spent for both recreation and refreshments represented 7.4 per cent. The expenditures for refreshments tended to center around $15, but those for recreation were concentrated within a range of from $16 to $24. Both showed a tendency to vary directly with total expenditures.

EXPENDITURES BY MEN AND WOMEN

The figures below show that in 1940-41 the median amount spent by men for recreation and refreshments was almost twice that of women.

Group	Number in Sample	First Quartile	Median	Third Quartile
Men	586	$30.55	$51.06	$97.68
Women	687	16.66	26.78	53.46

Reduced to a weekly basis, the median expenditure of the men amounted to $1.42 and of women to 74 cents.[9] The men estimated that they spent 83 cents out of the $1.41 for the items included under recreation and 58 cents for refreshments and tobacco. The median estimated amount spent by the women for recreation out of the total of 74 cents was 46 cents and for refreshments 28 cents. In the case of both men and women the variation in expenditures for these items was noticeably great. The greater spread between the median expenditures and the third quartile than between the first quartile and median expenditures indicated that the student may vary his expenditures for these items as his economic status changes.

9 The cards for two students were rejected by the machines because of inconsistencies in punching when the cards were sorted for data relative to recreation and refreshments.

The relative importance of recreation and refreshments in the budgets of men and women is perhaps best shown by the proportion of their total expenditures allotted to the two items. In the budget of the men, the amounts spent for recreation represented 6.6 per cent of their total expenditure and that for refreshments 3.7 per cent. Collectively these percentages which included sums spent for treats for both women and men friends represented 10.3 per cent of the budget and ranked in fifth place in importance. Recreation in the women's budget represented 2.4 per cent and refreshments 2.6 per cent, making a total for the two items of 5.0 per cent, or slightly less than half the proportion spent by the men. In the budgets of all single men and women studied by the National Resources Committee, all expenditures for any kind of food, including refreshments and " snacks," were listed under the heading of food; but amounts spent for recreation were treated separately. For items listed under this latter heading, the single men spent 4.5 per cent of their budget and the women 1.9 per cent of theirs. The smaller importance of recreation in these budgets than in those of the student men and women is largely explained by the greater variation in the ages of the men and women studied.[10] In the study made by the National Resources Committee dues to social and recreational clubs were also included under recreational expenditures and not treated as a separate category as in the study of student spending.[11] This fact makes the smaller proportion of their budgets spent for recreation by single men and women even more pronouncd when compared with those of the students.

The median number of soft drinks purchased for their own consumption by the men and women in the sample was the same, amounting to six per week. In view of the larger median total budget expenditures of women students, this similarity in consumption of soft drinks seems to indicate that men economize

10 National Resources Committee, *Consumer Expenditures in the United States*, pp. 82-83.

11 *Ibid.*, p. 97.

relatively less on this item than women.[12] Reasons why this is so are that more men than women work in places where soft drinks are sold and the existence of the custom among men living in groups of purchasing a dozen bottles of Coca Cola at a time. Much of the consumption of soft drinks by women students is explained by a desire for an excuse to go to the Commons or a restaurant to " joe " and possibly make new acquaintances, since women as a rule are more hesitant than men about going into a restaurant without buying anything. It is doubtful, however, whether the consumption of soft drinks by women students was as great prior to 1940-41 when vending machines were first placed in the women's dormitories.

When the number of packages of cigarettes consumed by men and women students were compared, it was found that the proportion of men who smoked was almost twice as large as that of women, amounting to over 46 per cent in contrast to 28.1 per cent of the women. At least part of this difference is explained by the attitude of Hoosier men, especially those in Southern Indiana who are inclined to be conservative in their views relating to women's smoking. Evidence of such an attitude among some of the students on the campus of the University is found in the following editorial which appeared in the *Indiana Daily Student* on September 24, 1941.

Co-eds: Cut Out the Smoking

For many students, Indiana University is an awfully swell place to be. Especially for the Juniors and Seniors, it's a real pleasure to get back in the fall and look the place over again.

Outside of the modernizing program that is constantly being carried on, there is no real drastic change in the campus. It still has all the wooded paths that so characterize it, the red brick buildings that have stood for many years. In fact, it's pretty hard to find a change ... that is on the campus itself.

12 In common with other colleges and universities the University discourages the use of liquor. In collecting and analyzing the data collected under the heading of recreation and refreshments, no attempt was made to study the consumption of liquor as a separate item, although any expenditure for it was reported under the heading of refreshments.

This year, however, there is a noticeable change at Indiana University. More than one student has noticed it and not been afraid to comment on it. It is something that was not a part of campus life last year, two years ago or twenty-two years ago. It is new and if student opinion has any power, should get old pretty fast.

For the first time since we have been in Indiana University, co-eds have taken it upon themselves to light cigarettes and smoke to their hearts' content, no matter where they might be. In front of Kirkwood, Wylie, Science . . . it doesn't seem to make a bit of difference.

According to many co-eds, who feel the same as we do, this was and should again be tabooed. Certain of these co-eds think that there is a University ruling against it.

Concerning this last fact, we have no information. All we can say is that the mass of student opinion is against it and think that steps should be taken by one of the co-ed guidance groups to curb it immediately.

We do not feel that any habit, fad, or whatever one wished to call it can continue to be practiced when student opinion is so strong against it. That is exactly how the majority of students feel about Indiana University co-eds ' puffing " on the campus.

While the effects of an editorial such as this could not be measured accurately, conversations with several women students revealed the importance to them of what men thought about their smoking.

The men consumed more cigarettes per week than the women, their median number of packages purchased per week being five in comparison with three for women. More than 25.1 per cent of the men in the sample for 1940-41 averaged a pack of cigarettes per day, while only 11.6 per cent of the women purchased an equivalent amount. A much larger proportion of the women than of the men smoked only one package of cigarettes a week or any number up to and including three packages per week. However, the consumption of more than three packages a week was greater among men than women, since only about 9.1 per cent of the women purchased four packages or more per week, while 18.8 per cent of the men reported the regular purchase of more than four packages per week.

ORGANIZED AND UNORGANIZED STUDENTS

Table 45 shows that both organized and unorganized men spent appreciably more on recreation and refreshments than did the sorority and unorganized women. This was probably because they not only spent more for themselves but also more in entertaining co-eds. The smaller difference between the expenditures of unorganized men and women suggests that unorganized women pay for relatively more of their own recreation and refreshments than do the sorority girls, since, in general, fraternity men do not date unorganized women. Further evidence for this conclusion is found in the smaller differences between the amounts spent by the two groups of women than for most items in their budgets.

TABLE 45

MEDIAN AND QUARTILE EXPENDITURES FOR RECREATION, REFRESHMENTS AND TOBACCO BY INDIANA UNIVERSITY STUDENTS, 1940-41

Group	Number in Sample	First Quartile	Median	Third Quartile
Men				
Organized	205	$40.97	$79.12	$146.45
Unorganized	381	26.37	45.93	85.44
Women				
Organized	234	20.88	39.20	65.53
Unorganized	453	12.24	26.30	44.52

The interquartile ranges in the expenditures of organized men and women and unorganized men are all wider than that in the amounts spent by the unorganized women. From this difference we see that it is the unorganized women who economize most on recreation and refreshments.

When reduced to a weekly basis, the median amount spent for recreation by the fraternity man was $1.50 and for refreshments and tobacco 70 cents. Similar expenditures for non-member men were 74 cents and 53 cents respectively. For the sorority women the median weekly expenditure for recreation was 62 cents and for refreshments and tobacco 47 cents. These same expenditures for unorganized women were 58 cents and 15 cents respectively. One-fourth of the unorganized women spent 34 cents or less per week for all of these items. In general, unorganized women were more apt to go "dutch treat" than organized women, because the sororities tend to frown on the practice, and because the sorority members usually feel that their escorts can afford to pay their expenses.

The proportion of the organized men in the sample who said they smoked was 54.6 per cent and that of the unorganized 41.8 per cent. The difference in the proportion of the two groups of women who reported they smoked was considerably greater than that between fraternity men and non-members. The lower percentage of unorganized women who smoke may be accounted for by more conservative early conditioning of those students than in general was experienced by the organized women. In spite of the fact that sorority girls tend to be social pacesetters on the campus and a relatively large proportion of them smoke, the unorganized women have been relatively slow to follow their lead in adopting the practice.

The median number of packages of cigarettes consumed per week by the organized women in the sample who smoked was four, or one package more per week than were consumed by the unorganized women. The median number of packages consumed by both organized and unorganized men was greater than that of the women, although the six packages smoked by the fraternity men was one package a week more than were smoked by the men who did not belong to Greek-letter societies.

Organized Sophomore men and women spent more for recreation and refreshments than organized Freshmen.[13] This differ-

13 For median expenditures for recreation and refreshments by organized and unorganized men and women in all college classes, see Tables 81 and 82, pages 247 and 248.

ence is doubtless due to the supervision of sorority and fraternity pledges to prevent their social programs from interfering
with their academic records. Before the Freshman women were
moved to the dormitories, study tables were maintained in the
chapter houses for Freshmen. Now, the whereabouts of the
pledge is checked frequently during the day. Fear of failure to
secure marks that will meet the university requirement for initiation helps to keep Freshman pledges at work and prevents
their spending as much time at the movies or on trips to Indianapolis as they might otherwise do. Besides, the new experience
of living with a group of young people keeps them amused between study hours and dates, and lessens their interest in recreation outside the house which would involve expenditures.

The organized Sophomores, safely initiated and enjoying a
sense of freedom of release from Freshman rules, begin to
branch out and take more time for recreation outside the houses
in which they live.

There is less difference between the expenditures of unorganized Freshmen and Sophomores than between the organized
students in these classes. This is probably explained by the fact
that the unorganized Freshmen who live out in town are subject
to less supervision than those pledged or recently initiated by
Greek-letter societies. Because of the greater freedom in the
allotment of time and the lack of definitely planned social schedules such as those of the students pledged to the sororities and
fraternities, the unorganized Freshmen tend to spend as much
or even more in the Freshman year than in the Sophomore year.

The fact that the median number of soft drinks purchased by
organized women per week was twice as large as that purchased
by unorganized women was consistent with the smaller total
expenditure of the latter. As shown in the figures on page 162,
the difference between the organized and unorganized men in
the weekly consumption of soft drinks was less than in the
case of women.

Organized women spent more on Coca Colas and other types
of soft drinks than organized men, primarily because of the
tendency to gather in their sorority houses for " gabfests " in

TABLE 46

MEDIAN NUMBER OF SOFT DRINKS ORDINARILY PURCHASED EACH WEEK
BY 524 MEN AND 627 WOMEN STUDENTS AT INDIANA
UNIVERSITY, 1940-41

Group	Number in Sample	Number of Soft Drinks
Men		
Organized	192	6
Unorganized	332	4
All	524	6
Women		
Organized	192	8
Unorganized	435	4
All	627	6

the late afternoons or at night after they had finished studying
or had come in from dates. The practice of having hot coffee
and sandwiches sent in is more common among the fraternity men than among sorority women. The fact that the total
expenditure of the unorganized women was larger than that of
unorganized men suggests that of these two groups women
economized relatively more on their consumption of cold drinks
in spite of the fact that the median number consumed by each
group was four per week.

Thus we see that the consumption of both soft drinks and
cigarettes by organized men and women was greater than by the
unorganized students. The median number of soft drinks consumed by the unorganized men and women was the same, but
as between the organized men and women, the median number
consumed by the women was greater.

CLASS MEMBERSHIP AS A FACTOR AFFECTING EXPENDITURES

In the table below are presented the median expenditures
for recreation, refreshments, and tobacco as related to college
class membership.

A comparison of the amounts spent by men and women in the
different university classes shows an increase in the median
amounts spent by both men and women students through the
Junior year. In the Senior year the expenditures of men show
a sharp rise while those of the women decline. This difference

TABLE 47

MEDIAN EXPENDITURES OF MEN AND WOMEN IN THE FOUR COLLEGE
CLASSES FOR RECREATION AND REFRESHMENTS, 1940-41

Class	Number in Sample	Men	Women
Freshman	446	$46.60	$28.78
Sophomore	323	52.35	29.97
Junior	288	55.45	36.90
Senior	214	63.38	34.93

suggests that by the time a man reaches his last year in college he tends to spend a larger share of his income on recreation and refreshments for women. As a consequence, the expenditures of the women students which show a tendency to increase up to their Senior year begin to decline.

The percentages shown below seem to indicate that one's college class membership affects the degree of generality of smoking, but after the Freshman year has no effect on the amount of smoking per student.

TABLE 48

MEDIAN NUMBER OF PACKAGES OF CIGARETTES SMOKED PER WEEK
BY STUDENTS IN DIFFERENT COLLEGE CLASSES AT INDIANA
UNIVERSITY, 1940-41

Class	Number in Sample	Median Number of Packages Smoked Per Week	Percentage of Students in Sample Who Smoke
Freshman	446	4	28
Sophomore	323	5	37
Junior	288	5	41
Senior	214	5	40

A larger proportion of the students who had been in college a year or two smoked than of these just entering college, possibly because Sophomores and Juniors tend to regard smoking as evidence of maturity and social sophistication. The slight drop in the proportion of the Seniors who smoked was explained in several ways by students in that class who were questioned. One girl said she stopped because she was engaged and her fiance didn't want her to smoke. Two girls said they really

didn't enjoy smoking but had been afraid not to when they were
underclassmen for fear they would be considered ultra-conserva-
tive or unsociable. One man said he stopped smoking when he
was a Senior because he felt he smoked so much it prevented
his doing his best work. Need for economy was also given as a
reason by both men and women who were questioned.

<h2 style="text-align:center">EXPENDITURES BY SCHOOLS</h2>

The expenditures of the students in the sample enrolled in
the different schools of the University were examined to see if
there were any noticeable differences in their expenditures for
recreation and refreshment. Because the samples from the
Schools of Music, Law, Medicine, and Dentistry were too small
to be very significant, conclusions could be drawn regarding
only three schools, namely the College of Arts and Science, the
School of Educaton, and the School of Business. Among students in the latter three schools, the median expenditures for
recreation and refreshments of those in the School of Business
were highest, probably because of the predominance of men in
this school. Those of the students in the College of Arts and
Sciences ranked next in amount, and those of men and women
enrolled in the School of Education ranked third. The amounts
of the medians together with the first and third quartile expenditures for both recreation and refreshments of the students in
each of these schools and those of the limited number of students
representing the Schools of Music, Law, and Medicine are given
in Table 49.

TABLE 49

MEDIAN AND QUARTILE EXPENDITURES FOR RECREATION AND REFRESHMENT
OF 1263 STUDENTS ENROLLED IN DIFFERENT SCHOOLS
OF INDIANA UNIVERSITY, 1940-41

School	Number in Sample	First Quartile	Median	Third Quartile
Arts and Sciences	481	$18.97	$35.83	$58.71
Education	159	14.72	29.67	53.77
Business	519	25.62	45.30	89.80
Music	38	15.59	27.36	50.75
Law	9	21.25	55.00	78.75
Medicine	57	32.96	49.88	93.24
	1263			

STUDENTS WHO EARN PART OF THEIR COLLEGE EXPENSES

The relative amounts spent for recreation and refreshment by students who earn different proportions of their own college expenses and by those who earn none are especially interesting because of the relatively non-essential character of these items. These figures provide an answer to the question, " Does the student who earns none of his own expenses spend more or less for recreation and refreshments than the student who earns part or all of them? " An examination of the figures in Table 50 indicates that the median expenditure by students who earned none of their own expenses was lower than that of the students who earned less than a fifth of their expenses.

TABLE 50

MEDIAN EXPENDITURES FOR RECREATION AND REFRESHMENTS OF
1195 STUDENTS EARNING DIFFERENT PROPORTIONS OF
THEIR COLLEGE EXPENSES IN 1940-41

Proportion of Total College Expenses Earned	Number in Sample	Median
None	517	$38.59
Under 20%	288	46.00
20–39%	157	38.49
40–59%	89	32.96
60–79%	45	31.85
80–99%	43	34.85
All expenses	56	35.40

This difference is partly explained by the tendency for the majority of students who depend on their parents to finance their college expenses to feel that they must lighten the burden by reducing their expenditures for non-essentials as much as possible; while, on the other hand, the parents of many of the students who earn a small part of their own expenses can afford to pay the minimum amounts required for necessities in the student budget. If their children spend more, they must earn it. If they do so, these students are inclined to regard their earnings as their own " spending money " to be used as they please. Although a few prefer to add what they earn to the amounts given them by their parents to secure better food, rooms, and clothing than they could have otherwise, others prefer to spend their earnings on such non-essentials as recreation and refreshment.

Students who earn more than 60 per cent of their own expenses spend more for refreshments but less for recreation than those who earn 40 to 59 per cent. One possible explanation for the greater expenditure for refreshment is that many of these students work at places where such food is sold.

There was relatively little difference between the median expenditures for the two items of the students who earned none and all of their own expenses. This was because many of the students who earned all of their own expenses played in bands or were engaged in work which influenced what they spent for these items. In addition, the student engaged in work which pays enough to cover all of his expenses often earns an amount sufficient to give him as much if not more purchasing power than the median student who earns none of his own expenses.[14]

On the whole, the expenditures for recreation and refreshments of the students who earn any part of their own expenses show less variation than was found in the amounts spent by these same students for clothing and food, in spite of the fact that these two items are generally considered non-essentials. Therefore, we are forced to conclude that the student's demand for these items is less elastic than that of the average person. Furthermore, similarity in the amounts spent by students who earned different proportions of their own expenses suggests that if a student has to earn a large proportion of his own expenses and economize more than the student who earns less, he will not economize noticeably on recreation, refreshments, and tobacco.[15]

14 In 1941-42 some of these students had to pay incomes taxes.

15 The fact that the median expenditures for recreation and refreshment of the NYA men students shown below were almost twice as great as that of the women indicates that they also spent part of their incomes for recreation and refreshments for women. The median amounts spent by the NYA men and women were considerably lower than those of all men and women in

STUDENTS FROM FARMS, SMALL TOWNS, AND CITIES

Table 51 shows that men and women students from farms spent the least for recreation and refreshments and those from cities the most. As judged from their median expenditures, the men from cities spent more than twice as much as the men from farms and considerably more than men from small towns. The greater difference between expenditures of men and women from cities than from other types of localities indicates that the city men spent relatively more for recreation and refreshments for women. Another reason for this difference is that men students from cities are accustomed to spending more for these items than the men from small towns and farms. Because women from farms had more food sent from home for "snacks" and parties than students from small towns or cities and because their need to economize was greater, they spent the least for recreation and refreshments. The women from all three types of localities spent less than the men. The median expenditure for recreation for women from cities was greater than those of women from the other two types of communities, amounting to 94 cents per week as compared with 61 cents for women from farms and 86 cents for those from small towns.

the sample, indicating that these items are ones in the student budget on which the NYA student tends to economize.

Group	Number in Sample	First Quartile	Median	Third Quartile
NYA Men	78	$20.01	$33.44	$50.52
NYA Women	51	9.12	18.24	31.03

The extent of their economy is shown by the fact that the fourth of the NYA women who economized most on these items spent 25 cents or less per week for both recreation and refreshments and one-half spent 50 cents or less. The larger weekly first quartile and median expenditures of the NYA men for the two items which amounted to 55 cents and 93 cents respectively were explained by the amounts spent on recreation and refreshments for women students, their interest in spectator sports, and their tendency to stop in places where cold drinks and refreshments were sold. The range in the expenditures of the NYA men was also narrower than was that of the women.

TABLE 51

Median Expenditures for Recreation, Refreshments, and Tobacco by 739 Indiana University Students from Farms, Small Towns, and Cities, 1940-41

Group	Number in Sample	Median
Farms		
Men	55	$35.94
Women	93	22.02
	148	
Small Towns		
Men	142	51.53
Women	121	31.07
	263	
Cities		
Men	136	80.42
Women	192	33.77
	328	

SUMMARY

From the data presented in this chapter we see that men at Indiana University spend about twice as much for recreation, refreshments, and tobacco as women, largely because the men pay for part of these items consumed by women. Organized students spend more than unorganized, but the difference between the median expenditures of organized men and women was greater than between those who were not members of Greek-letter social societies. The amounts for recreation and amusement spent by both men and women students tend to increase from year to year up to the Senior year when the expenditures for men show a sharp rise and those of women begin to fall. This suggests that by that time a greater number of men have found women students with whom they are willing to share a part of their current income.

Students from cities spent more for these items than students from farms and small towns, probably because they were more accustomed to spending larger amounts on recreation and refreshments. The median amount spent by women from farms was only slightly greater than that spent by NYA women. Of the students in the sample enrolled in different colleges of the University, the students in the Schools of Business, Law, and Medicine tended to spend the most for recreation and refreshments. These are all schools in which men predominate.

Among the students who earned part or all of their own expenses, the median expenditure of the NYA women was the least. While the median expenditures of all other students who earned any part of their own expenses were slightly below the median for all students, the difference was not great.

In general, the students at Indiana University who have the least to spend do exercise some economy in their purchase of recreation and refreshments, but the typical student tends to regard a certain amount of such items as necessary and prefers to economize on items other than these. For this reason, the demand of the student for the goods and services listed under the general heading of recreation and refreshments tends to be fairly inelastic.

CHAPTER VIII
UNIVERSITY FEES, ORGANIZATION DUES, AND TEXTBOOKS

UNIVERSITY FEES

OF the items of student expenditure which, for convenience of analysis, are grouped in this chapter; university fees are least flexible and least affected by individual choice. In contrast, the amounts spent for organization fees and dues vary widely. If a student belongs to a social fraternity or sorority, the dues he pays may constitute an important item in his budget. If he is not a member of a Greek-letter society, his expenditures may be negligible. Although the amount a student spends for textbooks would seem to be fixed by the courses he takes, this is not always true. Instead, the amount he spends for this purpose may vary according to his means, his living arrangements, and his scholarly interests.

Since Indiana University is a state institution, tuition is provided by the commonwealth. A Contingent fee is charged, however, to cover in part the cost of the physical maintenance of the University, including the library and gymnasium. The amount of these basic fees charged in the different schools of the University are shown in Table 52. All fees are assessed on the basis of the number of hours listed on the student's enrollment card, and if special courses or extra hours are taken by the student the total paid will be greater than the regular amount.

In addition to the regular Contingent fees, the average student at Indiana University pays at least one additional fee related to his academic program.[1] Such fees are levied for the

---

1 A more complete list of fees of this type that were charged in 1940-41 is as follows:

Training as an Air Pilot	$40 fee to cover insurance and examinations
Horseback riding	$8 for 9 lessons
Typewriting Courses for all Arts and Sciences Students	$5 a semester for use of machine

170

TABLE 52

FEES CHARGED UNDERGRADUATE STUDENTS IN DIFFERENT
SCHOOLS AT INDIANA UNIVERSITY, 1940-41

School	Resident (Semester)	Nonresident [a] (Semester)
Arts and Sciences	$ 44.75	$ 62.50
Business		
Freshmen and Sophomores	46.00	63.70
Juniors and Seniors	52.50	70.00
Dental (First Year) First Semester	128.00	153.00
Second Semester	103.00	153.00
Law (First Year)	52.25	106.25
Medicine (First Year)	108.75	211.25

[a] In the second semester of 1940-41 the enrollment included 669 out-of-state students, representing every state in the Union except Rhode Island, and including students from nine foreign countries.

use of equipment in sciences and in other courses such as aviation, typing, music, or in some phase of physical education.

The cost of attending the University is definitely reduced for the student who receives a scholarship, a fellowship, or a money award. Students not eligible for one of these grants are often enabled to go to college or, if already there, to remain by means of loans available to students from one of the loan funds of the University. In each county in Indiana at least two state scholarships paying $71.50 per year in Contingent fees are granted annually on the basis of scholastic records and aptitude examinations. These scholarships which represent the greatest source of financial aid are offered to high school seniors and students already attending college who qualify for them. The total num-

Supervised Teaching, Nursing and Safety Education	$5 fee
Dietetics (One Year)	$25 per semester for both resident and nonresident students
Golf on Country Club Course	$6 for 7 lessons
Golf on University Campus	$1 per season
Practice Piano	$5, $7.50, or $10 a semester for each hour's use daily during a semester, depending on instrument
Practice Room	$3 a semester (without piano)
Orchestral Instrument	$5 a semester

ber offered in the state is 200. A limited number of Special Merit Scholarships designed primarily for new students are granted each year for the remission of $50 in Contingent fees. Besides, numerous scholarships are awarded by campus organizations, foundations, and individiuals. About thirty scholarships covering the cost of Contingent fees are given each semester to the children of men who served in the First World War.[2] In addition, awards and prizes in the form of money ranging from $5 to $400 help some students to pay their university fees and purchase their textbooks. For advanced students, several fellowships amounting to $500 to $900 are granted each year.

The economic status of the student probably affects his expenditure for university fees less than for any other item in his budget. Unless a scholarship or fellowship or some monetary award is secured by means of which the cost of trainng in a chosen field of work can be reduced, the young man or woman with relatively little money must pay the same amount for this expense as the student with more.

In submitting the estimates of their expenditures for university fees, the students who received scholarships or other stipends to cover their Contingent fees were asked to include their total expenditures for these items regardless of the source from which they were paid.

ALL STUDENTS

In the budget for all students the amount spent for fees represented 13.9 per cent and ranked fourth in importance from the standpoint of amounts spent. Because of the narrow variation in the amounts paid for university fees, the proportion of the

2 The scholarships given to the children of men in the World War are known as Noyes scholarships. These are also offered to any man who was in the World War. Other scholarships offered at Indiana include the William Lowe Bryan grants of $125 each, the Army and Navy Scholarship of $71.50 for Contingent fees for one year which is awarded to the son or daughter of an officer of the Army or Navy, two scholarships awarded to girls enrolled in the State Fair Girls' School, and four scholarships to students participating in the Hoosier Music Festival.

budget spent for them tends to decrease as the total expenditure increases. The median expenditure for university fees for the academic year by students in the sample in 1940-41 was $98.43, which amounted to $49.21 for a semester or $2.73 per week.[3] The interquartile range in annual expenditures was $91.16 to $108.13.

MEN AND WOMEN

As shown below, the median amount spent for university fees by men students was $6.86 more than that spent by women students, a difference explained by the predominance of men in the schools in the University in which the fees are highest and by the greater tendency for men to take laboratory courses for which the largest fees were charged.

Group	Number in Sample	First Quartile	Median	Third Quartile
Men	586	$91.45	$102.15	$109.12
Women	689	90.23	97.29	105.37

The men students spent 15.0 per cent of their total expenditure for university fees and the women 13.01 per cent. Expenditures for education in the National Resources Committee's study included tuition and special fees at schools and colleges with the exception of athletic and infirmary fees.[4] They also included books and supplies such as pens, ink, and notebooks used at school. Fees for all correspondence courses and special lessons of all kinds were also included. As would be expected among single men and women in general, the expenditure for education was much less important in their budgets than in those of groups composed solely of university students. Even when the amounts spent for textbooks and supplies and the

3 For the median and mean expenditures and the proportion of their budgets spent for university fees by all students and groups within the sample, see Table 83, page 249.

4 National Resources Committee, *Consumer Expenditures in the United States*, pp. 82-83.

amounts paid for lessons not strictly intellectual in character were added to the sums spent for tuition and fees, the proportion of the budget of single men spent for the items listed under the general heading of education amounted to only 0.5 per cent and those of single women to 0.3 per cent.[5] The absolute amount spent in twelve months by these men was $6 and by the women $3.

ORGANIZED AND UNORGANIZED STUDENTS

Table 53 shows that university fees are one item in the student budget for which the unorganized students frequently spend the most. The difference among the expenditures of the four groups in Table 53 suggest that, in general, the unorganized students tend to take more hours of work or more laboratory courses while in college than the organized students. The difference may also help to explain the lower expenditures of the unorganized students for recreation. As was true of all fairly rigid costs, the expenditures for fees took a larger proportion of the funds of the unorganized students than of the organized because of their lower total expenditures. See Table 83 in Appendix B.

TABLE 53

MEDIAN AND QUARTILE AMOUNTS PAID IN UNIVERSITY FEES BY
THE ORGANIZED AND UNORGANIZED MEN AND WOMEN
STUDENTS AT INDIANA UNIVERSITY, 1940-41

Group	Number in Sample	First Quartile	Median	Third Quartile
Men				
Organized	205	$92.38	$101.25	$110.52
Unorganized	381	92.39	102.54	108.75
Women				
Organized	236	90.63	96.79	107.00
Unorganized	453	91.13	99.08	104.84
	1275			

5 National Resources Committee, *Consumer Expenditures in the United States*, pp. 82-83.

EXPENDITURES BY STUDENTS IN DIFFERENT CLASSES

As may be seen from Table 54, the amount spent for university fees tends to rise between the student's Sophomore and Junior years as he moves into advanced work in his major field or enters a professional school.

TABLE 54

MEDIAN AND QUARTILE AMOUNTS PAID IN UNIVERSITY FEES
BY THE STUDENTS IN DIFFERENT CLASSES AT
INDIANA UNIVERSITY, 1940-41

Group	Number in Sample	First Quartile	Median	Third Quartile
Freshman	446	$84.29	$ 94.69	$104.41
Sophomore	323	91.40	95.59	103.63
Junior	291	91.81	102.86	109.24
Senior	215	94.90	105.80	123.12

ORGANIZATION DUES

It is frequently said that Americans are a nation of joiners, and one finds little evidence on the American university campus to disprove such a statement. Membership in honorary, academic, and social clubs and societies is important to American college students and is often an important social and economic influence in later life. Not until the variety and number of organizations found on the typical university campus are known can their effect on student spending be realized. For this reason it has seemed worth while to describe some of those found at Indiana University before discussing the amounts spent for dues.

THE INDIANA UNION

All men students in the University are required to be members of the Indiana Student Union, paying fees of seventy-five cents per semester. The stated purpose of the organization, which is housed in the Indiana University Memorial Union Building, is to provide a " varied and wholesome social and recreational program for all students, faculty and friends of the University."

THE ASSOCIATION OF WOMEN STUDENTS

Similarly, all women students are required to be members of this organization which has its headquarters in the Student Building, the center of women's activities on the campus. Fees, levied to cover the cost of operating the Student Building and of the social functions and conferences sponsored by the Association, are seventy-five cents a semester.

HONORARY ORGANIZATIONS

Selection for membership in an honor society or as a leader in a departmental club often proves beneficial; since a business man, interviewing a student with the thought of employing him, is usually impressed by such evidence of ability. Such distinctions are also an aid in obtaining fellowships and scholarships which make advanced training possible.

The significance of membership in Phi Beta Kappa and Sigma Xi is quite generally known. Election by one of these is one of the most coveted goals of the more ambitious and capable students in the field of scholarship.[6] Other honorary organizations and Greek-letter societies which issue invitations for membership on the basis of academic achievement or proficiency in skill are described in the following list published in the Indiana University Bulletin:

Law students constitute the membership of the Order of the Coif. Phi Delta Kappa, for men, and Pi Lambda Theta, for women, are organizations composed of students in the School of Education.

6 Sigma Xi is a national scientific society to which a student who meets the qualifications for membership may be elected in his Senior year. The purpose of this society "is to encourage the investigation of science, pure and applied." Phi Beta Kappa is a society for "the promotion of scholarship and friendship among students and graduates of American colleges." At Bloomington, where a chapter was established in 1911, the society elects not over 10 percent of the seniors who have given evidence of high scholarship, made no substitutions for required work, and have been in residence for two full years. *Indiana University Bulletin,* XXXIX, (1941), p. 119.

Organizations in the School of Business are Beta Gamma Sigma, the national business fraternity for men and women; Alpha Kappa Psi and Delta Sigma Pi, national professional fraternities for men; Omicron Delta and Chi Gamma, local clubs for women in the School. In the School of Music Alpha Delta Chi is for men, and Sigma Alpha Iota is a national organization for women. There are two organizations among the students in the Department of Journalism: Sigma Delta Chi for men and Theta Sigma Phi for women. Phi Lambda Upsilon, Alpha Chi Sigma, and Iota Sigma Pi are for chemistry students, the last named for women. Eta Sigma Phi is for students in Latin or Greek. Alpha Omega Alpha is a medical scholarship society. Omicron Kappa Upsilon is an honor fraternity in dentistry. Kappa Kappa Psi fosters interest in advanced band work. Omicron Nu is a national honor society for students of home economics. Pershing Rifles and Scabbard and Blade are organizations for students proficient in military work. Sigma Delta Psi is open to students who pass a series of tests in track and gymnasium work. Alpha Lambda Delta (Women) and Phi Eta Sigma (men) are scholastic societies for Freshmen. Sigma Gamma Epsilon is the organization for geology and geography students and faculty. Tau Kappa Alpha is a national honorary oratorical and debating organization. Theta Alpha Phi is a national dramatics organization for both men and women.... Delta Phi Alpha is a national society for German students. Phi Epsilon Kappa is a national fraternity in physical education. Alpha Kappa Delta is a national scholarship society in sociology, and Pi Sigma Alpha in political science.[7]

On joining many of these organizations the student is charged an initiation fee and required to purchase a key or pin. After induction annual fees amounting to $1 to $5 are sometimes collected.

ACADEMIC CLUBS SPONSORED BY SCHOOLS AND DEPARTMENTS

The membership of the clubs sponsored by schools and departments of the University usually consists of both faculty members and advanced students. Such organizations include:

7 *Ibid.*, p. 120.

Student Affiliates of the American Chemical Society, Physics Seminar, History Club, Euclidean Circle, Le Cercle Français, Spanish Club, Der Deutsche Verein, English Club, Home Economics Club, Classical, Skeleton Club, University Theatre (dramatics organization), Economics Club, Philosophy Club, Sociology Club, Pro-Music Club, Taps (dramatics), Dolphin Club (men's swimming), Education Club, Future Teachers of America, Advertising and Merchandising Club, Accounting Club, Insurance Club, Management Club, Collegiate Chamber of Commerce, the Law Club.

Other clubs open to students in different departments are: the Cosmopolitan Club, designed to promote international understanding and friendship; the International Relations Club; the Men's Glee Club; the Girls' Glee Club; the Symphony Orchestra; the Concert Choir; and the R.O.T.C. Band. Fees charged by clubs in this group tend to be nominal.

RELIGIOUS ORGANIZATIONS

The Union Building houses the headquarters of the University Committee on Religion, which is an administrative committee of faculty members, church leaders, and students. This committee is representative of various faiths and coördinates the religious activities on the campus.

YMCA AND YWCA

In the same bulding is the YMCA which takes an active part in the religious, social, and service activities on the campus and in the city.

The YWCA headquarters, as those of other women's organizations, are located in the Student Building where monthly meetings are held for Freshmen and for all other members. The YWCA conducts study and discussion groups, sponsors literary and musical programs, teas, and parties. The members also participate in welfare work in the community.

CHURCHES

Most of the churches in Bloomington have special programs for work with students. In addition to special societies and Sunday School classes for the students, one church maintains a social and recreatonal center. Another sponsors a cooperative rooming house. For its program for Jewish students the Hillel Foundaton not only maintains a building adjoining the campus but also a full-time Director. For the Catholic students the local church sponsors a Newman Club which is affiliated with a national federation of Catholic clubs. The national office of the Christian Science church also sponsors a campus organization.

In general, membership in student activities provided by the churches does not involve the payment of dues. The programs designed for work with the students are usually subsidized by district, regional, or national organizations of the church. The student's contribution is voluntary and depends on what he is able or willing to give. Most of the sororities and fraternities compel their pledges to attend church and instruct them to put money in the collection plate. The attendance of unorganized students is entirely voluntary.

SOCIAL FRATERNITIES AND SORORITIES

All of the organizations described above are open to both members of Greek-letter social organizations and to non-members. Only the exceptional non-member, however, joins a sufficient number of clubs and societies of this type to make his annual expenditure for dues amount to as much as those paid by the members of a social fraternity or sorority. For this reason the contrast between the median expenditure for dues by the fraternity members and non-members is greater for dues than for expenditures listed under any other heading in the student budget.

In the fraternity and sorority chapters on the Indiana campus, students pay a fee of from $5 to $25 when they are pledged. Following the pledge service, the pledges pay dues which in most cases are the same in amount as those paid by the members of the chapter who have already been initiated. In some organizations these pledge dues are paid by the month and in others in flat sums for the year. In one sorority, the total amount of $90 for the year was paid in monthly installments of $10. At another house, the annual payment amounted to only $3. Still another chapter collected only 10 cents a week from its pledges.

The initiation fees paid by Freshmen in 1940-41 ranged from $30 to $65, but in certain of the sororities the amount paid included the cost of a pin. The prices of pins began at $3.75 and rose to $16.50. In all but two sororities initiated members paid monthly dues to their local chapters. In some organizations these dues were as low as $2 per month and in others as much as five times that amount. In addition to the local dues, most fraternities and sororities paid dues to the national organization. As in the case of pledge dues, both the amount and method of payment of this levy differed considerably. At one sorority, where it was paid only once a year, the amount paid per member was only $1, while at three others it amounted to $10 per month. Some chapters assessed their members for special purposes such as for insurance; social events, including dances; charity; and for life membership in the organization. Others imposed levies of from $5 to $100 per year on their members for building funds.

AMOUNTS SPENT FOR ORGANIZATION FEES AND DUES

Under the heading of organization dues the students in the study were asked to state what they paid during 1940-41 to the clubs and societies to which they belonged. The members of Greek-letter chapters were instructed also to include all amounts paid to their organizations except for board and room. When the amounts submitted in answer to this request were thrown into a frequency distribution and the median amounts spent by different groups computed, it was found that for no item in the student budget did the amounts spent by the organized and unorganized students vary as greatly as for those spent for dues. As may be seen from Table 55, the median amounts spent for dues by the unorganized students are almost negligible when compared with those of the sorority and fraternity members.[8]

8 The median and mean expenditures and proportions of their budgets spent for dues by all students and by groups within the sample are shown in Table 85, page 251.

As a consequence, the expenditure for dues occupies one of the least important positions in the budgets of the unorganized students, representing less than one per cent, while for the organized students it ranked in fifth place in importance, representing 8.7 per cent of their entire expenditure. Dues to social and recreational clubs, but not business associations, were listed under the heading of recreation in the National Resources Committee's study of single men and women.[9] For this reason, the proportions of their budgets spent for these items are not available for comparison with those spent by the university students in whose budgets expenditures for dues seemed important enough to warrant placing them in an individual category.

TABLE 55

MEDIAN AND QUARTILE EXPENDITURES FOR ORGANIZATION FEES AND
DUES BY ORGANIZED AND UNORGANIZED MEN AND WOMEN
AT INDIANA UNIVERSITY, 1940-41

Group	Number in Sample	First Quartile	Median	Third Quartile
Men				
Organized	205	$38.33	$78.00	$100.00
Unorganized	380	1.80	3.60	6.75
Women				
Organized	228	30.84	76.67	101.19
Unorganized	451	1.67	3.23	4.99
	1264 a			

a Eleven students did not report whether or not they spent anything for dues.

College class membershp appeared to have relatively little influence on the amount a student spent for dues except for the organized Freshmen. Because of pledge and initiation fees and accompanying expenditures, the organized Freshmen spent on an average more for dues than the upper classmen. It should be pointed out, however, that pledges whose marks do not permit them to be initiated in the Freshman year frequently qualify in their Sophomore year.

9 National Resources Committee, *Consumer Expenditures in the United States*, p. 97.

EXPENDITURES FOR TEXTBOOKS

In 1940-41 the students in the sample spent on an average $26.83 for textbooks and other supplies related to their class work, an amount representing 3.8 per cent of their budgets.[10] Data collected by means of personal interviews seemed to justify the conclusion that between one-third and one-half of the money spent for books was spent for new books and the rest for second-hand books and other supplies.

MEN AND WOMEN

The women spent slightly more for texts than men in spite of the fact that the latter showed a greater tendency to take courses in such fields as Law, Medicine, Dentistry, Business, and Physics, in which the cost of textbooks was relatively high.[11] The difference is largely explained by the greater conscientious-ness on the part of women in the purchasing of textbooks for the courses they take and by their preference for new texts. Women students who were questioned were inclined to regard a used book as " second-hand " and to prefer a new one to a " good buy " in a used one. In general the men seemed to have no hesitancy in using a used text, if it were intact and cheaper. Many students complained that books were changed so often that they brought relatively little when sold second hand.

The amount spent for textbooks represented 3.9 per cent of the men students' budget and 3.7 per cent of the women's be-cause of their larger total expenditure. In the National Re-sources Committee study of single men and women, expendi-tures for textbooks and supplies were included under the general heading of education (see page 173).[12]

10 For the median and mean amounts and proportion of the budget spent for textbooks by all students in the sample and by groups within the sample see Table 84, page 250.

11 The median amount spent by men was $26.16 and by women $27.38.

12 The National Resources Committee, *Consumer Expenditures in the United States*, p. 97.

ORGANIZED AND UNORGANIZED STUDENTS

In spite of the fact that the organized students spent less than the unorganized on university fees they spent more on textbooks. This was probably because they purchased fewer second-hand books and because more of them purchased individual copies of the texts used. As shown in Table 56, however, the difference in the median expenditures of the organized women, who had the highest expenditures, and the unorganized men, who had the lowest, was not great enough to be highly significant.

TABLE 56

MEDIAN AND QUARTILE EXPENDITURES FOR TEXTBOOKS BY
ORGANIZED AND UNORGANIZED MEN AND WOMEN
AT INDIANA UNIVERSITY, 1940-41

Group	Number in Sample	First Quartile	Median	Third Quartile
Men				
Organized	205	$20.92	$26.17	$32.79
Unorganized	381	18.97	25.76	33.91
Women				
Organized	233	21.70	28.66	34.78
Unorganized	453	20.44	27.16	34.61
	1272 a			

a Three students did not report any expenditure for textbooks.

EXPENDITURES BY STUDENTS IN DIFFERENT CLASSES

As would be expected, the textbooks used in the Junior and Senior years tend to cost more than those used in the first two years. The similarity found among the first quartile expenditures in all four classes suggests that the upper classmen are better bargainers than the underclassmen. The median expenditure of Freshmen shows a definite tendency on their part to purchase new and individual copies of the texts used in their classes. In all classes, however, including the Freshman class, it is not uncommon for two or even three students who live in the same house or neighborhood to purchase and use a common text. The median and quartile amounts spent for textbooks by students in the different college classes were:

TABLE 57

MEDIAN AND QUARTILE EXPENDITURES FOR TEXTBOOKS BY 1272 INDIANA
UNIVERSITY STUDENTS IN THE FOUR COLLEGE CLASSES, 1940-41

Group	Number in Sample	First Quartile	Median	Third Quartile
Freshman	446	$20.97	$26.91	$34.00
Sophomore	322	18.97	25.37	31.72
Junior	289	20.89	27.46	34.35
Senior	215	20.39	28.72	40.42

SUMMARY

University fees were found to be the most important of the categories of expenditure considered in this chapter. The median expenditures for this item by all students in the sample amounted to $98.43 and ranked fourth in order of importance in the student budget. Men were found to spend somewhat more than women because they took more laboratory courses and were found in greater numbers in the professional schools. Membership in Greek-letter societies was found to make little difference in the amount spent for fees. University fees paid by upperclass students tended to be higher than those paid by Freshmen and Sophomores.

Expenditures under the heading of organization dues were of two kinds which differed greatly in amount. Dues paid to general organizations open to all students and to honorary, academic, and departmental clubs were relatively small in amount and the median for all unorganized students was only $3.60 for the men and $3.23 for the women. Fees and dues paid by members of fraternities and sororities were much larger—the median payments being $78 for men and $76.67 for women.

The median expenditure for textbooks and supplies by all students in the sample was $26.83. Women were found to spend slightly more than men because of greater conscientiousness and a more pronounced preference for new books. Members of fraternities and sororities were found to spend slightly more for books than the unorganized students. Median expenditures for textbooks by all students were slightly higher in the last two years of college because books used in advance courses tend to cost somewhat more than those used in the first two years.

The categories in the student budget which remain to be considered in the next chapter are transportation, health, gifts and contributions, and general reading.

CHAPTER IX

TRANSPORTATION, HEALTH, AND MIS-CELLANEOUS EXPENDITURES

THE items in the student budget which remain to be studied are relatively minor in importance when judged from either the standpoint of the proportion of the budget involved or of the absolute amount spent. Because of their heterogeneous character each category is treated separately.

EXPENDITURES FOR TRANSPORTATION

The homes of the great majority of the students attending Indiana University are within the state and many are within a fairly short distance of the campus. As a result, students traveling back and forth to school at Bloomington find many ways to reduce their transportation costs. One way is for the parents of four or five students from one community to take turns driving them to and from school. Since a different family makes the trip each time, none of the students are charged for their transportation. Another plan is for one father to make the trip and several families contribute to the cost. From the standpoint of expense and convenience either of these ways of getting home is regarded as preferable to taking a train or bus. It is not unusual to find students who have never ridden on a train.

It is also usually fairly easy for students to find someone with whom they may ride home on week-ends. Transportation for week-ends is advertised on various bulletin boards around the campus. Some men students earn part of their school expenses by driving home every week-end and taking paying passengers with them. At the beginning of vacations, however, it is not so easy to find cheap transportation because everyone is looking for a way to get home. Some of the men depend entirely on hitchhiking. Others spend money for transportation only when thumbing their way involves waiting too long or a delay that would interfere with their reaching their destinations in time to carry out their plans or make them reach Bloomington too late to be counted present in their classes on the day following a vacation.[1]

In recent years, the number of students attending Indiana University from states along the Eastern seaboard has increased.[2] Some of these students when interviewed said they came to Indiana because they had relatives living in the state. A few wanted a taste of " country life " and others wanted to go to college away from home. The most important reason given by most of these students for attending Indiana University, however, was the belief that even after paying the higher fees charged students whose homes were outside the state and taking into account the cost of transportation their expenses were less than they would have been at a school of similar academic standing nearer home.

To get to and from the University, groups of these students sometimes charter private cars or buses, which reduces the cost of the trip to a nominal amount. Some travel via railroad or a regular commercial bus. A few in the group have purchased cheap used cars for the purpose of driving to and from Bloomington. Some hitchhike back and forth, sometimes leaving Bloomington with very little money in their pockets. Expenses mentioned by students who had hitchhiked from Bloomington to New York City or Philadelphia amounted to between $1.50 to $3 depending upon their luck and whether or not they had to sleep in a hotel or tourist cabin. Trolley or bus fare through the larger cities amounted to 10 to 25 cents. One boy from New Jersey said he found it so easy to get rides to Bloomington that once there he decided to see as much of the Middle West as possible. Success on these trips caused him to decide to return to New Jersey in June via California.

1 A student at Indiana University loses one half-hour's credit if he cuts class on the day before or after a vacation.

2 In 1940-41, the enrollment from the states of Connecticut, Maine, Massachusetts, New York, New Jersey, and Pennsylvania was 253 in comparison with 174 from the same states in 1935-36 and 92 in 1930-31.

Neither men nor women students were permitted to have cars on the campus in 1940-41 unless they could show evidence of need for them because of illness, business necessities, commuting, or some other urgent need. Only eleven of the 1275 students in the sample reported that they owned cars and kept them in Bloomington during the entire school year. Sixty-two said they kept a car at school much of the time, and fourteen said they sometimes had one. As may be seen from these figures, the maintenance of a car is a relatively unimportant item in the budget of an Indiana student. When students were interviewed on the subject of having a car while at the University many said that even if they could have one they would not want it. In general the reasons given by these students were similar to that of one man who said:

I wouldn't want a car down here. If a fellow has one he has to use it as a taxi. The fellows at the house all pile in and make him take them to their classes. By the time the fellow who owns the car has hauled the others over the campus he is usually late for his own class. Besides, on week-ends, the fellows either cook up a trip some place and make the fellow who owns the car take them or make him lend them his car.

One boy said that when he brought his car back to Bloomington with him he often left it parked on a side street across town from the fraternity house so that his fraternity brothers would not know it was in town. The only women students who had cars at the University in 1940-41 were those who received permission from the Dean of Women because of a definite need for a car.

Since Bloomington is a small city and most of the students are housed within walking distance of the campus, local transportation costs are relatively unimportant. In rainy weather students make some use of the city buses and of taxicabs. For formal dances the latter are largely used; but, since the fare in 1940-41 was only fifteen cents per person for any distance between stops within the city limits, the amount spent in a year by the ordinary student was not great. In the statistical analysis that follows, no attempt was made to segregate these purely local transportation expenditures from those involved in traveling to and from Bloomington and outside points.

Only 6.9 per cent of the 1230 students who reported how they traveled to and from Bloomington indicated that they usually traveled by train. About three times as many women as men used this means of transportation. A larger proportion of organized than unorganized students used railroad services. Almost 19 per cent of all the students depended on buses, and again, as in the case of trains, the women who used them were about three times as numerous as the men.. A slightly larger proportion of unorganized than organized students rode in buses. About 22 per cent of all the students in the sample and slightly more women than men regularly rode back and forth from school in cars owned by friends or their parents. About the same proportion of organized and unorganized students traveled in this way. More than 23 per cent of the 538 men who reported how they traveled to and from home said they ordinarily hitchhiked. Of these about one-third were organized students and two-thirds unorganized. In noting the above figure, however, it should be kept in mind that over a third of all the students in the sample in 1940-41 reported that during the year they used more than one means of transportation and that the estimates of expenditure for transportation from which the medians used in the chapter were computed include amounts spent for travel in all kinds of public conveyances as well as in privately owned automobiles.

EXPENDITURES BY ALL STUDENTS

The median expenditure for transportation to and from home and while at college of all students in the sample who reported transportation costs in 1940-41 was $20.23 and the interquartile range $11.03 to $29.46.[3] In the budget for all students the pro-

3 For the median and mean amounts spent for transportation by the groups studied, see Table 86, page 252.

portion spent for transportation represented 3.4 per cent. Three and three tenths per cent of the budgets of the single men in the National Resources Committee's study was spent for transportation other than for the use of an automobile and 4.5 per cent of that of single women.[4] The expenses represented by these percentages covered transportation to and from work but not outlays deductible as business expenses. The students at Indiana University had very little expense for transportation to and from jobs and the types of transportation available to them on their way to and from Bloomington and while in Bloomington were more limited than those available to men and women at large. These differences help to explain the slightly greater importance of the expenses listed under the general heading of transportation in the budgets of the single men and women studied by the National Resources Committee even though their expenses for the use of an automobile were listed under a separate heading.

EXPENDITURES BY MEN AND WOMEN

During the year 1940-41 the median and quartile amounts spent for transportation by men and women students were:

Group	Number in Sample	First Quartile	Median	Third Quartile
Men	586	$ 9.04	$20.67	$56.11
Women	686	12.51	20.17	29.97

As may be seen, the median expenditures for travel by men and women were very similar.[5] The interquartile range in the amounts spent by men was much wider than in that of the women, amounting to $9.04 to $56.11 as compared with $12.59 to $29.97 for women. The greater range in the case of men is explained by a tendency for some of them to hitchhike,

4 National Resources Committee, *Consumer Expenditures in the United States*, pp. 82-83. For a more complete list of the types of transportation and related expenses included under the general heading of transportation, see p. 97 *ibid*.

5 For the median and mean amounts spent for transportation by the groups studied, see Table 86, page 252.

while on the other hand a larger proportion of them than of women came from distant states. About twenty per cent of the 686 women students left the campus every week-end and an even larger percentage of the men, many of whom went to see girls in their home towns or at other colleges. But even though they traveled more during the school year than the women, the men spent very little more because so many of them hitchhiked. The proportion of the average total expenditure of men spent on transportation was 3.2 per cent and that of women 3.6 per cent.

EXPENDITURES BY ORGANIZED AND UNORGANIZED STUDENTS

The organized students spent on an average more for transportation than the unorganized for several reasons. One of these is the greater tendency for the unorganized men to hitchhike, many of whom actually travel back and forth from home to school without paying anything for transportation. The other reason is that many of the unorganized students do not leave the campus except for the Christmas and Spring vacations, or if they do, only when free transportation is available. Besides frequently spending week-ends at the homes of roommates or other friends, it is not uncommon for sorority members to go by bus to Indianapolis on Saturday to shop or to see a play. Organized men find countless reasons for visiting girls or fraternity brothers at other colleges. The median expenditures of the organized and unorganized students for transportation in the sample in 1940-41 are shown in Table 58.

Because of the larger total expenditure of the organized students the proportion of their budget spent for transportation, which was 3.4 per cent, was practically the same as that spent by the unorganized students.[6] The difference in the amounts spent by the two groups is explained by the number of trips away from Bloomington rather than by differences in the mode of transportation used by the two groups.

6 For the median expenditure for transportation by all organized and all unorganized students, see Table 86, page 252.

TABLE 58

MEDIAN AND QUARTILE EXPENDITURES FOR TRANSPORTATION
BY ORGANIZED AND UNORGANIZED MEN AND WOMEN
AT INDIANA UNIVERSITY, 1940-41

Group	Number in Sample	First Quartile	Median	Third Quartile
Men				
Organized	205	$13.42	$24.15	$38.59
Unorganized	381	7.58	15.88	27.02
Women				
Organized	233	22.38	24.29	36.21
Unorganized	453	11.88	18.63	28.08
	1272			

EXPENDITURES BY STUDENTS IN DIFFERENT CLASSES

As judged from their median expenditures shown in Table 59 both men and women in the Senior class spent more for transportation than the underclassmen, although the median amounts spent by students in all classes were too similar to warrant the belief that class membership was an important factor in determining expenditure for travel (see Table 86, page 252. Among the women, the lowest expenditures were found in the first two years. The interquartile as well as the median expenditure by each class are given below:[7]

TABLE 59

MEDIAN AND QUARTILE EXPENDITURES FOR TRANSPORTATION BY 1272 INDIANA
UNIVERSITY STUDENTS IN THE FOUR COLLEGE CLASSES, 1940-41

Group	Number in Sample	First Quartile	Median	Third Quartile
Freshman	446	$10.65	$18.77	$28.55
Sophomore	322	10.05	17.86	37.86
Junior	286	11.36	18.99	22.65
Senior	215	12.95	21.86	35.57

7 For differences in the median and mean expenditures of organized and unorganized men and women in all four college classes, see Table 86, page 252.

EXPENDITURES BY STUDENTS IN DIFFERENT SCHOOLS
OF THE UNIVERSITY

When the amounts spent for transportation by students in the different schools in the University were compared, it was found that the students in the College of Arts and Sciences spent the most. The median for these students was $23.36 while that of the School of Business which ranked next in amount was $20.56. The median expenditure of the students in the School of Music was $18.64 and ranked third in amount. These medians and those of the other schools are shown below.

TABLE 60

MEDIAN EXPENDITURES FOR TRANSPORTATION BY STUDENTS IN
DIFFERENT SCHOOLS OF INDIANA UNIVERSITY, 1940-41

School	Number in Sample	Median
Arts and Sciences	482	$23.36
Business	519	20.56
Education	159	17.80
Medicine and Dentistry	59	15.73
Music	38	18.64
Law	9	18.00
	1266	

In spite of the reduction in the average cost per mile traveled by students in recent years the amounts actually spent by the majority of students have risen because of the greater tendency to move about while in college.[8] At Indiana, the practice of going home for week-ends is much more common than formerly.

8 The tendency in recent years to move from place to place more frequently than formerly is not confined to students. A recent report of the U. S. Bureau of Labor Statistics showed that American families now spend almost as much for transportation as for clothing; a change largely attributed to the spread in the ownership of automobiles. In this report, it was pointed out that an automobile has become far more than a means of transportation. It is now a " prestige symbol " in the minds of most Americans as well as an important means of recreation. At least one-half of the urban families with yearly incomes on an average of above $1,500 owned an automobile. All families spent more on the automobile than on public conveyances for either local or distant travel. The report points out that in 1917 automobile ownership was so uncommon among moderate income families that expenditures for automobiles were tabulated with those for

EXPENDITURES FOR HEALTH

Since the fall of 1939 the University has maintained a Student Health Center on the campus which in 1940-41 was staffed by four full-time physicians, an x-ray technician, four graduate part-time nurses, and two nurse's aids. For students entering the University for the first time, whose preliminary physical examinations indicate the need for a more complete physical check-up or special tests, such services are provided. During the academic year any student may secure first aid, the diagnosis of ailments or treatment of minor ones at the Health Center. An infirmary is provided for students having minor illnesses which require them to stay in bed not more than four days. To help meet the costs of these services a charge of $3 a semester is included in the Contingent fee paid by all students.

In the case of major illnesses, the student's parents are notified and consulted regarding the choice of a physician. When hospital care beyond the facilities of the university infirmary is required, the Student Health Service pays up to a maximum of $20 toward the cost.

In addition to the services outlined above, a trained nurse, supervised by the staff at the Student Health Center, is housed in each of the women's dormitories.[9] From these women several interesting facts relating to student health were learned. Evidence of the benefit of balanced meals planned by dieticians is found in a comparison of the experiences of these nurses. Many of the girls living at Forest Hall, the coöperative dormitory where there is no dining room, take their meals at restaurants. As a consequence, relatively more cases of gastric disturbances

bicycle and motorcycles in the study of expenditures of wage earners and clerical workers made by the Bureau of Labor Statistics in 1917-19. In 1935-36 the average expenditures for transportation by the families studied was below food expenditures for all income levels but generally exceeded those for clothing. The proportion of car owners in smaller cities was greater than in New York and Chicago. United States Bureau of Labor Statistics Bulletin 648, Vol. VI, *Family Expenditures in Selected Cities: Trade and Transportation*, pp. 3-6, 31.

9 These nurses are usually graduate nurses who have come to the University for training in public health nursing.

and digestive illnesses have been reported among them than at the dormitories having dining rooms and well balanced meals. In 1940-41, however, the number of cases of illnesses of this type was reduced at Forest Hall by the introduction of an educational program. At house meetings the nurse talked to the girls on the importance of a balanced diet and the consumption of specific types of foods.

Certain other differences between the girls living at the coöperative dormitory and the other university residences were mentioned by the nurses who were interviewed. While in each instance the nurse reported that she treated approximately half the girls in the dormitory in which she lived, the causes for treatment were somewhat different. Besides showing a greater tendency for gastric and digestive disturbances, the Forest Hall girls showed a somewhat greater propensity for colds. This latter tendency, the nurse pointed out, was probably at least partially due to the lack of a proper amount of fresh fruits and vegetables in the girls' diet. In general, however, the greater differences in the demands made on the nurses by the women students were due to their previous conditioning and current way of living rather than the nature of their illness. At Forest where a large proportion of the girls work to earn a part or all of their college expenses, they were apt to be in a hurry when they visited the nurse for treatment necessary for a sore throat or cold and had no time to wait for sympathy. The nurse in that dormitory remarked: " They come to get their throats painted and are away in a minute. They have not time for a half hour discussion of their illness." But at the other dormitories, more girls went to the nurse for sympathy than for medical care. One nurse in commenting on this tendency said: " Many come from well-to-do families and have been very much babied. They want me to do the same thing." The girls in these dormitories have colds, sore throats, and headaches, too; but practically none have gastric disturbances due to food. Sprains, scratches, and blisters take them to the nurse. Others go to her to have blemishes on their faces cured before dances.

EXPENDITURES BY ALL STUDENTS

The expenditures for health represent amounts students paid to physicians, dentists, and occulists and for medicine during the academic year 1940-41 in addition to the university fee of $3 per semester.[10] The median amount spent for these items by all students in the sample was $7.27 for the year, or less than 81 cents a month. A fourth of all the students spent $3.63 or less, while the upper fourth spent $13.23 or more. For a month these sums amounted to 40 cents and $1.47 respectively. The proportion of the budget spent for the maintenance of health was 1.1 per cent.

A recent study of doctor and dentist bills for the families of urban wage earners and clerical workers made by the U. S. Department of Labor showed that the average aggregate expenditure for health protection for each member of the family amounted to $16.[11] This sum, even when the fees of $6 for the regular school year that were paid for the services of the Health Center were added to the expenditures reported by the students, was greater than amounts listed by more than half of the students in the sample studied at Indiana in 1940-41.[12] The low median expenditure for health by Indiana University students is probably explained in part by the fact that students are of an age when expenditures for health are normally low and partly by the fact that the university medical service reduces the expense of colds and other minor ailments. Parents tend to supply their children with medicine before they leave home, and to replenish their supplies when they go home. Many students also have dental work done during the summer vacations.

10 This fee was included in those listed by the students under the heading of university fees.

11 "Doctor Bills of City Workers," *The Monthly Labor Review*, L (May, 1940), p. 1063. This study covered 14,469 white and negro families in 42 cities with populations of over 50,000 in 1934-35. No families having an income of less than $500 or on relief were included in the study. The investigation showed that the absolute amount spent for medical care tended to increase as the family income increased.

12 For a list of the median and mean amounts spent for health services by different groups of students, see Table 87, page 253.

MEN AND WOMEN

Contrary to what might be expected, the women students spent only about 39 cents more per year in 1940-41 for the maintenance of health than the men students. The median and quartile expenditures of the men and women in the sample were:

Group	Number in Sample	First Quartile	Median	Third Quartile
Men	575	$3.53	$7.06	$12.36
Women	659	3.73	7.45	14.15

On a monthly basis, the men's median expenditure of $7.06 for the year amounted to 78 cents, while $7.45, the median for the women, amounted to 82 cents per month. Above the third quartile expenditures of both men and women students there were several amounts of $150 or more reported for hospitalization.

In the budget of the men students the amount spent for health maintenance represented 1.2 per cent. In that of women, it amounted to 1.1 per cent. In contrast, the single men studied by the National Resources Committee spent 2.8 per cent of their budget for medical care and single women 3.1 per cent. As judged from a comparison of these figures, it would seem that, because of the services supplied by the University and the youth of the students, the amounts spent for health services by the students were reduced to a relatively less important expense in their budgets than in that of single men and women in general.[13] It is probable that the difference in the expenditures of the two groups for medical care would have been still greater had it not been that many of the single men and women included in the National Resources Committee study were covered by group health and accident insurance plans.

13 The costs listed under medical care in the National Resources Committee's study included such services as those of physicians, dentists, optometrists, nurses, hospitals, clinics, and laboratories; medicines; drugs such as aspirin and rubbing alcohol; and devices such as eyeglasses, elastic stockings, braces, listed under the heading of medical care; see National Resources Committee, *Consumer Expenditures in the United States*, p. 96.

EXPENDITURES BY ORGANIZED AND UNORGANIZED STUDENTS

Table 61 shows that a student's expenditure for the maintenance of health is affected relatively little by whether or not he belongs to a Greek-letter organization although the median amounts spent by both the organized men and women were slightly higher than those spent by the unorganized students. The unorganized women spent the least, getting along on a median monthly expenditure of 74 cents as compared with 92 cents per month spent by organized women.

TABLE 61

MEDIAN AND QUARTILE EXPENDITURES FOR THE MAINTENANCE OF HEALTH BY ORGANIZED AND UNORGANIZED STUDENTS AT INDIANA UNIVERSITY, 1940-41

Group	Number in Sample	First Quartile	Median	Third Quartile
Men				
Organized	200	$3.75	$7.52	$13.95
Unorganized	375	3.42	6.84	11.10
Women				
Organized	222	4.14	8.28	17.07
Unorganized	437	3.33	6.66	9.99
	1234			

EXPENDITURES BY STUDENTS IN DIFFERENT CLASSES

As judged from the median and quartile expenditures shown in Table 62, a student's expenses for the maintenance of health were somewhat affected by his class ranking.

TABLE 62

MEDIAN AND QUARTILE EXPENDITURES FOR THE MAINTENANCE OF HEALTH BY STUDENTS IN DIFFERENT CLASSES AT INDIANA UNIVERSITY, 1940-41

Group	Number in Sample	First Quartile	Median	Third Quartile
Freshmen	420	$3.31	$6.62	$ 9.94
Sophomores	317	3.60	7.20	12.82
Juniors	286	3.95	7.90	15.23
Seniors	211	4.03	8.05	15.68

Not only was the median expenditure of the students in each succeeding class greater than that in the preceding, but the first and third quartile expenditures also increased in the same fashion.

EXPENDITURES FOR CONTRIBUTIONS AND GIFTS

Amounts spent for contributions to churches and charity, for gifts, and for flowers were grouped under one heading. Because of this grouping, the figures did not show how the students in different groups apportioned their expenditures among the various items within the categories. Data collected by interviews with students indicated, however, that the non-fraternity members contributed relatively more of their total expenditures to churches and charity than fraternity members and that women gave more than men. Non-members of Greek-letter organizations spent less for gifts and flowers than the members. Women spent more than men for gifts but they gave most of them to women friends as birthday, Christmas, Valentine's Day, or Easter gifts. Most of the men's gifts went to women. Amounts spent by students for Christmas presents after they went home for the vacation were not included in their estimates.

EXPENDITURES BY ALL STUDENTS

In 1940-41, the median amount spent for contributions, gifts, and flowers by all students was $12.21 and the interquartile range $6.69 to $21.46.[14]

EXPENDITURES BY MEN AND WOMEN

The median expenditure for contributions and gifts for the women was $13.21 and for the men $11.27. The interquartile range for women was $6.99 to $23.20, and for men $6.38 to $19.03. When questioned regarding his observations relating to the purchase of gifts by men students, a clerk in a shop popular with students and regularly patronized by them said that they buy fewer boxes of candy and bottles of perfume than they

14 For median and mean expenditure and proportion of their budget spent for contributions and gifts by all students and by groups within the sample, see Table 88, page 255.

did a decade ago. As judged by the comments of some of the students who were interviewed, flowers are now considered more " correct " by fraternity men whose precedent in this matter appears to be followed by non-members.

The university women spent 2.1 per cent of their budget for contributions and gifts and the men 1.9 per cent. Items included in the student budget under the heading of gifts and contributions were not treated as one of the main categories of consumption in the National Resources Committee's study of single men and women. Instead, amounts spent for them were lumped with sums paid for personal taxes and shown as a percentage of the income spent.[15] The inclusion of taxes prevents the results from having significance for purposes of comparison with the amounts spent by the students.

EXPENDITURES BY ORGANIZED AND UNORGANIZED STUDENTS

The median amount spent by the members of Greek-letter organizations for contributions and gifts shown in Table 63 was $15.17 and that of non-members $10.67. The interquartile ranges of the two groups were $5.38 to $18.23 and $8.80 to $27.86 respectively. From Table 63 we see that with the exception of the lower fourth of their respective groups the sorority women spent the most on contributions and gifts and the unorganized the least.

TABLE 63

MEDIAN AND QUARTILE EXPENDITURES FOR CONTRIBUTIONS AND
GIFTS BY ORGANIZED AND UNORGANIZED MEN AND WOMEN
AT INDIANA UNIVERSITY, 1940-41

Group	Number in Sample	First Quartile	Median	Third Quartile
Men				
Organized	204	$8.78	$14.17	$26.74
Unorganized	381	9.13	9.62	16.14
Women				
Organized	236	8.71	18.41	29.72
Unorganized	453	6.15	11.67	119.54
	1274			

15 National Resources Committee, *Consumer Expenditures in the United States*, pp. 81-83.

TRANSPORTATION 201

As may be seen from the figures shown in Table 64, the amounts spent for gifts and flowers by fraternity members and non-members rise as the student approaches graduation:

TABLE 64

MEDIAN AND QUARTILE EXPENDITURES FOR CONTRIBUTIONS AND GIFTS BY ORGANIZED AND UNORGANIZED MEN AT INDIANA UNIVERSITY, 1940-41

Group	Men	
	Organized	Unorganized
Freshman	$12.78	$ 8.75
Sophomore	13.75	9.44
Junior	14.04	10.95
Senior	26.88	11.25

The sharper rise in the median expenditure of organized Senior men is at least partially explained by the greater tendency for Senior men to "put out their fraternity pins." At such times it is customary for the man to buy a box of " good " cigars to pass around among the members of the fraternity and to send a box of candy to the girl and flowers to her sorority. For some men this expense is increased when the procedure is repeated during the year. Women students frequently win honors and hold offices in their Senior year which calls for flowers from men friends. Some Senior men and women who have not attended many dances in other years realize that it is their last year in college and begin to attend more social functions. For the men this frequently involves the purchase of flowers or dance favors.

Sorority pledges lived in the dormitories in 1940-41 where there is less precedent for giving gifts in case of illness or for birthdays or special days than in the sorority houses. As a consequence, the average expenditure of the organized Freshman women was lower than for women in other classes. In the dormitories, birthdays are usually celebrated by " spreads " or dinner parties financed by all the girls who attend. There was little difference in the amounts spent by the unorganized women in the different classes because of the absence of the factors which caused the difference in the case of the other groups.

GENERAL READING

On the whole the students at Indiana University spend very little for newspapers, magazines, and books. Except for the *Indiana Daily Student,* which is often subscribed to by roommates or as many as three or four students collectively, relatively few students take a newspaper regularly. A much larger number usually reads a daily paper, however. Papers having a state or national circulation are also available in the university library, and at least one such paper is provided for the students in each dormitory. The family copy of the home town paper is often mailed to the student at school, particularly during his Freshman year. In case such a practice is not followed, a student may read his local paper at the university library.

Magazines are subscribed to by the dormitories and Greek-letter organizations. Moreover, students returning from home frequently bring copies of magazines that have been purchased and read by other members of their families. At college, students living in the same house sometimes pool their funds to purchase a current issue of a magazine. A very common habit, particularly among men students, is to go into a restaurant, take a magazine from the rack, read it while drinking a cup of coffee or " coke," or eating a meal, and then return it to the rack. A check at several restaurants on what the students choose to read on such occasions shows that periodicals containing " comics " such as " *Superman,*" " *Dr. X,*" etc., were surprisingly popular.

The students at Bloomington, however, apparently have little taste for " pulp " magazines. One of the most popular newsstands near the campus does not even carry the types of periodicals generally known as " westerns," " love stories," " mysteries," or " thrillers." Its largest sales are of *Colliers, Saturday Evening Post,* and *Liberty. Time* is also exceedingly popular. At this one newsstand about 20 copies of *Esquire* are sold each month, in spite of its high price of 50 cents. But usually in the purchase of a magazine of this price several students either pool their funds to purchase it collectively or take turns in purchasing one issue. The average expenditure for books, magazines, and newspapers by students from the East who were interviewed was somewhat higher than that for all students in the sample. It is the exceptional student who purchases many books other than textbooks and the university yearbook, the *Arbutus,* while attending Indiana University.

EXPENDITURES BY ALL STUDENTS

In the sample studied, the median amount spent for books (other than textbooks), magazines, and newspapers for the year was $2.81, or about 31 cents a month.[16] A fourth of all the students spent less than $1.24 a year for general reading matter and three-fourths of the students less than $5.44 per year. In the budgets of all groups the proportion spent for general reading was less than that spent for any other item, amounting to about one-half of one per cent.

EXPENDITURES BY MEN AND WOMEN

The median expenditures for men and women in 1940-41 were:

Group	Number in Sample	First Quartile	Median	Third Quartile
Men	578	$1.30	$2.92	$5.51
Women	676	1.18	2.73	5.42

As may be seen from these figures, there was very little difference in the amounts spent by men and women students. In the budgets of the men, this expenditure amounted to 0.5 of one per cent and in those of women 0.4 of one per cent. There were, however, several differences in the kinds of current publications read by the students in each group. More of the men than women students read newspapers having a state or national circulation. The women preferred magazines. At one of the dormitories where they were asked to vote for magazines which

16 For the median and mean expenditures and proportion of their budget spent for general reading by all students and groups within the sample, see Table 89, page 255.

were to be subscribed to for the year, the choices of the women in the order of the number of votes cast were:

1. *Madamoiselle*
2. *Esquire*
3. *Vogue*
4. *Ladies Home Journal*
5. *Readers' Digest*
6. *McCalls*

The single men and women at all income levels studied by the National Resources Committee listed their expenses for newspapers, magazines, and all books except textbooks under the general heading of reading.[17] They also included under this heading expenses associated with circulating libraries such as fees for membership, the renting of books, and fines for overdue books. For these items single men and women each spent 1.4 per cent of their budget.[18] As judged from a comparison of the proportions of their respective budgets spent for reading, the expenditures for reading represented a more important part of the budgets of single men and women than of those of students. This difference is largely accounted for by the greater accessibility to students of books, newspapers, and magazines that could be read without cost.

EXPENDITURES BY ORGANIZED AND UNORGANIZED STUDENTS

As may be seen from Table 65, the median amount spent for general reading by organized men was less than that spent by unorganized men. This difference is interesting for several reasons. Although in general the organized students tend to have more money to spend than the unorganized for the different items in the students budget, this difference does not show up in their expenditures for general reading material. This suggests

17 National Resources Committee, *Consumer Expenditures in the United States*, p. 97.

18 National Resources Committee, *Consumer Expenditures in the United States*, pp. 82-83.

that the greater expenditures by the organized students for other
items may have been made at the expense of general reading
matter. It may also be true that the fuller social program of the
organized students makes them more indifferent to such purchases or that more newspapers, magazines, and books may be
available at the chapter houses than in other types of dwellings.
Among the women, the sorority members spent more for books
and magazines than the non-members because they had more
extra money to spend and partly because the possession of new
books and magazines has a certain amount of prestige value in
a sorority house. In the budgets of all organized students the
expenditure for general reading represented 0.4 per cent and
in those of the unorganized students 0.6 per cent.

TABLE 65

MEDIAN AND QUARTILE EXPENDITURES FOR GENERAL READING BY
ORGANIZED AND UNORGANIZED MEN AND WOMEN AT
INDIANA UNIVERSITY, 1940-41

Group	Number in Sample	First Quartile	Median	Third Quartile
Men				
Organized	205	$ .86	$2.48	$5.27
Unorganized	373	1.56	3.15	5.48
Women				
Organized	223	1.20	3.15	5.80
Unorganized	453	1.61	1.71	4.72
	1254			

EXPENDITURES BY CLASSES

When the median expenditures for general reading of the
students in each of the different classes were compared, it was
found that the Sophomores spent the least and the Seniors the
most. The medians of the Freshman and Juniors were very
similar in amount. The amounts of these medians are given
in Table 66.

TABLE 66

MEDIAN AND QUARTILE EXPENDITURES FOR GENERAL READING
OF 1254 STUDENTS IN DIFFERENT CLASSES AT
INDIANA UNIVERSITY, 1940–41

Group	Number in Sample	First Quartile	Median	Third Quartile
Freshman	440	$1.17	$2.80	$5.35
Sophomore	317	1.19	2.53	5.29
Junior	288	1.20	2.78	5.35
Senior	209	1.66	3.89	5.80

SUMMARY

Median expenditures for transportation for all students in the sample were found to be $19.02 for the year and to rank eighth among the items of the budget. Median amounts spent by men and women were almost identical although the quartile expenditures differed much more from the medians in the case of the men than of the women. This was probably because men in the lower fourth of the sample did much of their traveling by hitchhiking and more men than women in the upper fourth came from out of the state.

The expenditures of both organized men and women were somewhat higher than those of the unorganized students; but, because their total expenditures were also higher, those for transportation formed a relatively smaller proportion of the total budget than in the case of the unorganized students.

Median expenditures for health by all students in the sample were $7.27 for the school year. This was in addition to the fee of $6.00 a year charged by the University for the support of the Student Health Center and reported in the study under university fees. The median yearly expenditure for the women was only 39 cents more than for the men. Fraternity and sorority members spent slightly more for items listed under the heading of health than did the unorganized students. Expenditures by members of the different classes showed a small but progressive rise from the Freshman through the Senior year.

Amounts spent for gifts and contributions by individual students varied widely. The median for all students was $12.21. The median for women was about two dollars higher for the year than for men. The expenditures of organized students in all classes were higher than those of the unorganized members of the same classes. Organized Senior men had the highest expenditure with a median of $26.88.

The least important category in the student budget was general reading, for which the median expenditure for all students in the sample was less than three dollars a year. When expenditures for the different classes were compared, those of the Seniors were found to be slightly higher than those of other classes.

The discussion of expenditures for general reading completes the description of student spending for individual categories in the student budget. In Chapter 10, the findings in the previous chapters will be summarized and the median and, in some instances the quartile, expenditures of different groups of students will be brought together to show the patterns of spending which characterize those groups. Finally such conclusions relating to the student budget as compared with that of single men and women in general as seem justified by the findings of this study will be presented.

CHAPTER X
SUMMARY AND CONCLUSIONS

In the preceding chapters the amounts spent for the various categories of goods and services in the student budget have been analyzed and compared. In doing this, account has also been taken of the various socio-economic factors which condition and affect the spending of individuals and of groups. These detailed discussions of particular items of expenditure have a specific interest for the student of consumer economics, the college administrator, and others dealing with special aspects of student spending. They are, however, of somewhat less concern to one whose primary interest is in knowing how much a student at a representative state university spends during an academic year and who is interested in the patterns of expenditure of the different groups on a single campus. It is the purpose of this final chapter to present a summary picture of such patterns of spending on the Indiana campus and to draw such general conclusions regarding student consumption as seem warranted by the facts of the study.

PATTERNS OF EXPENDITURE

When the expenditures of all the students in the sample were distributed by quartiles, it was found that the student body breaks roughly into three groups: about a quarter whose total expenditures were less than the first quartile of $514.89; those falling in the second and third quarters of the sample for whom the median total of $673.06 may be regarded as representative; and finally that quarter of the sample whose expenditures were above the third quartile of $842.83.

If the median student falling in the middle half of the sample may be regarded as representative of the student body as a whole, the expenditure pattern of a typical student may then be described as follows: of his total expenditures of $673.06 he spent $110.62 for room rent and $207.28 for his meals. His clothing cost him $74.78, his laundry $9.71, and the goods and

TABLE 67

THE MEDIAN AND QUARTILE AMOUNTS SPENT FOR ALL ITEMS IN THE STUDENT BUDGET BY ALL STUDENTS AT INDIANA UNIVERSITY, 1940-41

Group	Number in Sample	First Quartile	Median	Third Quartile
1. Rent	1275	$ 94.97	$110.62	$144.66
2. Food	1275	150.61	207.28	240.24
3. Clothing	1266	44.20	77.78	147.06
4. Personal Care	1272	6.33	9.94	14.94
5. Laundry	1269	5.47	9.71	17.41
6. Recreation	1273	12.79	21.83	38.16
7. Refreshments	1273	8.35	17.60	33.08
8. University fees	1275	91.16	98.43	108.13
9. Textbooks	1274	20.38	26.83	34.19
10. Dues	1264	2.46	4.93	40.88
11. Transportation	1272	11.03	19.02	29.46
12. Health	1234	3.63	7.27	13.23
13. Contributions	1274	6.69	12.21	21.46
14. General Reading ...	1254	1.24	2.81	5.44

services required for his personal care $6.33. His fees paid to the University amounted to $98.43 and his dues to organizations $4.93. For his textbooks he paid $26.83 and for general reading matter $2.81. Trips to and from college cost about $19.00 and services and supplies related to the maintenance of his health $7.27. For recreation he spent $21.83 and for refreshments and tobacco $17.60. Gifts including flowers and contributions cost him $6.69.

The fourth of the students in the sample who were most pressed financially and forced to skimp along on less than $514.89 were able to reduce their expenditures for rent to less than $94.97 and for board to an amount below $150.61. As may be seen by reference to Table 67 the students in this group tended to economize on all items in their budget. However, they were less successful in reducing their expenditures for such necessities as food, room, university fees, textbooks, laundry, and personal care below those of the median student in the sample than for the other items in the budget for which their demand was more elastic. They economized most on clothing, recreation, refreshments, general reading, health, dues and contributions. The smaller proportion of their budget allotted to recreation and refreshments is evidence of how little these students have to spend on the items most closely related to " college life " and offers a strong argument for the provision by the University of entertainment and recreational facilities for these students. Their need for the latter is emphasized when it is recalled that it is largely the students in this group who live in dwellings in which there is often no satisfactory place in which to entertain their friends.

At the other extreme were the fourth of all the students who spent $842.83 or more. Their expenditures for all categories in the budget were greater than those of the median student. This was true even in the case of university fees and textbooks, probably not because they took more courses or used more texts but because a larger proportion of them were financially able to take courses such as law and medicine requiring extensive training and for which textbooks are relatively expensive. In addition, the students in this group tend to use new textbooks rather than used ones. Their demand for the items in all categories, with the exception of housing, was more elastic than that of students in the first quartile. Practically all of the students in this group belonged to Greek-letter organizations, a fact which explains the large amount spent for organization dues in contrast with the amounts spent by the median student and the students in the lower quartile.

MEN AND WOMEN

In the examination of the patterns of group expenditures, let us consider first those of men and women students whose expenditures for each item in the student budget are shown in Table 68. The men spent more than the women for laundry, recreation, refreshments, university fees, dues, transportation, and general reading. It is customary for a large part of the women students to do at least a part of their own laundry at college, but no similar custom has developed among the men students who are usually still dependent upon others for such service. Men students share a part of their expenditures for recreation with the women and in addition tend to spend more of their time in places where soft drinks and supplementary kinds of food are sold. In general, they enjoy attending more types of sports events that require the purchase of tickets for admission and more equipment for active participation in sports than women.

TABLE 68

MEDIAN EXPENDITURES OF MEN AND WOMEN STUDENTS FOR ALL ITEMS
IN STUDENT BUDGET AT INDIANA UNIVERSITY, 1940-41

	Men		Women	
	Number of Students	Median Expenditure	Number of Students	Median Expenditure
1. Rent	586	$106.58	689	$119.83
2. Food	586	206.55	689	208.08
3. Clothing	584	57.93	682	111.14
4. Personal Care	586	9.17	686	11.23
5. Laundry	585	11.49	684	8.62
6. Recreation	586	30.01	687	16.41
7. Refreshments	586	21.05	687	10.37
8. University Fees	586	102.15	689	97.29
9. Textbooks	586	26.76	686	27.38
10. Dues	585	5.56	679	4.77
11. Transportation	586	20.67	686	20.17
12. Health	575	7.06	659	7.45
13. Contributions	585	11.27	689	13.21
14. General Reading	578	2.92	676	2.73

The dues charged for men's organizations on the university campus tend to be somewhat higher than those charged by women's clubs and societies. Men students frequently go home or to other college campuses to see girls and some even go home each week-end to work. Custom also permits men to move about at irregular hours and by more varied means of transit than women and makes it possible for them to get farther away from the campus during a week-end. Men spend more for general reading because convenience is more important to them than to women students who are more willing to pool their resources to purchase a daily paper or magazine and wait their turn to read it or to rent a book from a lending library.

The women students spent more than the men for food, clothing, personal care, rent, textbooks, health, and contributions. In general, the lowest priced rooms available to students in Bloomington are either not suitable for women because of their location, are not offered to women students because the proprietors prefer men students, or fail to meet the minimum requirements set by the University for rooms to be rented to women students. Service and the type of place at which meals were taken are more important to women than to men students. The additional costs of service which have to be covered by the prices charged for meals together with the fact that men occasionally purchase meals for women students more than compensate for the greater quantity of food eaten by the men.

Since women students tend to be nearer ready for marriage and aware of competition among themselves for the attention of men, clothing is a more important item in their budgets. For similar reasons women tend to spend more for personal care than the men; although the difference between them is much smaller than is generally assumed, because women can economize on beauty parlor service if they have to while men at least have to have their hair cut.

The women students spend slightly more for textbooks than men, partly because they tend to be more conscientious about owning a text for each course they take and partly because they are more inclined to be self-conscious about being seen with a second-hand book. These tendencies on the part of women become even more significant when one realizes that the texts required for many of the technical and professional courses, in which the enrollment consists almost wholly of men, are more expensive than those most commonly purchased by women students. In general, the larger aggregate amounts spent for contributions by women consist of a much larger number of small contributions and inexpensive gifts than do the smaller totals spent by the men.

As may be seen from Table 73, page 225, the relative importance of individual items varied considerably in the budgets of men and women. For both groups food ranked first and rent second in importance. But for the men university fees ranked third and clothing fourth, while for the women the order of importance of these last two items was reversed. Recreation and refreshments and laundry were relatively more important in the men's budgets than in those of women. Personal care, transportation, and contributions occupied relatively less important positions in the men's budgets than in the women's. Health, organization dues, and general reading held the same rank in both budgets. Because of smaller total expenditures the proportions of their budgets spent by men for textbooks, dues, and health were larger than those spent by women, even though the absolute amounts spent for these items by the latter were greater.

ORGANIZED AND UNORGANIZED MEN AND WOMEN

The budgets of fraternity and sorority members and of men and women non-members are shown in Table 69. From these we see that among these groups the organized women spent more for rent, clothing, personal care, laundry, textbooks, transportation, health, and contributions and gifts than any other group. With the exception of textbooks and room rent the demand for each of these items is elastic and consequently increases directly with total expenditures. Women in this group would not be expected to spend the most for recreation since they tend to measure social success in terms of the number of dates they have. The smaller expenditures for recreation and refreshments by the women as compared with their noticeably greater expenditure for clothing, which more than exceeds the difference between the total expenditures of fraternity men and sorority women, suggests that anything these women save on recreation is spent on clothing.

Organized men spent the most on food, recreation, refreshments, and dues. While their meals are served with somewhat less emphasis on detail and appearance than those of the sorority women, their demand for such things as steaks and larger quantities of meat and other foods makes their meals cost more. They spend more money for recreation and amusement for women than do the unorganized men and also more for recreation for themselves. Their dues which consist of fraternity dues and those of other all-college organizations to which they belong total up to a larger amount than do those of any of the other three groups.

The unorganized men spent the most for only one item in the student budget, university fees, although they tied with organized women for first place in expenditures for general reading. This suggests that in this group we tend to find the largest proportion of serious students. Unorganized women, whose total expenditures were the lowest for all four groups, did not spend the most for any item in the student budget.

With the exception of the organized women who spent the least of any of the four groups for university fees, the two groups of unorganized students spent less for each item in the student budget than the organized students. Of the two groups of the unorganized students, the men spent the least for clothing, textbooks, transportation, contributions, and general reading, and the women the least for the remaining items.

For all of the groups except the organized women the food, rent, university fees, and clothing ranked in importance in the order listed. Those women, whose total expenditures, it will be remembered, were the largest for any group studied, spent more for food, clothing, and room rent than for university fees and more for clothing than room rent. These differences suggest that as the total expenditures increase the relative importance of rent and university dues, for which the demand is relatively fixed and the prices practically uniform, drop to less important positions in the student budget.

TABLE 69

MEDIAN EXPENDITURES FOR ITEMS IN STUDENT BUDGET BY ORGANIZED AND UNORGANIZED MEN AND WOMEN AT INDIANA UNIVERSITY, 1940-41

| | ORGANIZED | | | | UNORGANIZED | | | |
| | MEN | | WOMEN | | MEN | | WOMEN | |
	Number of Students	Median Expenditures	Number of Students	Median Expenditures	Number of Students	Median Expenditures	Number of Students	Median Expenditures
1. Rent	205	$109.00	236	$144.58	381	$109.71	453	$105.66
2. Food	205	233.23	236	224.26	381	221.00	453	180.00
3. Clothing	205	94.16	230	203.32	379	48.30	452	77.76
4. Personal Care ...	205	11.02	233	13.34	381	9.50	453	8.74
5. Laundry	205	14.38	229	12.12	381	9.87	453	7.45
6. Recreation	205	54.12	234	22.31	381	26.80	453	14.53
7. Refreshments ...	205	25.00	234	16.89	381	19.13	453	11.77
8. University Fees ...	205	101.25	236	96.79	381	102.54	453	99.08
9. Textbooks	205	26.17	233	28.66	381	25.76	453	27.16
10. Dues	205	78.00	228	76.67	380	3.60	451	3.23
11. Transportation ...	205	24.15	233	24.29	381	15.88	453	18.63
12. Health	200	7.52	222	8.28	375	6.84	437	6.66
13. Contributions ...	204	14.17	236	18.44	381	9.62	453	11.67
14. General Reading ...	205	2.48	223	3.15	373	3.15	453	1.71

FOUR UNDERGRADUATE CLASSES

The budgets made up of median expenditures for all items by the students in the sample from each of the four undergraduate classes disclose several interesting differences. Not only were the total expenditures of the Freshmen the largest but the amounts they spent for food and clothing were also larger than those of the students in other classes, probably because they were less familiar with living conditions at college than the upperclassmen who had learned how to get the most for their money and because their parents tended to overestimate the amount of money a student would need for a year at college. Another reason for the larger expenditure of the Freshmen for food and clothing may be that parents regard these as necessities for which they are willing to make ample provision but hesitate to give their children much additional money during their first year away from home lest it interfere with their work.

The expenditures of the Sophomores for all items as well as in the aggregate were the lowest for any class. This suggests that in the second year students tend to let down on all expenditure rather than to change drastically the amounts they spend for any particular item. This tendency is consistent with the traditional notion of the college Sophomore who lives in accordance with a pattern suited to his own newly acquired tastes. Having finished Freshman year he no longer feels bound by the uncertainties which made him more of a conformist during his first year. Besides, by the beginning of Sophomore year, both men and women students have usually found out how to get the most for their money, particularly in housing and food. Usually most of the clothing and supplies purchased at the beginning of the Freshman year last through the Sophomore year. By their second year in college, men students usually have also learned the cheapest way to travel.

The only item for which the Juniors spent the most was dues. This was true because of the increased membership in all campus social and academic organizations by both organized and unorganized students in their Junior year when they enter professional schools and begin advanced courses rather than because of additional amounts paid by the fraternity and sorority members to their chapters.

The Seniors spent the most of any of the four groups for personal care, laundry, recreation, refreshments, university fees, textbooks, transportation, contributions and gifts, and general reading. As may be noted from the list several of these items are ones associated with a well-groomed appearance which in turn is generally related either to getting a job for the next year or to the additional responsibilities of leadership in the Senior year. A tendency for the social activities of the students to increase year by year and reach a maximum in the Senior year is indicated by the larger expenditure for recreation and refreshments by the Seniors.

Food ranked first and room rent second in order of importance in the budgets of all classes. Except in the budget of Freshmen, where their order was reversed, university fees ranked third and clothing fourth in all budgets. Textbooks, recreation, transportation, refreshments, and contributions occupied positions in the budgets of all students in the order listed and directly followed that of clothing. Personal care and laundry ranked tenth and eleventh in the budgets of all classes except in that of the Juniors, where the positions of these two items were reversed. The remaining items of health, dues, and general reading, followed personal care and laundry in the order listed in all four budgets.

Thus we see that the ranking of the different items in the student budget was practically the same for the members of all the classes with the exception of the Freshmen, who spent more for clothing than for university fees and in the case of the Juniors who spent more for laundry than for personal care.

Complete consumption patterns were not obtained for the other groups within the sample whose expenditures for some of the items were discussed in the preceding chapters. When the expenditures for the different items were brought together, they did suggest certain tendencies that seemed characteristic of vari-

TABLE 70

MEDIAN EXPENDITURES FOR ITEMS IN STUDENT BUDGETS BY STUDENTS IN THE FOUR UNDERGRADUATE CLASSES AT INDIANA UNIVERSITY, 1940-41

	Freshman		Sophomore		Junior		Senior	
	Number of Students	Median Expenditures	Number of Students	Median Expenditures	Number of Students	Median Expenditures	Number of Students	Median Expenditures
1. Rent	446	$136.85	323	$104.29	291	$106.30	215	$105.92
2. Food	446	231.41	323	201.67	291	197.63	215	199.38
3. Clothing	443	99.09	321	66.33	289	74.25	213	67.94
4. Personal Care	446	9.08	323	10.49	289	9.69	214	12.02
5. Laundry	444	8.25	323	10.19	288	10.41	214	11.67
6. Recreation	446	18.90	323	22.39	288	23.51	214	26.28
7. Refreshments	446	15.76	323	17.84	288	18.60	214	19.82
8. University Fees	446	94.69	323	95.59	291	102.86	215	105.80
9. Textbooks	446	26.91	322	25.37	289	27.46	215	28.72
10. Dues	436	4.26	320	5.29	285	7.39	214	6.67
11. Transportation	446	18.77	322	17.86	289	18.99	215	21.86
12. Health	420	6.62	317	7.20	286	7.90	211	8.05
13. Contributions	446	10.42	323	12.30	290	13.65	215	14.57
14. General Reading	440	2.80	317	2.53	288	2.78	209	3.89

ous groups. Students from farms spent less in the aggregate and for food, room, and clothing than the students from villages and small towns and cities. Those from small towns spent the most for food and rent. Small town women and city men spent the most for clothing and farm men and women the least. The expenditures for room and clothing of the students who earned a part of their college expenses decreased as the proportion of their expenses earned increased. But the amounts that they spent for food reached a minimum when the student earned 40-59 per cent of his total expenditure and from there on even showed a slight rise as the proportion earned increased.

EXPENDITURE AS RELATED TO ACADEMIC ACHIEVEMENT

In the analysis of expenditure patterns some interesting relationships were found between spending and academic achievement as measured by the number of " credit points " earned during a semester.[1] For the purpose of comparison, the median expenditures for the items in the student budget by students earning different numbers of credit points were computed.

The first categories considered were food and clothing, which although necessities are subject to more variability in amount spent than are such other items as housing and university fees.

The expenditure for food shown with those for other items in Table 71 tended to rise as the number of credit points earned by the students increased. But beginning with the students who earned 15 to 29.99 credit points the amount spent for clothing, recreation, and refreshments, and the total for all items decreased steadily as the number of credit points earned increased. This suggests that the amounts spent for these items are definitely influenced by the amount of spare time the student has and that the student who has no serious interest in his academic

---

1 Credit points are determined at Indiana University as follows: A (grade of 100-95), 3 credit points; B (grade of 95-85), 2 credit points; C (grade of 85-75), 1 credit point; D (grade of 75-65), no credit points; F (grade of below 65), -1 credit point. The number of hours of work ordinarily carried by a student during one semester is 15. Students who earn less than 15 credit points in a semester are those who fail in their courses or have less than a C average in 15 hours.

TABLE 71

EXPENDITURES FOR 11 ITEMS IN THE STUDENT BUDGET BY 1145 INDIANA UNIVERSITY STUDENTS AS RELATED TO CREDIT POINTS EARNED, 1940-41 [a]

	No Credit-points		1-14.99 Credit-points		15-29.99 Credit-points		30-44.99 Credit-points		45 Credit-points	
	No. of Students	Median	No. of Students	Median	No. of Students	Median	No. of Students	Median	No. of Students	Median
1. Food	12	$203.34	220	$206.66	604	$216.20	278	$204.00	31	$215.00
2. Clothing	12	76.66	220	92.00	604	76.24	278	65.88	31	42.50
3. Personal Care ..	12	9.17	220	10.36	604	10.00	278	9.14	31	8.54
4. Laundry	12	10.00	220	10.61	604	9.74	278	9.61	31	7.50
5. Recreation	12	21.25	220	21.06	604	21.82	278	21.30	31	17.14
6. Refreshments ...	12	25.00	220	18.96	604	18.23	278	12.75	31	11.43
7. University Fees..	12	92.50	220	97.86	604	100.06	278	96.07	31	92.81
8. Textbooks	12	25.00	220	26.55	604	26.73	278	25.98	31	25.41
9. Dues	12	5.00	220	9.17	604	4.56	278	6.88	31	4.96
10. Transportation ..	12	19.00	220	22.33	604	19.34	278	17.71	31	13.18
11. Health	12	8.57	220	7.24	604	7.51	278	7.47	31	10.45

[a] Figures for Rent, Contributions and General Reading were not computed.

program finds more time on his hands and hence more ways to spend his money on entertainment, refreshments, and clothing than the student who is more intent on his academic work. It should be remembered, however, that many of the more brilliant students are enabled to come to college because of scholarships and fellowships which do not allow for more than a minimum expenditure for necessities. In order to have such grants continued the student is usually required to maintain a good academic rating.

The fact that the students who earned the most credit points spent almost half of their total expenditures for food suggests that since they spent less for refreshments between meals they ate more at meal times.

CONCLUSIONS

The task which remains is to present the general conclusions regarding student spending which seem justified by the findings of the study and to see what distinguishes the student budget from that of the average single person as disclosed in such studies as those of the National Resources Committee. To do this it is necessary to pull away from the detailed treatment of the expenditures of different groups for individual categories and to look at the general tendencies and types of spending behavior which have been sufficiently persistent among the students covered by the study to warrant considering them as characteristic of student spending in general.

Circumstance and custom make certain categories of expenditure relatively less important in the student budget than in that of the average single person. Particularly is this true of food and rent. In addition, the range in prices at which these are offered is also much narrower than is found in the prices of board and room generally. Clothing is almost as important an item to the student as rent and more important than for the average single person. For the three essentials, food, shelter and clothing the student spends about three-fifths of his budget while the average single person spends over two-thirds. When the student's expense for university fees, another " must " expenditure for him, is added to the amounts spent for the other three items about three-fourths of his budget is required. As a consequence, his demand for the remaining items in his budget is less elastic than that of the average single person for items other than food, shelter, and clothing.

In spite of the traditionally heavy social programs of college students their expenditures for recreation account for approximately the same proportion of their budget as is generally true of single persons, probably because some expenses for recreation are included in the fees paid by organized students and because the University provides many kinds of entertainment at either a nominal cost or without charge. Still another reason is that the academic programs of students often prevent their attending dances or movies on school nights. The importance of " cokes " and other kinds of refreshments in the social life of the students makes their expenditures for such items important enough in their budgets to warrant treating them in a separate category. Expenditures in addition to those for food, rent, and recreation which are relatively less important for the student than for other single persons are personal care, transportation, and general reading. The medical services provided by the University make the student's expense for this proportionately less than it is in the average single person's budget.

On the other hand, college attendance causes expenditures for certain items to rise to positions of more importance in the student budget than in that of the average single person. Among those are: university fees, dues, textbooks, refreshments, contributions, and laundry. The greater importance of university fees and textbooks is too obvious to need explanation. The existence of Greek-letter social organizations which except for alumni chapters are found only on college campuses accounts for the position occupied by dues in the student budget. The frequency of " dates " at college which usually involve some expense for refreshments warrants placing the items listed under this heading in a separate category, since to combine expenditures for refreshments with those for meals would distort the student's expenditure for board at college.

Laundry and cleaning more frequently involve some definite payment for such services for the student than for the average single person whose expenses for laundry are often included in a general outlay for household operation. The prevalence of the practice of giving gifts and sending flowers at college and the fact that the student usually expects to receive financial aid from home rather than extend it to parents or relatives warrants considering the amounts spent by the students for gifts, flowers, and contributions as a part of his total consumption disbursement and placing them in a separate category.

TABLE 72

PERCENTAGE OF BUDGET SPENT FOR INDIVIDUAL ITEMS BY UNIVERSITY
STUDENTS AND SINGLE PERSONS IN GENERAL

Item	Students 1940-41		Single Persons,[a] 1935-36	
	Percentage of Budget	Rank in Budget	Percentage of Budget	Rank in Budget
1. Food	27.45	1	33.6	1
2. Rent	16.99	2	23.8	2
3. Clothing	16.09	3	12.0	3
4. University Fees	13.92	4		
5. Recreation	4.28	5	4.5	5
6. Dues	4.16	6		
7. Textbooks	3.77	7		
8. Transportation	3.40	8	4.5	5
9. Refreshments	3.10	9		
10. Contributions	2.02	10		
11. Laundry	1.70	11		
12. Personal Care	1.54	12	2.1	8
13. Medical Care	1.12	13	3.6	6
14. General Reading	.49	14	1.7	9
15. Household Operation			5.6	4
16. Automobile			4.5	5
17. Household Furnishings			.3	12
18. Tobacco			2.3	7
19. Education			.5	11
20. Other Items			1.0	10

[a] The National Resources Committee, *Consumer Expenditures in the United States*, p. 81.

When the expenditures of men and women students are considered separately and are compared with the corresponding expenditures of single men and women in general, it is evident that men students spend a smaller proportion of their budgets for food than is usual among single men, but women students spend more than the average single woman. Student men spend more for both rent and university fees than for clothing which is a relatively less important item for them than for single men in general. Women students spend more for clothing than for rent which is usually the most important expenditure for single women. Expenditures for university fees and textbooks takes a larger part of the total expenditure of men students than of that of the women, amounting to approximately 15 per cent for the men and 13 per cent for the women. In the budgets of the single men and women studied by the National Resources Committee all expenses related to education amounted to less than one half of one per cent and were among the least important items.

Recreation is a relatively more important item for women students than for single women generally. Men students spend more for refreshments including tobacco and soft drinks than women students but these items are either included under expenditures for food in the budgets of single men and women or treated separately as in the case of tobacco and consequently are not comparable with the student expenditures.

College men and women spend about the same proportions of their budgets for personal care as single men but less than single women. In their budgets expenditures in this category are less important than in those of single persons.

Women students spend only a slightly larger proportion of their total expenditure for transportation than men in spite of the fact that the men often hitchhike and have a better opportunity to find free rides home. However, the difference between the amounts the men and women spend is less than is commonly found among single men and women.

Even though it is customary for college men to send flowers and gifts to women friends on the campus, they do not spend as much for these and for contributions as do the women students who exchange more gifts among themselves and send more to relatives.

TABLE 73

Percentages of Budget Spent for Individual Items by Men and Women Students and Single Men and Women in General

Item	MEN				WOMEN			
	Students, 1940-41		All Single Men,[a] 1935-36		Students, 1940-41		All Single Women,[b] 1935-36	
	Percent-age of Budget	Rank in Budget	Percent-age of Budget	Rank in Budget	Percent-age of Budget	Rank in Budget	Percent-age of Budget	Rank in Budget
1. Food	28.58	1	30.1	1	26.54	1	21.2	2
2. Rent	16.83	2	23.0	2	17.11	3	26.1	1
3. Clothing	10.72	4	8.2	3	20.38	2	12.8	3
4. University Fees	15.02	3			13.05	4		
5. Recreation	6.60	5	4.5	5	2.44	9	1.9	7
6. Dues	4.20	6			4.13	5		
7. Textbooks	3.89	7			3.68	6		
8. Transportation	3.20	9	3.3	6	3.56	7	4.5	4
9. Refreshments	3.73	8			2.60	8		
10. Contributions	1.91	11			2.12	10		
11. Laundry	2.14	10			1.59	11		
12. Personal Care	1.47	12	1.4	9	1.47	12	2.3	6
13. Medical Care	1.19	13	2.8	7	1.06	13	3.1	5
14. General Reading	.51	14	1.4	9	.47	14	1.4	8
15. Household Operation			5.0	4			.9	9
16. Automobile								
17. Household Furnishings								
18. Tobacco			2.4	8			.6	11
19. Education			.5	11			.3	12
20. Other Items			.8	10			.7	10

[a] The National Resources Committee, Consumer Expenditures in the United States, p. 82.   [b] Ibid., p. 83.

College men and women spend smaller parts of their budgets for general reading material than is usual among single persons, but as in the case of single persons, the men spend the most. Men students also spend slightly more than the women for dues.

CHANGES IN THE PROPORTION OF BUDGET SPENT FOR INDIVID-UAL CATEGORIES AS TOTAL DISBURSEMENT INCREASES

The proportion of the student budget spent for food decreases as does that of the single person and family when the total expenditure increases. A similar change occurs in the student expenditures for rent, a fact explained by the fairly uniform rates charged for like kinds of housing accommodations at college. Clothing expenditures show an opposite tendency and take a larger proportion of the budget as total expenditures increase. Beyond a total expenditure of $1200 they account for the largest part of the additional expenditure. The amounts spent for personal care and laundry tend to decrease as total expenditures rise.

The proportion of the budget spent for refreshments tends to rise until the total reaches $1000 and then to decline as the total increases. Recreation tends to take a slightly smaller proportion of the total as the amount of the total rises. University fees, another uniform cost for most students, regardless of what they have to spend, represents a smaller proportion of the budget as the total amount grows larger. The same is true of the expenditure for textbooks. The amounts spent for dues and general reading tends to increase at a more rapid rate than total expenditures.

ELASTICITY AND VARIATION IN STUDENT SPENDING

The items in the student budget for which there was the greatest elasticity of expenditure were clothing, recreation, refreshment, dues, health, transportation, general reading, and contributions. The total expenditures of some students were raised or lowered by additional expenditures or economies for all items or the majority of items in the budget. Large total expenditures by others were explained by amounts spent for individual music lessons, an operation, or transportation from some exceptionally distant point. Most frequently, however, total expenditures of over $900 were largely accounted for by additional amounts spent for clothing, recreation, and refreshment.

Of course the range in individual spending on most items is great. As a result the individual patterns of spending varied considerably. In general, however, the individuals within the groups studied varied more in their expenditures for specific items in their budgets than in their total expenditures. Proof for this statement is found in a comparison of the coefficients of variation of the total expenditures of several groups of students (shown in Appendix A, p. 234) with those of expenditures for specific items in the budget. For total expenditures the coefficient of variation was in no instance above 39, while for the expenditures of some groups for specific items it rose to more than 100. In the case of food the coefficients of variation were much nearer those of total expenditures, for only one group amounting to as much as 40. The greatest variations in the items tested were found in the expenditures for recreation, refreshments, and clothing.

There are many items for which student demand is inelastic. Among these are university fees, textbooks, fees for health service, and for some students, rent. This is because the charges for these items are in the nature of administered prices which are uniform for all students and consequently do not increase as total disbursements increase and for the same reason represent a decreasing proportion of the total budget as the amount of the total expenditure increases. Such prices are relatively insensitive to changes in market prices.

Other items for which student demand is more elastic but for which prices tend to be determined in part at least by custom are those for personal care, refreshments such as " cokes," and hamburgers. The greatest elasticity is found in student expenditures for clothing, personal care, laundry, transportation, health, and contributions. As might be expected, the demand of the organized students showed a greater degree of elasticity than did that of the unorganized.

STUDENT FOLKWAYS

Student spending is conditioned by the usages and traditions generally accepted and adhered to by the members of individual groups on the campus and by the student body as a whole. Some of these student folkways are found among students on all campuses, some in a single college community. Some are associated with traditions of long standing, others pop-up in impulsive and unpremeditated fashion in response to particular situations. Many of the usages which materially affect spending are social rather than academic in nature. The question as to whether or not the member of a group is the " right " kind may arise from failure to adhere to the spending practices of the group. The practice of wearing a flower in her hair may become a " must " for the girl in the dormitory. Prestige comes from adherence rather than defiance. Changes when they come are usually initiated by previously recognized leaders.

Campus folkways may be responsible either for additional spending or in some instances for economies on the part of students. The obligation of a fraternity man to send flowers to the girl to whom he has given his pin and to her sorority sisters often costs him a considerable sum. On the other hand the wearing of senior " cords " reduces the clothing expenditure of the men in that class. While the economic status of the student is undoubtedly the major determinant of the amount he spends in college, the folkways of campus living have an important influence on how he spends that portion of his funds which is not required to meet certain uniform costs. It is the influence of these folkways and the relative homogeneity of student expenditures for such categories as university fees, which are peculiar to college life, that chiefly differentiate the student budget from budgets in general and make student spending a special problem in consumption.

APPENDICES

APPENDIX A

METHODS USED IN THE STUDY

METHOD OF OBTAINING INFORMATION

THE study was based on personal interviews and on estimates for the regular two-semester college year.[1] The estimates were collected on schedules distributed to the students in February, the first month of the second semester. This month was chosen because by then most students have paid for their room and board, textbooks, and university fees for the entire year. At that time the student usually knows what he has already spent, what he will have to spend during the remainder of the year, and how he expects to spend it. In making the estimates, the students were given an opportunity to refer to any records which they had kept.

In practically all the studies of student spending that have been made, including those of Professor Moffat of Indiana University, Professor James Yocum at Ohio State University, and Mr. Walter P. Kuenstler at the University of Pennsylvania, schedules have been used in collecting data. This technique of using estimates has the advantage of making it possible to obtain information from a greater number of students than the collection of detailed records would permit.

The writer is convinced from the experience of several years of working with estimates made by students that the average student has a good idea of the total amount he spends during the school year. If his parents finance his education, the amount set aside for the year for that purpose is usually decided upon in advance. Moreover, the student is usually sufficiently impressed by any change in that amount to remember it. If the student earns part of his own expenses he is even more apt to remember what he spends. Expenditures for many of the items

1 In 1940-41 this period extended from September 11 to June 2. During this period there were twenty-five and a half days of vacation.

in the student budget such as tuition, fees, room and board are fairly fixed amounts and therefore not hard to remember.

While there is some degree of error in the estimates submitted for such items as clothing, recreation, refreshments, and contributions; the writer believes that they are not any more serious than the errors in figures collected by an alternative method of having students keep a detailed record of expenditures for one month. For even if such accounts of the expenditures for a single month could be secured from a large enough number of students to make the sample representative, the amounts spent during any one month are likely to be too dissimilar to justify the assumption that a multiple of the average for one month would give a significant total for the entire academic year.

In a study sponsored by the Family Economics Bureau of the Northwestern National Life Insurance Company and made at the University of Minnesota, account books were distributed to students to keep detailed records for the month of May. Expenditures for the year were estimated on the basis of multiples of these figures. In a study made by the writer of weekly reports of a limited number of Indiana University students, it was found that the expenditures for March were 12 per cent greater than the expenditures for the same group for May, and those for April were 20 per cent higher than those for May. These differences lead to the conclusion that it is not safe to assume that the expenditures for a single month are typical of the amounts spent in the other months of the year.

VALIDITY OF ESTIMATES

In this study, in order to check on the validity of the estimates submitted, a small group of students were asked to estimate their expenditures for a stated period of time. When these estimates were collected the same students were asked to keep accurate detailed records for that time. Both estimates and records were finally obtained from a group of twenty-six students. These showed that the students frequently forgot to list their expenditures under separate headings. This was evident from the fact that the total amount spent each month, which was listed independently of the itemized account, was in excess of the total of the expenditures for the separate items. In the case of each student reporting, the total amount spent for the month was known because the student frequently received his allowance in the form of checks and knew that he had spent all of it. The total amount of money known to have been spent was 23 per cent greater than the total of the amounts recorded under the separate items.

In contrast to this discrepancy, the total of their itemized estimated expenditures differed from the total known expenditures by only 6 per cent. It appeared, then, that the estimates of expenditures were more indicative of the total amount spent than a sum of the itemized amounts recorded as having been spent by the student.

As to the question of whether or not the student had allocated the amounts correctly under separate headings, it is impossible to be certain. However, students in interviews expressed confidence in their estimates.

The difference between the sum of the recorded expenditures for individual items and the total amount reported spent was greater than the difference between the sums of the separate estimates and the total expenditure reported later. These differences meant that the totals were the most reliable figures. They raised the question as to whether the students had allocated the total correctly among the different items. Because of the fixed charges for several items in the student budget, doubt was limited primarily to those items for which there was considerable elasticity in demand.

DISPERSION OF DATA

In order to measure the dispersion of the data in the sample used for this study, the standard deviations of the estimates of expenditures for food, clothing, recreation, personal care, and for all items in the student budget by the fraternity men, sorority women, non-member men, and non-member women were computed. The formula used for these computations was:

$$\sigma = \sqrt{\frac{\sigma . X^2}{N} - M^2_x}$$

In this formula

σ = The standard deviation
X = Amount of the individual expenditure
N = Number of items
M_2 = Square of Mean of X

The results were as follows:

MEN

	ORGANIZED				UNORGANIZED			
	N	Mean	σ	σ_M[1]	N	Mean	σ	σ_M
Food	209	221.32	58.30	4.03	381	181.04	59.01	3.02
Clothing	205	102.09	72.77	5.08	381	55.99	42.96	2.20
Recreation	205	68.62	56.37	3.94	381	31.99	25.14	1.29
Refreshments ...	205	33.62	26.50	1.85	381	21.08	17.89	.92
Personal Care ...	205	11.22	7.19	.50	381	9.30	5.84	.30
Total	205	826.00	208.49	14.56	381	591.31	165.15	8.46

WOMEN

	ORGANIZED				UNORGANIZED			
	N	Mean	σ	σ_M	N	Mean	σ	σ_M
Food	233	218.70	50.51	3.31	456	176.90	67.81	3.18
Clothing	233	211.54	162.81	10.67	456	113.50	114.53	5.36
Recreation	233	21.45	15.95	1.05	456	15.53	13.33	.62
Refreshments ...	233	27.79	27.23	1.78	456	14.48	15.79	.74
Personal Care ...	233	15.72	14.70	.96	456	9.36	10.01	.47
Total	233	909.52	260.63	17.08	456	617.00	220.09	10.31

[1] σ_M = Standard error of the mean.

VARIABILITY OF DATA

In order to compare the variability of the data for these groups the coefficients of variation in the expenditures for the same items by the same groups as those for which the standard deviations were obtained were computed by means of the formula:

$$V = \frac{\sigma}{M} \times 100$$

V = the coefficient of variation
σ = standard deviation
M = Mean of X

The results showed:

	MEN				WOMEN			
	Fraternity Members		Non-Members		Sorority Members		Non-Members	
	N	V	N	V	N	V	N	V
Food	205	26.3	381	32.6	233	23.1	456	38.3
Clothing	205	71.3	381	76.7	233	77.0	457	100.9
Recreation	205	82.1	381	78.6	233	74.4	456	85.8
Personal Care	205	64.1	381	62.8	233	93.6	456	106.9
Total	205	25.2	381	27.9	233	28.7	456	35.7

TREATMENT OF DATA

The data on the schedules were transferred by means of coded symbols to cards designed for use on machines and the cards were sorted on the machines to obtain frequency distributions. From these distributions, averages, medians, and quartiles were computed. Expenditures for a month were obtained by dividing the median by 9 and for the week by 36.

Total expenditures and median amounts spent for separate items of the budget were studied. Each item in the budget was also studied in terms of the proportion of the total expenditures which it represented. To discover some of the factors influencing the amounts spent, the students were grouped in different ways and compared as to spending habits. The extent to which individuals within a group varied among themselves within a given year was indicated by means of frequency distributions and by medians and quartiles.

Throughout the study, the figures listed in all tables are medians unless otherwise designated. All proportions of budgets included in the text, however, are based on arithmetic means. These are shown in Tables 67-81 in Appendix B.

The formula used to obtain the medians computed in this study was: [2]

2 This formula is designed to express the method of obtaining a median presented in Mills, Frederick C., *Statistical Methods* (New York: Henry Holt and Co., 1939), p. 114.

$$Md = 1 + \frac{n}{f} \times i$$

1 = the lower limit of the interval containing the median value
n = the number of measures from this class added to the frequencies already totaled to give a number equal to the total number of cases divided by 2 (the number which must lie on each side of the point to be located)
f = the total number of cases in the class containing the median
i = the class interval

The formula used in computing the modes in the study was:[3]

$$Mo = 1 + \frac{f_2}{f_2 + f_1} \times i.$$

1 = lower limit of modal class
f_1 = frequency of class below modal class
f_2 = frequency of class above modal class
i = class-interval

In the relatively few instances in which individual students failed to list expenditures for one of the less important items, the median used was derived from the actual number of estimates for that item rather than one representing a median position in the general sample of 1275 cases. It was felt that such a method based upon estimates listed would give a more significant idea of typical expenditures of Indiana University students than one based upon the assumption that the students who omitted particular items spent nothing for them. This decision seemed further justified since the items under each heading of the budget were of such a character that they would have involved some expenditure on the part of each student with the possible exception of health, general reading, and contributions. In some instances omissions were probably made by individuals because they did not know exactly how much of their total to allot to some minor item in the budget, although as previously explained, they might be quite accurate in their estimates of their total expenditures.

GROUPS OF STUDENTS STUDIED

The groups studied included:

All students
Men and Women

3 *Ibid.*, pp. 118, 119.

Organized Men and Women (in each of four under-graduate
  college classes)
Unorganized Men and Women
Freshmen
Sophomores
Juniors
Seniors
Students in the School of Business
Students in the School of Education
Students in the College of Arts and Sciences
Students from Farms
Students from Small Towns and Cities
Students from Large Cities

BUDGET ITEMS STUDIED

Room Rent
Food
Clothing
Personal Care
Laundry and Maintenance of Clothing
Recreation
Refreshments
University Fees
Textbooks, Supplies, Equipment
Dues
Transportation
Health
Contributions, Gifts
General Reading

COMPARISON WITH OTHER STUDIES OF STUDENT SPENDING

1. The majority of studies previously published have stressed
the importance of the student body as a potential market for
retail sellers of goods and services. In the studies of this type,
preferences of students for individual brands and specific articles
of goods have been stressed more than the proportion of total
disbursements devoted to individual items in their budgets.
Among these studies are the following:

238 APPENDICES

(1) Kuentsler, Walter P. "Buying Habits of Women Students on the University of Pennsylvania Campus." (Unpublished Senior-Research Thesis, Wharton School of Finance and Commerce, University of Pennsylvania, 1940.)

(2) Sandage, Charles H. "Student Expenditures for Clothing," *Miami Business Review*, vol. VII, No. 3, December, 1934, pp. 1-4.

(3) "Seven Keys to an 80 Million Dollar Market." Prepared for Major College Publications, 101 Eshleman Hall, University of California, under the direction of Fred C. Fischer.

(4) Yocum, James Carleton, "Expenditures and Apparel Buying Habits of Ohio State University Students." The Bureau of Business Research, College of Commerce and Administration, The Ohio State University, Columbus, Ohio, January, 1934.

2. One survey was based on detailed records kept for only one month. Averages for the college year were based on the assumption that expenditures for that month were representative of all months in the academic year. This study was made by the Northwestern Life Insurance Company at the University of Minnesota.

3. Several of the more comprehensive studies have related to universities located in large cities, and having a large number of students whose homes are in the university community. This situation is not found at Indiana, where by far the larger number come from homes outside the college community. For this reason, room and board represent items of greater importance in the students' budgets than they do in the studies made at Ohio State University and the University of Minnesota.

4. Some of the studies have omitted certain items in the student budget. In the study made at the Ohio State University such costs as those of tuition, college fees, textbooks, supplies, and organization dues were not considered. In the study made at Miami University, clothing, barber shop services, tobacco, and health costs were omitted. Tuition was omitted in the study made at the University of Minnesota. In the present study all items in the student budget were included in an attempt to determine the total expenditure for a year at Indiana University.

APPENDIX B
SUMMARY TABLES

TABLE 74

The Percentage of the Total Enrollment of Organized and Unorganized Men and Women in Each of the Four Undergraduate Classes at Indiana University Represented in the Sample for 1940-41

	Freshman Class			Sophomore Class		
	Number enrolled in the University 2nd semester	Number in sample	Percentage of enrollment in sample	Number enrolled in the University 2nd semester	Number in sample	Percentage of enrollment in sample
Men						
Organized	262	58	22.14	254	64	25.20
Unorganized ..	562	120	21.35	429	113	26.34
Both	824	178	21.60	683	177	25.92
Women						
Organized	157	73	46.50	152	51	33.55
Unorganized ..	370	197	53.24	196	92	46.94
Both	527	270	51.23	348	143	41.09
Men and Women						
Organized	419	131	31.26	406	115	28.33
Unorganized ..	932	317	34.01	625	205	32.80
Both	1351	448	33.16	1031	320	31.03

	Junior Class			Senior Class		
Men						
Organized	233	47	20.17	250	36	14.40
Unorganized ..	423	74	17.49	389	74	19.02
Both	656	121	18.45	639	110	17.21
Women						
Organized	164	72	45.73	143	37	25.87
Unorganized ..	213	96	45.07	192	68	35.42
Both	377	168	45.35	335	105	31.34
Men and Women						
Organized	397	121	30.48	393	73	18.57
Unorganized ..	636	170	26.73	581	142	24.44
Both	1033	291	28.17	974	215	22.07

	All Classes		
Men			
Organized	999	205	20.52
Unorganized ..	1803	381	21.13
Both	2802	586	20.91
Women			
Organized	616	236	38.31
Unorganized ..	971	453	46.65
Both	1587	689	43.42
Men and Women			
Organized	1615	441	27.12
Unorganized ..	2774	834	30.06
Both	4389	1275	29.05

TABLE 75

THE MEDIAN AND MEAN TOTAL EXPENDITURE OF ORGANIZED AND
UNORGANIZED MEN AND WOMEN IN THE FOUR UNDERGRADUATE
CLASSES AT INDIANA UNIVERSITY, 1940-41

Group	Number of students	Median expenditure	Mean expenditure	Percentage of budget spent for tuition [a]
Freshman				
Men				
Organized	58	$800.00	$826.87	100.00
Unorganized	120	570.59	590.28	100.00
Women				
Organized	73	917.86	947.14	100.00
Unorganized	197	631.67	668.03	100.00
Sophomore				
Men				
Organized	64	890.91	825.84	100.00
Unorganized	113	541.89	555.17	100.00
Women				
Organized	51	879.17	918.14	100.00
Unorganized	92	540.62	603.03	100.00
Junior				
Men				
Organized	47	775.00	806.15	100.00
Unorganized	74	582.35	594.57	100.00
Women				
Organized	75	850.00	914.02	100.00
Unorganized	96	536.36	574.88	100.00
Senior				
Men				
Organized	36	942.86	950.09	100.00
Unorganized	74	625.00	659.41	100.00
Women				
Organized	37	843.75	719.44	100.00
Unorganized	68	560.00	598.21	100.00
All Classes	1275	673.06	703.41	100.00
Organized	441	852.05	881.09	100.00
Unorganized	834	574.10	610.81	100.00
Men	586	657.47	681.84	100.00
Women	689	687.63	721.59	100.00

[a] These percentages were computed on the basis of mean expenditures.

TABLE 76

THE MEDIAN AND MEAN EXPENDITURE AND PERCENTAGE OF BUDGET
SPENT FOR ROOM RENT BY ORGANIZED AND UNORGANIZED MEN
AND WOMEN IN THE FOUR UNDERGRADUATE CLASSES
AT INDIANA UNIVERSITY, 1940-41

Group	Number of students	Median expenditure	Mean expenditure	Percentage of budget spent for rent [a]
Freshman				
Men				
Organized	58	$133.75	$138.49	16.8
Unorganized ...	120	111.25	116.99	19.8
Women				
Organized	73	133.57	147.67	15.5
Unorganized ...	197	144.14	126.69	19.0
Sophomore				
Men				
Organized	64	115.83	114.26	13.8
Unorganized ...	113	96.83	102.66	18.5
Women				
Organized	54	121.88	132.28	14.4
Unorganized ...	92	102.25	114.86	19.1
Junior				
Men				
Organized	47	113.00	118.60	14.7
Unorganized ...	74	97.60	103.12	17.3
Women				
Organized	72	126.67	132.07	14.5
Unorganized ...	96	101.05	107.88	18.8
Senior				
Men				
Organized	36	120.00	118.60	14.7
Unorganized ...	74	98.89	111.31	16.9
Women				
Organized	37	113.57	101.13	14.1
Unorganized ...	68	102.22	109.60	18.3
All Classes	1275	110.62	119.49	17.1
Organized	441	128.92	130.64	14.8
Unorganized	834	103.36	113.73	18.6
Men	586	106.58	114.76	16.8
Women	689	119.83	123.48	17.1

[a] These percentages were computed on the basis of mean expenditures.

TABLE 77

THE MEDIAN AND MEAN EXPENDITURE AND PERCENTAGE OF BUDGET
SPENT FOR FOOD BY ORGANIZED AND UNORGANIZED MEN AND
WOMEN IN THE FOUR UNDERGRADUATE CLASSES AT
INDIANA UNIVERSITY, 1940-41

Group	Number of students	Median expenditure	Mean expenditure	Percentage of budget spent for food [a]
Freshman				
Men				
Organized	58	$240.00	$227.69	27.5
Unorganized ...	120	190.00	184.95	31.3
Women				
Organized	73	238.27	231.10	24.4
Unorganized ...	197	188.75	195.08	29.2
Sophomore				
Men				
Organized	64	228.83	211.37	25.6
Unorganized ...	113	173.12	172.12	31.0
Women				
Organized	54	221.25	206.37	22.5
Unorganized ...	92	159.38	169.11	28.0
Junior				
Men				
Organized	47	229.34	222.74	27.6
Unorganized ...	74	192.00	184.45	31.0
Women				
Organized	72	213.75	215.04	23.5
Unorganized ...	96	160.00	157.65	27.4
Senior				
Men				
Organized	36	213.67	226.60	23.9
Unorganized ...	74	184.62	184.08	27.9
Women				
Organized	37	222.14	190.32	26.5
Unorganized ...	68	158.84	166.00	28.4
All Classes	1275	207.28	193.06	27.5
Organized	441	228.95	220.29	25.0
Unorganized	834	184.22	179.00	29.3
Men	586	206.55	194.88	28.6
Women	689	208.08	191.53	26.5

[a] These percentages were computed on the basis of mean expenditures.

TABLE 78

The Median and Mean Expenditure and Percentage of Budget Spent for Clothing by Organized and Unorganized Men and Women in the Four Undergraduate Classes at Indiana University, 1940-41

Group	Number of students	Median expenditure	Mean expenditure	Percentage of budget spent for clothing [a]
Freshman				
Men				
Organized	58	$102.00	$111.71	13.51
Unorganized ...	119	54.23	64.93	11.00
Women				
Organized	71	215.00	220.60	23.29
Unorganized ...	195	107.14	134.29	20.10
Sophomore				
Men				
Organized	64	101.54	105.82	12.81
Unorganized ...	113	46.57	50.32	9.06
Women				
Organized	52	211.75	234.31	25.52
Unorganized ...	92	65.71	108.34	17.97
Junior				
Men				
Organized	47	75.00	85.55	10.61
Unorganized ...	74	47.27	53.27	8.96
Women				
Organized	72	180.00	220.48	24.12
Unorganized ...	96	67.69	91.94	15.99
Senior				
Men				
Organized	35	80.53	99.20	10.44
Unorganized ...	74	47.50	53.68	8.14
Women				
Organized	36	117.27	127.47	17.72
Unorganized ...	68	67.86	95.06	15.89
All Classes	1266	67.94	113.21	16.09
Organized	435	118.22	160.74	18.24
Unorganized	831	59.14	87.80	14.37
Men	584	57.93	73.09	10.72
Women	682	111.14	147.03	20.38

[a] These percentages were computed on the basis of mean expenditures.

TABLE 79

THE MEDIAN AND MEAN EXPENDITURE AND PERCENTAGE OF BUDGET
SPENT FOR PERSONAL CARE BY ORGANIZED AND UNORGANIZED
MEN AND WOMEN IN THE FOUR UNDERGRADUATE
CLASSES AT INDIANA UNIVERSITY, 1940-41

Group	Number of students	Median expenditure	Mean expenditure	Percentage of budget spent for personal care [a]
Freshman				
Men				
Organized	58	$10.94	$10.47	1.27
Unorganized	120	8.66	8.06	1.37
Women				
Organized	72	9.25	11.44	1.21
Unorganized	197	8.79	8.43	1.26
Sophomore				
Men				
Organized	64	11.95	11.97	1.45
Unorganized	113	9.89	9.79	1.76
Women				
Organized	51	13.54	18.96	2.07
Unorganized	92	8.61	10.61	1.76
Junior				
Men				
Organized	47	9.66	9.98	1.24
Unorganized	74	9.34	9.41	1.58
Women				
Organized	72	14.06	15.80	1.73
Unorganized	96	8.54	9.41	1.64
Senior				
Men				
Organized	37	13.75	14.23	1.50
Unorganized	74	10.89	10.41	1.58
Women				
Organized	37	16.75	16.45	2.29
Unorganized	68	9.17	10.35	1.73
All Classes	1272	9.94	10.82	1.54
Organized	438	12.73	13.70	1.55
Unorganized	834	8.92	9.34	1.53
Men	586	9.17	10.05	1.47
Women	686	11.23	11.48	1.59

[a] These percentages were computed on the basis of mean expenditures.

TABLE 80

THE MEDIAN AND MEAN EXPENDITURE AND PERCENTAGE OF BUDGET
SPENT FOR LAUNDRY BY ORGANIZED AND UNORGANIZED MEN
AND WOMEN IN THE FOUR UNDERGRADUATE CLASSES
AT INDIANA UNIVERSITY, 1940–41

Group	Number of students	Median expenditure	Mean expenditure	Percentage of budget spent for laundry [a]
Freshman				
Men				
Organized	57	$12.50	$15.51	1.88
Unorganized	120	10.00	11.95	2.02
Women				
Organized	73	7.75	8.45	.89
Unorganized	197	6.05	7.00	1.05
Sophomore				
Men				
Organized	64	15.00	20.48	2.48
Unorganized	113	9.46	10.87	1.96
Women				
Organized	51	14.72	15.80	1.72
Unorganized	92	8.40	8.25	1.37
Junior				
Men				
Organized	47	15.63	19.55	2.43
Unorganized	74	9.29	11.65	1.96
Women				
Organized	71	14.81	16.42	1.80
Unorganized	96	7.83	8.37	1.46
Senior				
Men				
Organized	36	15.71	20.97	2.21
Unorganized	74	12.14	15.70	2.38
Women				
Organized	37	14.50	12.29	1.71
Unorganized	67	8.45	8.90	1.49
All Classes	1269	9.71	11.96	1.70
Organized	433	13.26	16.00	1.82
Unorganized	836	8.60	9.87	1.62
Men	585	11.49	14.62	2.14
Women	684	8.62	9.71	1.35

[a] These percentages were computed on the basis of mean expenditures.

TABLE 81

THE MEDIAN AND MEAN EXPENDITURE AND PERCENTAGE OF BUDGET
SPENT FOR RECREATION BY ORGANIZED AND UNORGANIZED MEN
AND WOMEN IN THE FOUR UNDERGRADUATE CLASSES
AT INDIANA UNIVERSITY, 1940-41

Group	Number of students	Median expenditure	Mean expenditure	Percentage of budget spent for recreation [a]
Freshman				
Men				
Organized	58	$35.50	$53.44	6.46
Unorganized	120	24.29	28.98	4.91
Women				
Organized	71	16.94	16.78	1.77
Unorganized	197	14.69	15.37	2.30
Sophomore				
Men				
Organized	64	66.00	78.53	9.51
Unorganized	113	25.54	30.34	5.46
Women				
Organized	51	20.29	22.18	2.42
Unorganized	92	13.93	15.51	2.57
Junior				
Men				
Organized	47	55.62	68.23	8.46
Unorganized	74	26.80	36.26	6.10
Women				
Organized	72	23.60	24.13	2.64
Unorganized	95	15.00	15.38	2.68
Senior				
Men				
Organized	36	70.00	80.51	8.47
Unorganized	74	31.36	35.05	5.32
Women				
Organized	37	22.14	21.88	3.04
Unorganized	68	14.38	16.41	2.74
All Classes	1273	21.83	30.12	4.28
Organized	439	27.69	43.87	4.98
Unorganized	834	18.95	23.09	3.78
Men	586	30.01	45.00	6.60
Women	687	16.41	17.59	2.44

[a] These percentages were computed on the basis of mean expenditures.

TABLE 82

THE MEDIAN AND MEAN EXPENDITURE AND PERCENTAGE OF BUDGET
SPENT FOR REFRESHMENTS BY ORGANIZED AND UNORGANIZED
MEN AND WOMEN IN THE FOUR UNDERGRADUATE
CLASSES AT INDIANA UNIVERSITY, 1940-41

Group	Number of students	Median expenditure	Mean expenditure	Percentage of budget spent for refreshments [a]
Freshman				
Men				
Organized	58	$21.00	$27.95	3.38
Unorganized	120	18.06	19.62	3.32
Women				
Organized	71	16.59	22.15	2.34
Unorganized	197	12.77	14.27	2.14
Sophomore				
Men				
Organized	64	28.33	35.76	4.33
Unorganized	113	18.39	21.39	3.85
Women				
Organized	51	23.12	32.43	3.53
Unorganized	92	10.56	13.87	2.30
Junior				
Men				
Organized	47	33.57	34.32	4.26
Unorganized	74	18.42	20.46	3.44
Women				
Organized	72	24.29	28.72	3.14
Unorganized	95	11.30	14.34	2.49
Senior				
Men				
Organized	36	38.33	38.46	4.15
Unorganized	74	20.00	23.54	3.57
Women				
Organized	37	24.50	23.87	3.32
Unorganized	68	13.06	16.21	2.71
All Classes	1273	17.60	21.84	4.95
Organized	439	24.00	30.29	4.28
Unorganized	834	14.89	17.48	5.55
Men	586	10.37	25.46	4.11
Women	687	21.05	18.79	2.87

[a] These percentages were computed on the basis of mean expenditures.

TABLE 83

The Median and Mean Expenditure and Percentage of Budget Spent for University Fees by Organized and Unorganized Men and Women in the Four Undergraduate Classes at Indiana University, 1940-41

Group	Number of students	Median expenditure	Mean expenditure	Percentage of budget spent for University Fees [a]
Freshman				
Men				
Organized	58	$95.00	$88.85	10.75
Unorganized	120	95.00	91.25	15.46
Women				
Organized	73	95.68	93.33	9.85
Unorganized	197	94.11	92.61	13.86
Sophomore				
Men				
Organized	64	95.91	93.56	11.33
Unorganized	113	95.68	93.33	16.81
Women				
Organized	51	90.17	96.06	10.46
Unorganized	92	94.78	93.54	15.51
Junior				
Men				
Organized	47	106.61	98.09	12.17
Unorganized	74	107.05	101.97	17.15
Women				
Organized	75	93.21	100.07	10.95
Unorganized	96	94.44	91.12	15.85
Senior				
Men				
Organized	36	110.00	145.63	15.33
Unorganized	74	108.45	133.70	20.28
Women				
Organized	37	96.07	84.67	11.77
Unorganized	68	98.86	94.90	15.86
All Classes	1275	98.43	97.94	13.92
Organized	441	98.88	99.49	11.29
Unorganized	834	98.16	97.14	15.90
Men	586	102.15	102.38	15.02
Women	689	95.29	94.19	13.05

[a] These percentages were computed on the basis of mean expenditures.

TABLE 84
THE MEDIAN AND MEAN EXPENDITURE AND PERCENTAGE OF BUDGET
SPENT FOR TEXTBOOKS BY ORGANIZED AND UNORGANIZED MEN
AND WOMEN IN THE FOUR UNDERGRADUATE CLASSES
AT INDIANA UNIVERSITY, 1940-41

Group	Number of students	Median expenditure	Mean expenditure	Percentage of budget spent for text books [a]
Freshman				
Men				
Organized	58	$25.33	$23.44	2.83
Unorganized	120	25.93	24.87	4.21
Women				
Organized	73	25.23	24.70	2.61
Unorganized	197	28.47	27.72	4.15
Sophomore				
Men				
Organized	64	25.77	25.00	3.03
Unorganized	113	23.38	22.41	4.04
Women				
Organized	53	30.54	28.47	3.10
Unorganized	92	24.76	23.72	3.93
Junior				
Men				
Organized	47	26.04	24.55	3.05
Unorganized	74	27.50	25.49	4.29
Women				
Organized	72	29.38	27.97	3.06
Unorganized	96	26.67	25.75	4.48
Senior				
Men				
Organized	36	30.00	43.11	4.54
Unorganized	74	31.50	33.23	5.04
Women				
Organized	37	30.42	24.32	3.52
Unorganized	68	27.11	26.15	4.37
All Classes	1274	26.83	26.55	3.77
Organized	440	25.89	27.56	3.13
Unorganized	834	27.69	26.09	4.27
Men	586	26.16	26.52	3.89
Women	688	27.38	26.59	3.68

[a] These percentages were computed on the basis of mean expenditures.

TABLE 85

THE MEDIAN AND MEAN EXPENDITURE AND PERCENTAGE OF BUDGET
SPENT FOR DUES BY ORGANIZED AND UNORGANIZED MEN AND
WOMEN IN THE FOUR UNDERGRADUATE CLASSES AT
INDIANA UNIVERSITY, 1940–41

Group	Number of students	Median expenditure	Mean expenditure	Percentage of budget spent for dues [a]
Freshman				
Men				
Organized	58	$ 81.88	$ 84.16	10.18
Unorganized	120	3.07	2.18	.37
Women				
Organized	73	104.69	118.53	12.51
Unorganized	197	3.07	2.79	.42
Sophomore				
Men				
Organized	64	73.75	71.65	8.68
Unorganized	113	3.70	5.37	.97
Women				
Organized	49	80.62	65.47	7.13
Unorganized	92	3.41	3,21	.53
Junior				
Men				
Organized	47	84.50	73.04	9.06
Unorganized	74	4.02	10.54	1.77
Women				
Organized	72	65.00	60.03	6.64
Unorganized	96	3.24	2.54	.44
Senior				
Men				
Organized	36	52.50	52.37	5.51
Unorganized	73	3.86	6.91	1.05
Women				
Organized	34	8.00	55.31	7.69
Unorganized	66	4.45	4.99	.83
All Classes	1264	4.93	29.29	4.16
Organized	433	78.86	76.60	8.69
Unorganized	831	1.83	4.30	.70
Men	585	5.56	28.65	4.20
Women	679	4.77	29.83	4.13

[a] These percentages were computed on the basis of mean expenditures.

TABLE 86

THE MEDIAN AND MEAN EXPENDITURE AND PERCENTAGE OF BUDGET
SPENT FOR TRANSPORTATION BY ORGANIZED AND UNORGANIZED
MEN AND WOMEN IN THE FOUR UNDERGRADUATE
CLASSES AT INDIANA UNIVERSITY, 1940-41

Group	Number of students	Median expenditure	Mean expenditure	Percentage of budget spent for transportation [a]
Freshman				
Men				
Organized	58	$21.43	$22.33	2.70
Unorganized	120	16.41	17.38	2.94
Women				
Organized	73	22.50	24.32	2.57
Unorganized	196	18.38	23.79	3.56
Sophomore				
Men				
Organized	64	19.55	28.21	3.42
Unorganized	113	14.04	17.55	3.16
Women				
Organized	51	23.67	28.61	3.12
Unorganized	94	17.32	20.37	3.38
Junior				
Men				
Organized	47	18.93	21.98	2.73
Unorganized	74	14.23	15.97	2.69
Women				
Organized	72	24.44	39.42	4.31
Unorganized	95	19.85	33.94	4.16
Senior				
Men				
Organized	36	27.08	48.94	5.15
Unorganized	74	19.64	22.18	3.36
Women				
Organized	37	30.00	24.18	3.36
Unorganized	68	16.82	24.49	4.09
All Classes	1272	20.23	23.89	3.40
Organized	438	23.27	29.71	3.37
Unorganized	834	17.33	20.89	3.42
Men	586	20.67	21.79	3.20
Women	686	20.17	25.67	3.56

[a] These percentages were computed on the basis of mean expenditures.

TABLE 87

The Median and Mean Expenditure and Percentage of Budget
Spent for Health by Organized and Unorganized Men
and Women in the Four Undergraduate Classes
at Indiana University, 1940-41

Group	Number of students	Median expenditure	Mean expenditure	Percentage of budget spent for health [a]
Freshman				
Men				
Organized	57	$ 6.95	$ 4.96	.60
Unorganized	119	6.26	5.73	.97
Women				
Organized	63	7.88	9.01	.95
Unorganized	181	6.42	5.59	.84
Sophomore				
Men				
Organized	64	7.14	10.08	1.22
Unorganized	111	6.85	5.67	1.02
Women				
Organized	51	7.97	9.49	1.03
Unorganized	95	7.31	6.53	1.08
Junior				
Men				
Organized	47	8.39	8.36	1.04
Unorganized	73	7.30	9.09	1.53
Women				
Organized	71	8.26	8.66	.95
Unorganized	95	7.92	8.59	1.49
Senior				
Men				
Organized	37	8.18	16.03	1.69
Unorganized	66	7.50	11.47	1.74
Women				
Organized	36	9.74	11.06	1.54
Organized	72	7.86	6.96	1.16
All Classes	1234	7.27	7.86	1.12
Organized	422	7.90	9.47	1.07
Unorganized	812	6.98	7.02	1.15
Men	575	7.06	8.13	1.19
Women	659	7.45	7.63	1.06

[a] These percentages were computed on the basis of mean expenditures.

TABLE 88

The Median and Mean Expenditure and Percentage of Budget Spent
for Contributions and Gifts by Organized and Unorganized
Men and Women in the Four Undergraduate Classes
at Indiana University, 1940-41

Group	Number of students	Median expenditure	Mean expenditure	Percentage of budget spent for contributions [a]
Freshman				
Men				
Organized	58	$12.78	$15.45	1.87
Unorganized	120	8.75	9.30	1.58
Women				
Organized	73	12.18	15.16	1.60
Unorganized	197	10.19	11.18	1.67
Sophomore				
Men				
Organized	64	13.75	15.52	1.88
Unorganized	113	9.44	10.26	1.85
Women				
Organized	51	19.17	23.24	2.53
Unorganized	95	14.17	12.83	2.13
Junior				
Men				
Organized	44	14.04	18.26	2.27
Unorganized	74	10.95	9.93	1.67
Women				
Organized	75	19.44	21.58	2.36
Unorganized	96	13.24	14.83	2.58
Senior				
Men				
Organized	38	26.88	23.57	2.48
Unorganized	74	11.25	13.91	2.11
Women				
Organized	37	20.62	21.95	3.05
Unorganized	65	13.00	14.29	2.39
All Classes	1274	12.21	14.24	2.02
Organized	440	15.17	19.15	2.17
Unorganized	834	10.67	11.79	1.93
Men	585	11.27	13.02	1.91
Women	689	13.21	15.28	2.12

[a] These percentages were computed on the basis of mean expenditures.

TABLE 89

The Median and Mean Expenditure and Percentage of Budget Spent for General Reading by Organized and Unorganized Men and Women in the Four Undergraduate Classes at Indiana University, 1940-41

Group	Number of students	Median expenditure	Mean expenditure	Percentage of budget spent for general reading [a]
Freshman				
Men				
Organized	58	$ 1.83	$ 2.42	.29
Unorganized	119	3.86	4.08	.69
Women				
Organized	72	3.58	3.90	.41
Unorganized	190	2.49	3.22	.48
Sophomore				
Men				
Organized	63	3.00	3.63	.44
Unorganized	112	2.54	3.08	.55
Women				
Organized	50	2.65	4.47	.49
Unorganized	95	2.28	2.28	.38
Junior				
Men				
Organized	45	2.75	2.89	.36
Unorganized	74	3.00	2.96	.50
Women				
Organized	71	2.73	3.63	.40
Unorganized	93	2.70	3.14	.55
Senior				
Men				
Organized	33	4.38	4.24	.51
Unorganized	73	3.61	4.80	.64
Women				
Organized	36	5.12	3.54	.49
Unorganized	70	3.20	3.90	.65
All Classes	1254	2.81	3.45	.49
Organized	428	2.83	3.68	.42
Unorganized	826	2.81	3.33	.55
Men	577	2.92	3.51	.51
Women	677	2.73	3.40	.47

[a] These percentages were computed on the basis of mean expenditures.

TABLE 90

MEAN EXPENDITURE AND PERCENTAGE OF BUDGET SPENT FOR ITEMS IN STUDENT BUDGET BY ORGANIZED AND UNORGANIZED MEN AND WOMEN AT INDIANA UNIVERSITY, 1940-41

| | Organized | | | | Unorganized | | | |
| | Men | | Women | | Men | | Women | |
	Mean expenditure	Percentage of budget spent [a]	Mean expenditure	Percentage of budget spent [a]	Mean expenditure	Percentage of budget spent [a]	Mean expenditure	Percentage of budget spent [a]
Rent	$125.74	14.91	$134.90	14.76	$113.73	18.62	$117.70	18.85
Food	221.25	26.24	219.45	24.01	179.00	29.31	177.42	28.41
Clothing	101.50	12.04	212.23	23.22	87.80	14.37	114.08	18.27
Personal Care	11.48	1.36	15.62	1.71	9.34	1.53	9.38	1.50
Laundry	18.97	2.25	13.42	1.47	9.87	1.62	7.83	1.25
Recreation	69.51	8.24	21.59	2.40	23.09	3.78	15.56	2.49
Refreshments	33.73	4.00	27.29	2.99	17.48	2.86	14.49	2.32
University Fees	102.49	12.15	96.88	10.60	97.14	15.90	92.83	14.87
Textbooks	27.65	3.28	27.29	2.99	26.09	4.27	26.23	4.20
Dues	72.05	8.54	80.56	8.81	4.30	.70	3.15	.50
Transportation	28.76	3.41	30.54	3.34	20.89	3.42	23.21	3.72
Health	9.31	1.10	9.62	1.05	7.02	1.15	6.62	1.06
Contributions	17.56	2.08	20.53	2.25	11.79	1.93	12.76	2.04
General Reading	3.33	.39	3.98	.44	3.33	.55	3.11	.50
Total	$843.33	100.00	$913.90	100.00	$610.81	100.00	$624.37	99.99

[a] These percentages were computed on the basis of mean expenditures.

TABLE 91

MEAN EXPENDITURE, PERCENTAGE OF BUDGET SPENT, AND RANK OF
ITEMS IN STUDENT BUDGET BY 1275 INDIANA UNIVERSITY
STUDENTS, 1940-41

Item	Number of students	Mean expendi- ture	Percentage of total expenditure [b]	Rank in budget
1. Rent	1275	$119.49	16.99	2
2. Food	1275	193.06	27.45	1
3. Clothing	1275	113.21	16.09	3
4. Personal Care	1275	10.82	1.54	12
5. Laundry	1275	11.96	1.70	11
6. Recreation	1275	30.12	4.28	5
7. Refreshments	1275	21.84	3.10	9
8. University Fees	1275	97.94	13.92	4
9. Textbooks	1275	26.55	3.77	7
10. Dues	1275	29.29	4.16	6
11. Transportation	1275	38.89	3.40	8
12. Health	1275	7.86	1.12	13
13. Contributions	1275	14.24	2.02	10
14. General Reading	1275	3.45	.49	14
Total	1275	$703.41 [a]	100.00	

[a] This total is the mean of the totals and consequently the sum of the
means for all items listed above.

[b] These percentages were computed on the basis of the mean expenditures.

TABLE 92

MEAN EXPENDITURE AND PERCENTAGE OF BUDGET SPENT FOR ITEMS IN
STUDENT BUDGET BY 586 MEN AND 689 WOMEN STUDENTS
AT INDIANA UNIVERSITY, 1940-41

	All Men			All Women		
	Mean expenditure	Percentage of total expenditure [b]	Rank in budget	Mean expenditure	Percentage of total expenditure [b]	Rank in budget
1. Rent	$114.76	16.83	2	$123.48	17.11	1
2. Food	194.88	28.58	1	191.53	26.54	3
3. Clothing	73.09	10.72	4	147.03	20.38	2
4. Personal Care .	10.05	1.47	12	9.71	1.35	12
5. Laundry	14.62	2.14	10	11.48	1.59	11
6. Recreation ...	45.00	6.60	5	17.59	2.44	9
7. Refreshments .	25.46	3.73	8	18.79	2.60	8
8. University Fees	102.38	15.02	3	94.19	13.05	4
9. Textbooks	26.52	3.89	7	26.59	3.68	6
10. Dues	28.65	4.20	6	29.83	4.13	5
11. Transportation	21.79	3.20	9	25.67	3.56	7
12. Health	8.13	1.19	13	7.63	1.06	13
13. Contributions .	13.02	1.91	11	15.28	2.12	10
14. General Reading	3.51	.51	14	3.40	.47	14
Total	$681.84 [a]	100.00		$721.59 [a]	100.00	

[a] These totals are means of the totals and consequently the sums of the means for all items listed above.

[b] These percentages were computed on the basis of mean expenditures.

TABLE 93

Median Expenditures for Items in Student Budget by 441
Organized Students and 834 Unorganized Students
at Indiana University, 1940-41

	All Organized Students		All Unorganized Students	
	Number of students	Median expenditure	Number of students	Median expenditure
Rent	441	$128.92	834	$103.36
Food	441	228.95	834	184.22
Clothing	435	118.22	831	59.14
Personal Care	438	12.73	834	8.92
Laundry	433	13.26	836	8.60
Recreation	438	27.69	834	18.95
Refreshments	438	24.00	835	14.89
University Fees	441	98.88	834	98.16
Textbooks	438	27.89	834	27.69
Dues	433	78.86	831	1.83
Transportation	438	23.27	834	17.33
Health	422	7.90	812	6.98
Contributions	440	15.17	834	10.67
General Reading	428	2.83	826	2.81
Total	441	$852.05	834	$574.10

TABLE 94

MEAN EXPENDITURE, PERCENTAGE OF BUDGET SPENT, AND RANK OF
INDIVIDUAL ITEMS IN BUDGET OF ORGANIZED AND UNORGANIZED
STUDENTS AT INDIANA UNIVERSITY, 1940-41

	All Organized			All Unorganized		
	Mean expenditure	Percentage of total expenditure [b]	Rank in budget	Mean expenditure	Percentage of total expenditure [b]	Rank in budget
1. Rent	$130.64	14.83	3	$113.73	18.62	2
2. Food	220.29	25.00	1	179.00	29.31	1
3. Clothing	160.74	18.24	2	87.80	14.37	4
4. Personal Care .	13.70	1.55	12	9.34	1.53	11
5. Laundry	16.00	1.82	11	9.87	1.62	10
6. Recreation ...	43.87	4.98	6	23.09	3.78	6
7. Refreshments .	30.29	3.44	7	17.48	2.86	8
8. University Fees	99.49	11.29	4	97.14	15.90	3
9. Textbooks	27.56	3.13	9	25.92	4.27	5
10. Dues	76.60	8.69	5	4.30	.70	13
11. Transportation	29.71	3.37	8	20.89	3.42	7
12. Health	9.41	1.07	13	7.02	1.15	12
13. Contributions .	19.15	2.17	10	11.79	1.93	9
14. General Reading	3.68	.42	14	3.33	.55	14
Total	$881.09 [a]	100.00		$610.81 [a]	100.00	

[a] These totals are means of the totals and consequently the sums of the means for all items listed above.

[b] These percentages were computed on the basis of mean expenditures.

BIBLIOGRAPHY

SELECTED BIBLIOGRAPHY

Babcock, F. Lawrence. *The U. S. College Graduate.* New York: The Macmillan Company, 1941.

Consumer Expenditures in the United States. National Resources Committee, Washington: Government Printing Office, 1939.

Consumer Incomes in the United States. National Resources Committee, Washington: Government Printing Office, 1938.

Crawford, Mary M. "Student Expenses at Indiana University," *Indiana University News-Letter.* Vol. XXVI (August, 1938).

——, "Student Expenditures at Indiana University," *Indiana University News-Letter.* Vol. XXVIII (July, 1940).

Croxton, Frederick E. and Cowden, Dudley J. *Applied General Statistics.* New York: Prentice-Hall, Inc., 1940.

"Doctor Bills of City Workers," *The Monthly Labor Review,* L (July, 1940), 1062-1079.

Ezekiel, Mordecai. *Methods of Correlation Analysis.* New York: John Wiley and Sons, Inc., 1930.

Family Expenditures in the United States. National Resources Planning Board, Washington: Government Printing Office, 1941.

Greenleaf, Walter J. *The Cost of Going to College.* Office of Education, U. S. Dept. of the Interior, Washington: Government Printing Office, 1938.

Howard, William Luther. *A Personnel Study of NYA Students of Indiana University.* (Unpublished Thesis.) Bloomington: Indiana University, 1940.

Indiana Daily Student.

Kuenstler, Walter P. "The Buying Habits of Women Students on the University of Pennsylvania Campus." (Unpublished Senior-Research Thesis), Wharton School of Finance and Commerce, Philadelphia: University of Pennsylvania, 1940.

Latzke, Esther. "A Study of the Diets Selected by College Students from a College Cafeteria." *Journal of Home Economics,* XXVI (February, 1934), 107-114.

Lazarsfeld, Paul F. "Some Remarks on the Typological Procedures in Social Research," *Zeitschrift für Sozialforchung.* Jahrgang VI, Heft 1, Paris: Librairie Félix Alcan, 1937.

Lough, William H. *High-Level Consumption.* New York: McGraw-Hill Book Co., 1935.

Lundberg, George A. *Social Research.* New York: Longmans, Green and Co., 1942.

Lynd, Robert S. and Helen M. *Middletown in Transition.* New York: Harcourt, Brace and Co., 1937.

——, *Middletown.* New York: Harcourt, Brace and Co., 1929.

Lynd, Robert S. and Hanson, Alice C. "The People as Consumers," *Recent Social Trends*. A Report of the President's Research Committee on Social Trends. New York: McGraw-Hill Book Co., Inc., 1933, pp. 857-912.

Mills, Frederick C. *Statistical Methods*. New York: Henry Holt and Co., 1939.

Moffat, James E. "Student Budgets," *School and Society*, XXXVI (October 1, 1932), 432-434.

——, "Student Expenditures and the Depression," *Indiana University News-Letter*, XXII (July, 1934).

——, "Student Expenses at Indiana University," *Indiana University Alumni Quarterly*, XX (October, 1932), 476-486.

Monroe, Day and Pennell, Maryland Y. *How Professional Women Spend Their Money*. Bureau of Home Economics, U. S. Dept. of Agriculture, Washington: Government Printing Office, 1939.

Monroe, Day. "Analyzing Families by Composition Type with Respect to Consumption," *American Statistical Association Journal*, XXXII (March, 1937), 35-39.

Peixotto, Jessica B. *Getting and Spending at the Professional Standard of Living*. New York: The Macmillan Co., 1927.

Recent Economic Changes. Vol. I, A Report of the Committee on Recent Economic Changes of the President's Conference on Unemployment. New York: McGraw-Hill Book Co., 1929.

Recommended Dietary Allowances. A Report Prepared by the Committee on Food and Nutrition. Washington: National Research Council, 1940.

Sandage, Charles H. "Student Expenditures for Clothing," *Miami Business Review*, VII (December, 1934), 1-4.

——, "What it Costs to Go to College," *Miami Business Review*, VII (November, 1934), 1-4.

Stouffer, Samuel and Lazarsfeld, Paul F. *Research Memorandum on the Family in the Depression*. Bulletin 29, A Report Prepared under the Direction of the Committee on Studies in Social Aspects of the Depression. New York: Social Science Research Council, 1937.

Study of Consumer Purchases
  Urban Series
    Williams, Faith M. and Hanson, Alice C. *Money Disbursements of Wage Earners and Clerical Workers in the East North Central Region, 1934-36*. U. S. Dept. of Labor, Bull. No. 636. Washington: Government Printing Office, 1940.

    ——, *Money Disbursements of Wage Earners and Clerical Workers in the North Atlantic Region, 1934-36. Vol. I*. U. S. Dept. of Labor, Bull. No. 637. Washington: Government Printing Office, 1939.

    ——, *Money Disbursements of Wage Earners and Clerical Workers in the North Atlantic Region, 1934-36. Vol. II*. U. S. Dept. of Labor, Bull. No. 637. Washington: Government Printing Office, 1939.

——, *Money Disbursements of Wage Earners and Clerical Workers, 1934-36. Summary Volume.* U. S. Dept. of Labor, Bull. No. 638. Washington: Government Printing Office, 1941.

Family Income in Chicago, 1935-36. Vol. I. U. S. Dept.. of Labor, Bull. No. 642. Washington: Government Printing Office, 1939.

Family Expenditure in Chicago, 1935-36. Vol. II. U. S. Dept. of Labor, Bull. No. 642. Washington: Government Printing Office, 1939.

Family Income and Expenditure in New York City, 1935-36. Vol. I. U. S. Dept. of Labor, Bull. No. 643. Washington: Government Printing Office, 1941.

Family Expenditure in New York City, 1935-36. Vol. II. U. S. Dept. of Labor, Bull. No. 643. Washington: Government Printing Office, 1939.

Family Income in Nine Cities of the East Central Region, 1935-36. Vol. I. U. S. Dept. of Labor, Bull. No. 644. Washington: Government Printing Office, 1939.

Family Expenditure in Nine Cities of the East Central Region, 1935-36. Vol. II. U. S. Dept. of Labor, Bull. No. 644. Washington: Government Printing Office, 1941.

Family Expenditure in Seven New England Cities, 1935-36. Vol. II. U. S. Dept. of Labor, Bull. No. 645. Washington: Government Printing Office, 1941.

Family Expenditure in Three Southeastern Cities, 1935-36. Vol. II. U. S. Dept. of Labor, Bull. No. 647. Washington: Government Printing Office, 1940.

Family Expenditures in Selected Cities, 1935-36. Vol. I, *Housing.* U. S. Dept. of Labor, Bull. No. 648. Washington: Government Printing Office, 1941.

Family Expenditures in Selected Cities, 1935-36. Vol. II, *Food.* U. S. Dept. of Labor, Bull. No. 648. Washington: Government Printing Office, 1940.

Family Expenditures in Selected Cities, 1935-36. Vol. III, *Clothing and Personal Care.* U. S. Dept. of Labor, Bull. No. 648. Washington: Government Printing Office, 1941.

Family Expenditures in Selected Cities, 1935-36. Vol. IX, *Furnishings and Equipment.* U. S. Dept. of Labor, Bull. No. 648. Washington: Government Printing Office, 1941.

Family Expenditures in Selected Cities,, 1935-36. Vol. IV, *Medical Care.* U. S. Dept. of Labor, Bull. No. 648. Washington: Government Printing Office, 1940.

Family Expenditures in Selected Cities, 1935-36. Vol. VI, *Travel and Transportation.* U. S. Dept. of Labor, Bull. No. 648. Washington: Government Printing Office, 1940.

Family Expenditures in Selected Cities, 1935-36. Vol. VII, *Recreation, Reading, Formal Education, Tobacco, Contributions, and Personal Taxes.* U. S. Dept. of Labor, Bull. No. 648. Washington: Government Printing Office, 1941.

Family Expenditures in Selected Cities, 1935-36. Vol. VIII. *Changes in Assets and Liabilities.* U. S. Dept. of Labor, Bull. No. 648. Washington: Government Printing Office, 1941.

Rural Series

Monroe, D. and others. *Family Expenditures for Furnishings and Equipment; Five Regions.* U. S. Dept. of Agric. misc. pub. no. 436; Consumer Purchases Study. Washington: Government Printing Office, 1941.

——, *Family Income and Expenditures; Middle Atlantic and North Central Region and New England Region Part 1, Family Income.* U. S. Dept. of Agric. misc. pub. no. 370; Consumer Purchases Study. Washington: Government Printing Office, 1940.

Brady, D., and others. *Family Income and Expenditures; Southeast Region; Part 1, Family Income.* U. S. Dept. of Agric. misc. pub. no. 375; Consumer Purchases Study. Washington: Government Printing Office, 1940.

Martin, D., and others. *Family Income and Expenditures; Middle Atlantic, North Central and New England Regions; Part 1, Family Income.* U. S. Dept. of Agric. misc. pub. no. 383; Consumer Purchases Study. Washington: Government Printing Office, 1940.

Kyrk, H., and others. *Family Housing and Facilities; Five Regions.* U. S. Dept. of Agric. misc. pub. no. 399; Consumer Purchases Study. Washington: Government Printing Office, 1940.

Hollingsworth, H., and others. *Family Expenditures for Medical Care; Five Regions.* U. S. Dept. of Agric. misc. pub. no. 402; Consumer Purchases Study. Washington: Government Printing Office, 1941.

Stiebeling, H., and others. *Family Food Consumption and Dietary Levels; Five Regions.* U. S. Dept. of Agric. misc. pub. no. 405; Consumer Purchases Study. Washington: Government Printing Office, 1941.

Monroe, D., and others. *Family Expenditures for Automobile and Other Transportation; Five Regions.* U. S. Dept. of Agric. misc. pub. no. 415; Consumer Purchases Study. Washington: Government Printing Office, 1941.

Kyrk, H., and others. *Family Expenditures for Housing and Household Operation; Five Regions.* U. S. Dept. of Agric. misc. pub. no. 432; Consumer Purchases Study. Washington: Government Printing Office, 1941.

" Seven Keys to 80 Million Dollar Market." Prepared for Major College Publications, 101 Eshleman Hall, University of California, under the direction of Fred C. Fischer.

Structure of the American Economy, Part 1, Basic Characteristics. National Resources Committee, Washington: Government Printing Office, 1939.

Tunis, John Roberts. *Choosing a College.* New York: Harcourt, Brace and Co., 1941.

"*U*" *Students Report Their Expenditures.* Prepared by the Family Economics Bureau of the Northwestern National Life Insurance Co. Minneapolis: (Mimeographed), 1939, p. 3.

United States Bureau of Foreign and Domestic Commerce, *Survey of Current Business.* XXI (May, 1941), 18, 162.

Walters, Raymond. "Statistics of Registration in American Universities and Colleges, 1940," *School and Society,* December, 1940.

Woodburn, James A. *The History of Indiana University, 1820-1902.* Bloomington: Indiana University, 1940.

Yocum, James Carleton. *Expenditures and Apparel Buying Habits of Ohio State University Students.* The Bureau of Business Research, College of Commerce and Administration, The Ohio State University, Columbus, Ohio, Jan., 1934.

INDEX